THE LIFE of MOHAMMAD

CW01669283

Racim Mohammed. Alger.

راسم محمد بالجزائر

THE LIFE OF MOHAMMAD

Prophet of Allah

Sliman Ben Ibrahim
and
Etienne Dinet

Illustrations by Etienne Dinet

STUDIO EDITIONS
LONDON

Originally published as *La Vie de Mohammed, Prophete D'Allah*
by L'Edition D'Art, Paris, 1918, and as *The Life of Mohammad* London, 1919

This edition published 1990 by Studio Editions Ltd,
Princess House, 50 Eastcastle Street,
London W1N 7AP, England.

Copyright © Studio Editions Ltd., 1990

Reprinted in hardback 1992
First published in paperback 1992

All rights reserved. No part of this publication
may be reproduced, stored in a retrieval system,
or transmitted in any form or by any means, electronic,
mechanical, photocopying, recording or otherwise,
without the prior permission of the copyright holder.

ISBN 1 85170 220 2 (Hardback)
ISBN 1 85170 929 0 (Paperback)

Printed and bound in Singapore.

CONTENTS

LIST OF ILLUSTRATIONS

MEANING OF ARAB QUOTATIONS

TRANSLATION OF THE ARABIC CALLIGRAPHY

TITLE: *ALLAH.*

CHAPTER THE FIRST. — Page 13: *In the name of Allah, the Compassionate, the Merciful.*
Page 19: *Then when ye have ended the prayer, make mention of Allah, standing, and sitting, and reclining.* (the Qur'an, iv, 104.)

CHAPTER THE SECOND. — Page 23: *Have we not opened thy breast for thee? * And taken off from thee thy burden?* (the Qur'an, xciv, 1–2.)

CHAPTER THE THIRD. — Page 45: *Verily, we have caused It (the Qur'an), to descend on the night of Power.* (the Qur'an, xcvii, 1.)

CHAPTER THE FOURTH. — Page 77: *Ye shall assuredly be tried in your possessions and in yourselves.* (the Qur'an, iii, 183.)
Page 100: *And before them have We set a barrier and behind them a barrier, and We have shrouded them in a veil, so that they shall not see.* (the Qur'an, xxxvi, 8.)

CHAPTER THE FIFTH. — Page 105: *And fight for the cause of Allah against those who fight against you.* (the Qur'an, ii, 186.)

CHAPTER THE SIXTH. — Page 137: *And be not faint-hearted, and be not sorrowful; For ye shall gain the upper hand if ye be believers.* (the Qur'an, iii, 133.)
Page 166: *Nay, rather Allah is your liege lord, and He is the best of helpers.* (the Qur'an, iii, 143.)

CHAPTER THE SEVENTH. — Page 171: *Verily, We have won for three an undoubted victory.* (the Qur'an, xlviii, 1.)

CHAPTER THE EIGHTH. — Page 207: *Accomplish the Pilgrimage and the Visitation of the Holy Places in honour of Allah.* (the Qur'an, ii, 192.)
Page 227: *Say: Go through the earth, and see how He hath brought forth created beings.* (the Qur'an, xxix, 19.)

CHAPTER THE NINTH. — Page 231: *Thou truly art mortal, O Mohammad, and they truly are mortal.* (the Qur'an, xxxix, 31.)
Page 239: *Mohammad is no more than an apostle; other apostles have already passed away before him; if then he dies, or be slain, will ye turn upon your heels?* (the Qur'an, iii, 138.)

CHAPTER ONE — Decorative plate.

CHAPTER THE FIRST

THE MOSLEM PRAYER

A rosy ray lit up the horizon; the stars paled, and a voice cried out in cadence, in the silence of dawn:

"Allah is the greatest! There is no God but Allah, and Mohammad is the Prophet of Allah! Come and pray! Come to Salvation!"

High up above the flat housetops and the palm-trees of the oasis, the last notes of the Muazzin's call, wafted from the balcony of the slender minaret, died away in the infinite space of the Desert. . . .

Mohammedans who were still slumbering, enwrapped in the white folds of their shroudlike mantles, sprung to their feet with a start, like dead men coming to life. They hurried to fountains where they performed their ablutions; and then, with clean skins and pure thoughts, they gathered together in long processions, elbow to elbow, all turned in one direction: that of the Holy Ka'bah of Makkah (Mecca).

Standing erect, heads slightly bent, eyes downcast, perfectly still in the long folds of their garments, they seemed as if metamorphosed into a crowd of statues. Following the example of the Immam, in front of them, but in the same direction, and announcing each phase of the prayer by the Takbir: *"Allah is the greatest!"* they all lifted their open hands on a level with their foreheads, bearing witness to their ecstasy in the presence of the Almighty power of the Master of the Worlds. Then, every man made the same movement, bending their backs and bowing low before the throne of His Supreme Majesty.

But this did not suffice to express all the humility of their souls, so they dropped to the ground and prostrated themselves, piously pressing their faces against the earth. For a few moments they remained in this supplicating posture, as if crushed by the weight of the entire firmament which might have been prostrated with them.

They held up their heads at last and rose to a sitting posture, both knees on the ground, their heads bowed under the burden of their fervour. The prayer, terminated by salutation, accompanied by the face being turned first to the left, was addressed to the two recording angels who unceasingly attend every true Believer.

Generally, however, the Faithful who ask nothing from Allah, not even their daily bread, remain a little longer on their knees, and placing breast-high their open palms under their eyes, as if reading a book, they implore Divine Mercy for the salvation of their souls, for their relatives, and for Islam.

Only a few parts of the Prayer: the Takbir, the Fatihah and the final salutation are loudly intoned by

Praying around the Holy Temple of the Kaaba in Mecca.

the Imam. The congregation pray inwardly; the Takbir alone is murmured in whispers that are barely audible.

Such half-silence enhances the grandeur of their gestures, so expressive and simple, in which dignity is closely allied to humility; and being totally devoid of affectation, constitutes the most poignant display of adoration imaginable.

Every day, each time the rays of the sun change colour: at rosy dawn; flaming noon; during gilded sunset, when it descends below the horizon in all the yellow sadness of its disappearance; and at the moment it is enshrouded in the blue veiling of night, not only in the Mosques, but also in the houses and streets, in *cafes* and market-places, in the country or the desert, all Moslems, alone or grouped together, wherever they may be, without needing to be called by the Muazzin or led by the Imam, are bound to stop short in t heir work and even interrupt their trend of thought, for a few minutes, thus glorifying the Benefactor.

For more than thirteen centuries, from the Atlantic's African shore as far as the Chinese coast-line of the Pacific, more than two hundred millions of the Faithful turn five times daily in the direction of the Holy Ka'bah of Makkah; their millions of prayers being garnered there to be offered up to the Most High, bearing witness to the undying gratitude of the souls of Islam.

DESCRIPTION OF MAKKAH *(Mecca)*

This mysterious town, upon which the aspirations of so many human beings close in, was almost unknown in ancient times. What is it like?

Is it one of those cities, picturesquely situated, where ostentatious kings built splendid palaces, accumulating therein all the treasures of creation? Is it one of those vast commercial boroughs dominating land and sea routes to which the riches and produce of the universe came in abundance? Or was it an extensive imperial capital whose valiant warriors bent neighbouring peoples beneath their yoke?

Makkah has nothing in common with all this, being established in one of the most arid and forsaken spots on earth; and in olden times its only commerce consisted in desert caravan traffic, so that it was neither rich nor powerful. Nevertheless, many opulent towns are jealous of its glory, for it shelters in its midst the Holy Temple of the Ka'bah, besides being the birthplace of Our Lord Mohammad, the Prince of Prophets!

In our own times, despite gifts brought from the furthermost corners of the world by the hundred thousand pilgrims who come each year to prostrate themselves in its temple, Makkah, "The Mother of Cities," by the splendour of its palaces and mosques, cannot vie with any great capital. In the eyes of the True Believers, its treasures are radiant with incomparable brilliancy, but which is not terrestrial.

As a matter of fact, the aspect of Makkah—"Allah's Delight"— is no different from other Arab desert centres. There are more numerous and loftier dwellings, better decorated than in general, but its characteristics, on the whole, are unchanged.

From the top of the Jabal Abi-Kubeis which dominates it on the eastern side, it can be viewed stretching from north to south in a narrow valley. At first, it seems to form part of the earth on which it stands, because the bare and rocky mountains surrounding it are not separated from these heights by any oasis or verdant strip, and the terrace-roofs of the houses do not stand out from the heaps of stony fragments that have rolled down from the crags. The spectator's eyes gradually get used to the landscape and pick out architectural lines; mysterious entrances to dwellings; lace-work of tall, straight minarets; and then, astonished at the sudden apparition of a big town that he never thought was there, he sees it, as in a kind of mirage, increasing excessively. Now it is the turn of the rocks to look as if changed into houses; hills becoming immense suburbs extending boundlessly.

If, in this chaos of sharply-outlined shapes, it is difficult for the eye to distinguish dwellings from steep rocks, one cannot fail to be startled at once by the strange aspect of a great cube of masonry, built up in the middle of a spacious quadrangular courtyard and veiled by black silk, shining in violent contrast to the dull tints of the entire sun-scorched landscape.

This black cube is the Holy Ka'bah, the veritable heart of Islam, and like so many veins bringing blood to the heart to vivify the body, all the prayers of Islam flow towards this Temple to vivify souls. It is the only spot on earth where Moslems, when adoring the Eternal, can meet face to face.

THE TEMPLE OF THE KABAH AND THE BLACK STONE

The Ka'bah is not the tomb of the Prophet, nor an object to be worshipped, as many Europeans imagine. It is a temple called "Beit Allah al Haram" (the Holy House of Allah), and its origin can be traced to the most distant days of antiquity.

According to the Arab tradition, it was built by Adam, the father of the human race. Destroyed by the Flood, it was rebuilt on the same foundations by the Prophet Abraham, with the help of his son, Ishmael, the ancestor of the Arabs. Since then, often repaired, but retaining the same lines and proportions, the Ka'bah became the goal of Arab pilgrims flocking to adore Allah, the Only One, and perform seven ritual circuits instituted by their forefathers under the title of "Tawaf."

Little by little, the worship of Allah, the Only One, having degenerated in the memory of the pilgrims who added the practice of idolatry, Mohammad was sent to destroy the three hundred and sixty images they adored.

In the east angle of the monuments is encrusted the famous black stone "Hajaru'l-Aswad", framed in a silver circle.

This stone, which came down from Paradise, was brought by the angel Jibra'il (Gabriel) to Abraham and his son, during the rebuilding of the Temple, and they placed it where it is still to be seen this day, in order to serve pilgrims as a starting-point for their ritual circuits. Primitively as white as milk, its present characteristic ebony tint is due to the pollution of the sins of the pilgrims who come to touch and kiss it, while imploring the Merciful to pardon them.

Close to the Ka'bah is the well of Zamzam. Its miraculous water gushed forth from the earth to save Ishmael from the tortures of thirst when lost in the desert with his mother, Hajar (Hagar). Neglected by the Arab tribes, in the dark Days of Ignorance, it became choked up by sand and was dug anew by Abdul Muttalib, a few years before the birth of Mohammad. The water, ever since, is revered by pilgrims who use it for drinking purposes and for their ablutions, thereby sanctifying themselves by the remembrance of their ancestors.

The two functions of "Siqayah," (Management of Water Supply), and of "Hajaba," (Superintendence of the Ka'bah) were posts greatly sought after on account of their prerogatives. At the epoch at which our story begins, they were both united in the hands of Abdul Muttalib bin Hashem, of the Quraish tribe, the grandfather of the future Prophet.

THE MARRIAGE OF ABDULLAH, FATHER OF THE PROPHET

One day, Abdul Muttalib, custodian of the Ka'bah, set forth from the Sanctuary, his favourite son, Abdullah, holding his hand.

On the threshold of the temple was seated Quotila, a woman of the Bani Asad tribe. On catching sight of the lad, she started to her feet, evincing sudden surprise. She stared at him with strange persistence because she was fascinated by a supernatural light that radiated from his brow. 'Whither art thou going?' she called to him.—'To where my father leadeth me.'—'Stop and listen to me. I offer thee a hundred camels, being as many as thy father was bound to sacrifice to save thy life, if thou wilt consent to throw thyself upon me, now at once.'—'I am in my father's company and cannot disobey him, nor leave him,' replied Abdullah, petrified at such shamelessness, especially in the presence of such a respectable person as Abdul Muttalib.

The young man turned away, filled with confusion, and rejoined Abdul Muttalib who took him to the house of Wahb ibn Abdi Manaf, whose daughter the Superintendent of the Well thought would make a good wife for his boy.

Wahb was one of the chieftains of the Bani Zahrah tribe and Abdul Muttalib being numbered among the princes of the Quraish, a most noble tribe, an alliance between two such authentically aristocratic families would be easily brought about and so the marriage of Abdullah, with Aminah, daughter of Wahb, took place without further loss of time.

Abdullah went off with his bride to the dwelling of Abu Talib, his uncle. There the marriage was consummated during the young couple's sojourn of three days and three nights. When the newly-married young man went out of the house, he came face to face again with Quotila, the woman who had previously hailed him with such lack of decency and he was surprised at her complete indifference as she saw him pass by. Abdullah was considered to be the handsomest youth in Makkah. His manly bearing had aroused the sensual passions of most of the women of the city to such an extent that, when his marriage was announced, they fell ill by dint of jealousy and disappointment. Quotila, however, was not a victim to vulgar lust, being the sister of Waraqah ibn Taufal, the learned man renowned throughout Arabia for his knowledge of the Sacred Books. From him she had learnt how, in that part of the country, a Prophet was about to come into the world, whose father would be known by rays of light illuminating his face with a pearly or starry sheen. This sign she had detected on the brow of Abdullah, and was haunted by the ambitious desire of becoming the mother of the coming Apostle. Her hopes dashed to the ground, she no longer heeded Abdullah, notwithstanding his good looks.

Knowing nothing of all this, he felt hurt at her indifference, following so quickly on her great ardour. 'How comes it that thou dost not ask me again for what thou hungered for but a little while ago?' he asked Quotila.—'Who art thou?' she replied.—'I am Abdullah bin Abdul Muttalib.'—'Art thou the stripling whose brow seemed to me to be surrounded with a luminous aureola which has now disappeared? What hath befell thee, since we first met?'

He apprised her of his marriage, and Quotila guessed that the radiance surrounding the future Prophet had passed away from the forehead of Abdullah into the womb of Aminah, his wife.—'By Allah, I made no mistake!' she told him. 'On thy brow I discovered the pure light that I would have dearly liked to possess in the depths of my body. But now it belongeth to another who will be delivered of "The Best Among Created Beings, and there remaineth naught of thee that I care for.'

Thus it came about that Abdullah, by the words that fell from the lips of this learned woman, got to hear of his wife's pregnancy and the future in store for his son. Abdullah did not live long enough to have the happiness of knowing his offspring, for Mohammad's father died at Yasrib two months before Aminah was delivered.

Aminah, mother of Allah's Chosen One, spoke thus:

"Since the day I carried my son in my womb, until I brought him forth, I never suffered the least pain. I never even felt his weight and should not have known the state I was in, if it had not been that after I conceived and was about to fall asleep, an angel appeared to me, saying: 'Dost thou not see that thou art pregnant with the Lord of thy Nation, the Prophet of all thy people? Know it full well.' At the same instant, a streak of light, darting out of my body, went up northwards—yea, even unto the land of Syria.

"When the day of my deliverance came due, the angel appeared to me again and gave me a warning: 'When thou shalt bring forth thy child into the world, thou must utter these words: 'For him I implore the protection of Allah, the Only One, against the wickedness of the envious,' and thou shalt call him by the name of Mohammad which means The Lauded, as he is announced in the Taurat and the Injil, for he will be lauded by all the inhabitants of Heaven and Earth.' "

When the planet Al-Moushtari passed, a line of light darted for the second time from Aminah's body in the direction of faraway Syria and it illuminated the palace of the town of Busra. At the same time, other prodigies astonished the world: the Lake Sowa suddenly dried up; a violent earthquake made the palace of Chosroes the Great tremble, and shattered fourteen of its towers; the Sacred Fire, kept alight for more than a thousand years, went out, in spite of the exertions of its Persian worshippers, and all the idols of the universe were found with their heads bowed down in great shame.

All these portents caused fear in the hearts of those who witnessed them; but, despite the predictions of Al Moudzenab, the Parsee sorcerer, who had been warned in a dream that a great upheaval in the destiny of the universe would be caused by an event to take place in Arabia, the occurrence was unperceived: the birth of a child of the Quraish tribe at Makkah, a tiny town lost in the midst of the wilderness, unknown to the gorgeous monarchs of East and West alike, or else despised by them.

فَإِذَا قَضَيْتُمُ الصَّلٰوةَ فَاذْكُرُوا
اللّٰهَ قِيَامًا وَقُعُودًا وَعَلَىٰ جُنُوبِكُمْ

CHAPTER TWO — *Decorative plate.*

ألم نشرح لك صدرك ووضعنا عنك وزرك

CHAPTER THE SECOND

THE BIRTH OF MOHAMMAD

Our Lord Mohammad (May Allah shower His Blessings upon Him and grant Him Salvation!) was born a few seconds before the rising of the Morning Star, on a Monday, the twelfth day of the month Rabi-ul-Awwal of the first year of the Era of the Elephant. (August 29th A.D. 570).

When he came into the world, he was devoid of all pollution, circumcised naturally, and the umbilical cord had been cut by the hand of the angel Jibra'il.

The atmosphere of the city being fatal to infants, the leading citizens were in the habit of confiding their children to Bedouin wet-nurses who brought them up in their Badyaland, where dwelt the Bedouin, or nomads. Shortly after the birth of Mohammad, about a dozen women belonging to the tribe of the Bani Sad, all bronzed by the bracing breezes of their country, arrived at Makkah, to seek nurslings. Upon one of them devolved the honour of suckling the Prophet of Allah. And she was Halimah, signifying "The Gentle".

MOHAMMAD'S CHILDHOOD WITH THE BANI SAD TRIBE IN THEIR BADYA LAND

Quoth Halimah bint Zuib: "It was a barren year, and both my husband, Haris bin Abdul Ozza and myself, were plunged in dire distress. We made up our minds to go to Makkah where I proposed to seek a foster-child whose grateful parents would help us out of our miserable plight. We joined a caravan where there were many women of our tribe, bound likewise on the same errand.

The she-ass I was riding was so thin and exhausted by privation that she came nigh upon breaking down on the road and we did not get a wink of sleep all night by reason of our poor child being tortured by the pangs of hunger. Neither in my breasts, nor in the udder of a female camel driven by my husband, did there remain one drop of milk to relieve my baby's pain.

All sleepless as I was, I fell a prey to despair. In my parlous state, could I hope to take charge of a suckling?

Lagging far behind the caravan, we arrived in Makkah at last, but all the new-born babies had already been allotted to the other women, except one child and that was Mohammad.

His father being dead and his family far from rich, despite the high rank it held in Makkah, none of the wet-nurses cared to take charge of the baby boy.

We likewise turned away from him at first, but I was full of shame at thinking I should have to journey back empty-handed, for I feared the mockery of my friends luckier than I. Besides, my feelings were deeply stirred when I gazed upon that fine infant, bound to wither away in the unwholesome air of the town.

My heart became filled with compassion; I felt my milk welling up miraculously in my breasts, so I said to my husband: 'I swear by Allah that I have a good mind to adopt that orphan boy, notwithstanding that we have but slight hopes of ever earning anything worth talking about by so doing.'—'I cannot say thou art wrong,' he replied. 'Perhaps with him, the blessing of Allah may once more favour our tent.'

Scarcely listening, I could no longer restrain myself and rushed towards the handsome baby fast asleep. I placed my hand on its pretty little breast; he smiled and opened his eyes sparkling with light. I kissed his brow between them. Holding him tightly in my embrace, I made my way back to where our caravan was encamped. Once there, I offered him my right breast so that he should enjoy such nourishment as Allah chose to grant him. To my extreme astonishment, he found enough milk to satisfy his hunger. I proffered my left breast, but he refused it, leaving it to his foster-brother and he always behaved in like fashion.

A greater marvel still was when from our she-camel's teats, dried-up that morning, my husband drew enough milk to appease the hunger that gnawed my entrails, and for the first time for many a month, the shades of night brought us refreshing sleep. 'By Allah, O Halimah!' exclaimed my husband, next day, on awaking, 'thou hast adopted a child that is verily blessed!'

With the little boy, I mounted my she-ass who started off at a rapid pace. She was not long in coming up with my surprised companions and even trotted in front of them. Thereupon they cried out: 'O Halimah! pull up thy ass, in order that we may journey home all together. Is that the same animal you bestrode when we departed?'—'Aye, tis she and no other.'—'Then she is under some spell that we cannot unravel!'

We reached our tents of the Bani Sad. I know no more arid soil than ours and our flocks had been mowed down by famine. But we marvelled at finding them in more thriving condition than during the most prosperous seasons, and the swollen teats of our ewes yielded more milk than we knew what to do with.

Our neighbours' flocks, on the contrary, were in a grievous state and their masters threw the blame on their shepherds. 'Woe to ye all, stupid serving-men!' cried the sheep-owners. 'Lead our lambs to graze with those of Halimah!'

The men obeyed, but all in vain: the sweet grass that seemed to spring up out of the earth offering its tender sprigs to our sheep, withered immediately they were gone on their way.

Prosperity and blessings remained in our tent unceasingly. Mohammad attained his second year and it was then I weaned him. His disposition was truly uncommon. At the age of nine months, he talked in a charming way with accents that touched all hearts. He was never dirty; nor did he ever sob or scream, except peradventure when his nakedness chanced to be seen. If he was uneasy at nights and refused to close his eyes, I would bring him out of the tent, when he would fix his gaze immediately with admiration on the stars. He showed great joy, and when his glances were sated with the sight, he let his eyelids droop and allowed slumber to claim him.

But when he was weaned, Halimah was obliged to take Mohammad back to his mother who was eager to have him with her. What grief therefore for the poor wet-nurse! She could not resign herself to such cruel separation. As soon as she got to Makkah, she threw herself at Aminah's feet and burst out supplicating as she kissed them. 'See how the bracing air of the Badya hath profited thy child. Think that those breezes will do him still greater good now that he is beginning to walk. Fear the pestilential air of the city! Thou wouldst see him waste away before thine eyes and remember my words when it was too late'.

Moved by these touching prayers and thinking only of her son's health, Aminah stifled her motherly feelings and finished by consenting to let Halimah take Mohammad back to the Badya. His good-hearted nurse, buckling him securely to her loins, went off, overjoyed, on the road leading to her encampment.

Home again at the Badya of the Bani Sad, Mohammad's first footsteps were printed on the ripple-marked carpet of the immaculate sands, where he inhaled with welcome nostrils the sweet odours of the aromatic plants growing on the hillocks. And there it was he slept under the dark blue tent of the star-studded sky and his chest expanded, breathing the limpid air of desert nights. He grew strong thanks to the healthy, wholesome food of the nomads: milk and cheese, with unleavened bread baked under hot ashes and, now and again, camel's flesh or mutton, devoid of the sickening smell of wool-grease that comes from animals bred in confined stabling.

Such moral and physical well-being, that he owed the Badya, was of great help to him, during ordeals later in life. He was always pleased to refer to his childhood's days. 'Allah granted me two inestimable favours,' he would often say. 'First came the privilege of being born in the most noble of all the Arab tribes, the Quraish; secondly, that of being brought up in the Bani Sad region, the most salubrious of the entire Hijaz.'

Never were there effaced from his mind those pictures of the desert which were impressed on his earliest glances when, in company with other nomadic lads, he would climb to the top of a rock to watch over a grazing flock.

Notwithstanding, being inclined to dream and meditate, he did not agree very well with the turbulence and high spirits of the little Bedouins of his own age, and preferred to hide away from them, and ramble in solitude not too far from the tents.

MOHAMMAD AND THE TWO ANGELS

He went out, one morning, with his foster-brother leading the flocks of his foster-father to the pasturage.

All of a sudden, about the middle of the day, Mohammad's young companion went back alone. 'Come hither quickly!' he shouted to his father and mother, his voice hoarse with affright. 'My brother, the Quraish, having slipped away from us, according to his wont, two men, clothed all in white, seized hold of him on the ground and split his chest open.'

In mad fear, poor Halimah, followed by her husband, ran as fast as her legs would carry her, following the road pointed out by the youthful shepherd. Mohammad was found seated on the top of a hill. He was perfectly calm, but his face had taken on the sinister tint of the dust and ashes to which we must all return. They fondled him gently and put question after question to him. 'What ails thee, O child of ours? What hath befell thee?'—'While I was intent upon looking after the grazing sheep,' he replied, 'I saw two white forms appear. At first, I took them to be two great birds, but as they drew nearer, I saw my mistake: they were two men clad in tunics of dazzling whiteness.'—'Is that the boy?' said one of them to his companion, pointing to me. 'Yea! Tis he!' 'As I stood stupefied with fear, they seized me; threw me down and cut my breast open. They drew out of my heart a black clot of blood which they cast far away; and then closing up my chest, they disappeared like phantoms.'

The words of Allah, in the Qur'an, seem to allude to this incident: "*Have we not opened thy breast for thee? And taken off from thee thy burden. Which galled thy back?*" (the Qur'an, xciv. 1, 2, 3).

This story, together with many others to be met with in the pages of this work, must be taken to be a parable, which, in their case, signifies that Allah opened Mohammad's breast when quite young, so that the joy of monotheistic truth should penetrate therein and permeate his being, relieving him of the heavy burden of idol-worship.

Mohammad's foster-parents continued to live in a state of bewilderment and Haris said to his wife: 'I fear the boy is a prey to falling sickness, evidently due to spells cast by neighbours, jealous of the prosperity and the Blessing that the child hath brought into our tent. But whether possessed by the Evil One who conjured up this hallucination; or because, on the contrary, the boy's vision is a true one and pointeth to a glorious future, our responsibility is none the less heavy. Let us give him back to his family, before his disease becometh more violent.'

Halimah was regretfully obliged to agree with such wise arguments and, taking Mohammad with her, she turned in the direction of Makkah.

The boy, now four years of age, walked by her side, and, on the outskirts of the town, they found themselves in the midst of a great crowd wending their way to the market or the Temple pilgrimage. Night had come on. Hustled in the dense throng, Halimah was soon separated from her foster-son and was unable to find him in the dark, despite her active search and desperate shouts. Without losing time, she hurried to apprise Abdul Muttalib, whose high social position made it easy for him to send out clever men on the track of his grandson, while he rode on horseback to head the searchers.

In the Tihamamh water-course, one of the trackers soon found a child seated among some shrubs. He was amusing himself by pulling the branches. 'Who art thou, child?' he was asked. 'I am Mohammad' son of Abdullah bin Abdul Muttalib.'

Well pleased at having found the boy he was looking for, the man lifted up the child and carried him to the arms of his grandfather following behind. Abdul Muttalib embraced Mohammad affectionately, sat him on the pommel of his saddle in front of him and brought him back to Makkah. To show his joy, the old man slaughtered some sheep and distributed their flesh to the poor of the city. Then, taking his grandson astride on his shoulder, he performed the ritual circuits round the Ka'bah in token of gratitude.

Accompanied by poor Hamilah, now recovered from her anguish, he led Mohammad into the presence of Aminah, his mother. After she had given way to the effusive joy of a loving mother, she turned to Halimah: 'What doth this signify? O nurse, thou wast so desirous of keeping my son by thy side, and now thou dost bring him back to me, all of a sudden?'—'I considered that he had reached an age when I could do no more for him than I have done; and fearing unlucky accidents, I bring him back to thee, knowing how thou wert longing to set eyes on him again.'

Nevertheless, perplexity and sadness were only too clearly to be read on the kind nurse's features. Not being deceived by her explanations, Aminah continued: 'Thou dost hide from me the true motive of thy return. I wait to hear thee tell the whole truth.'

Halimah then thought it best to repeat what her husband had said, and Aminah's maternal pride was sorely wounded. 'Can it be that thou art afraid lest my son should fall a victim to the devil?' she quickly retorted.—'I confess that such is my fear.'—'Know then that the demon's wiles are powerless to do him harm, for a glorious destiny is in store for him.' Aminah made the nurse acquainted with the marvellous events that had happened during her pregnancy and lying-in. After having thanked and rewarded Halimah for her devotion, Aminah kept her child with her, and his health, fortified by life in the open air, had now nothing to fear from unhealthy conditions of town life.

Under the vigilant eyes of the most loving of mothers, Mohammad grew up handsome and intelligent; but he was not fated to long enjoy maternal affection which no other love can equal. On returning from a journey to Yasrib, whither she had taken him, Aminah died suddently, halfway on the road, in the straggling village of Al-Abwa, where she was buried.

AMINAH'S DEATH
(A.D. 576)

The sorrowing orphan boy, scarce seven years of age, was brought back to Makkah by a black slave-girl, Umm Aiman, entirely devoted to her young master and who, including five camels, constituted his sole inheritance.

He was taken in hand by his grandfather, Abdul Muttalib, who had always shown him great affection, and the old man's love increased daily, as he saw the lad growing up more and more like Abdullah, his father, so much regretted.

The following anecdote gives an idea of Abdul Muttalib's boundless affection for his grandson: in Makkah, where the streets are narrow and crooked like those of all the towns of the desert, there is only one open space of any size—the square in which stands the Ka'bah, and where, morning and evening, the citizens gathered together, resting and gossiping about their business as well as performing their devotions. Not a day passed without the servants of Abdul Muttalib throwing down a carpet in the Temple's shade; and round the rug sat his sons, grandsons and the leading townsmen, awaiting his coming. The respect shown to the Superintendent of "The House of Allah" was so great, that never did anyone ever dare to put his foot even on the outer edge of his carpet.

It came to pass one day that young Mohammad took up a position right in the middle of the revered carpet, scandalising in the highest degree his uncles who drove him away immediately. But Abdul Muttalib was coming and he had witnessed the conflict from afar. 'Let my grandson go back at once to where he was seated!' he called out. 'He is the delight of my old age and his great audacity ariseth from the presentiment he hath of his destiny, for he shall occupy higher rank than any Arab hath ever attained.'

So saying, he made Mohammad sit by his side and fondled his cheeks and his shoulders, while in ecstasies at the least thing the boy said or did.

Again the fates decreed that Mohammad should be deprived of gentle love: Abdul Muttalib died at the age of ninety-five, unanimously regretted by his fellow-citizens.

The unlucky orphan boy was received into the house of his uncle Abu Talib, who had been chosen for this kind succour by his grandsire, for the reason that, alone among his uncles, he was the brother of both the mother and father of Abdullah, Mohammad's father.

Having a large family and not being very well off, although the management of the Ka'bah had been bequeathed to him, Abu Talib was obliged to do business with the lands of Yaman and Syria.

Shortly after sheltering his newphew under his roof, he undertook the task of organising a caravan of Quraish men, and he was to lead them back to their tents.

MOHAMMAD'S FIRST JOURNEY IN SYRIA
(A.D. 582)

All was in readiness; the loads were shared and divided, corded and balanced on the pack-saddles of the kneeling camels, grunting according to their habit. Their drives began, by dint of blows and shouts, to force them to rise to their feet and direct their swaying stride in a northerly direction. This sight caused Mohammad to remember his beloved Badya, where caravans resembling this one about to depart passed to and fro continually. Fresh separation, this time from his beloved uncle, was about to plunge him into the sadness of solitude. He stood still, gloomy and silent. At last, heartbroken, he threw himself into Abu Talib's embrace, casting his young arms round him, and hiding his face in the folds of his uncle's mantle, to conceal his tears brought on by longing and despair.

SCENES FROM THE BADIA OR NOMADIC LIFE. *Camel keepers in the pastures.*

Greatly moved by this spontaneous manifestation of affection, and guessing how ardent was his nephew's wish to accompany him, Abu Talib declared: 'By Allah! we'll take him with us; he'll not leave me and I'll not leave him.'

Mohammad dried his tears and, joyfully, he busied himself in hastening the final preparations for the journey. At a sign from his uncle, he perched himself on the female camel, getting up behind him.

When the caravan began to pass along the tracks made by the Bedouin tribes, Mohammad's lungs, contracted by breathing the vitiated air of houses and streets, were deliciously dilated, revelling in liberally gulping down the life-giving air of the Badya to which he was accustomed. Being used to a nomadic existence from childhood, the young traveller was able to support most valiantly the exhausting privations and terrible fatigue of such an interminable journey in the midst of the Hijaz deserts.

For more than a year, the countries he passed through were so much alike in their sands and rocks, that the caravan seemed as if marking time. In the pitiless desert there was no other sign of life, except the presence of Him who is everywhere, eternally existent, but not to be seen by mortal eyes.

HOW MOHAMMAD MET THE MONK BAHIRA

On the terrace-roof of a convent, perched like a turban on a tall man's head, on the top of a steep hill, the lesser chain of the Jabal Hauran, the most learned monk, Bahira, looked out afar over the Syrian plains, stretching away in infinite space in the direction of Arabia. All of a sudden, his attention was drawn to the strange aspect of a solitary cloud, white and oblong, that stood out in bold relief on the immaculate blue background of the sky. Like some enormous bird, the cloud hovered above a small caravan winding its way northwards. The fleecy mass in the heavens covered the straggling procession with its azure shade and moved with the line of travellers.

At the foot of the hill on which the monastery was built, the caravan halted, close to a great tree that grew on the brink of a dried-up wadi, and began to organise the encampment. At that moment, the cloud stopped still and vanished in the celestial canopy, while the branches of the tree were bent, as if beneath the gusts of a breeze acting on those twigs and leaves, at the same time throwing their shade over one of the caravaneers, as if to protect him from the blazing rays of the sun. Seeing these prodigies, Bahira guessed that among these wayfarers coming from the Hijaz, would be found the man he had been awaiting so long: the Prophet (Peace be on him) announced by the Sacred Books. So Bahira hurried down from the flat roof, gave orders to prepare a bountiful meal and sent a messenger to invite all the folks of the caravan without exception, young or old, nobles or slaves.

The messenger returned, in company with the men of Makkah whose coming Bahira awaited on the threshold of his monastery. 'By Lat and Uzza! thy conduct doth puzzle me, O Bahira!' exclaimed one of the guests. 'Many a time and oft have we passed by the convent; yet, until now thou hast never heeded us; never didst thou dream of showing us the least sign of hospitality. What maggot biteth thee this day?'—'Thou dost not err,' replied Bahira. 'I have cogent reasons for behaving as I do. But ye are my guests at this hour and I pray that ye honour me by gathering together to partake of the repast that I have prepared for you all.'

While the people he had invited were enjoying the food with the appetites of men having recently been sorely deprived, Bahira scrutinised them all in turn, trying to find the one answering the description given in his Books. Much to his disappointment, he did not succeed. There was no one to be seen whose appearance agreed with the description. But as he had just witnessed marvels that could not be explained, otherwise than by the reason that one of Allah's elect was surely present, he refused to be discouraged. 'O men of the Quraish tribe!' he asked; 'is there not one of you remaining in your tents?'—'Aye, one only,' was the reply. 'We left him alone at rest on account of his extreme youth.'—'Why did ye not being him hither? Go, call him at once, so that he shareth the meal in your company.'—'By Lat and Uzza!' swore one of the guests; 'we give you right. Of a surety we are to blame for having left one of us behind, while we profit by thine invitation, especially as he is a son of Abdullah bin Abdul Mattalib.'

Rising, he went and fetched Mohammad and brought him into the midst of the group of guests. Bahira eyed the newcomer with great attention and when the men had done eating and drinking, the monk went to him, taking him on one side. 'O young man!' said the monk, 'I have a question to ask. By Lat and Uzza, wilt thou consent to answer?'

Bahira desired to put him to the test by invoking the idols Lat and Uzza, exactly as he had just heard his guests swearing, but Mohammad replied thus: 'Put no question to me in the name of Lat and Uzza, for there is nothing on this earth that I hate more than them.'—'Well then, by Allah! wilt thou answer me?'—'Question me and, by Allah! I'll answer thee!'

Thereupon Bahira interrogated him on everything that was of interest, such as his family, his position in life, his dreams that, now and again, disturbed his slumbers, and many other things. Finally, just as the youth, after having taken leave of the saintly scholar, turned to go away, the collar of his tunic yawned slightly and Bahira caught sight of the "Seal of Prophecy," imprinted on the lad's back, below the nape of the neck, on the exact spot indicated by the Sacred Texts. Bahira's last doubts vanished—here, indeed, standing in his presence, was the prophet (Peace be on him) whose advent had been foretold. Therefore, the monk went up to Abu Talib and spoke to him, saying: 'What relation is this lad to thee?'—'He is my son.'—'No! He is no son of thine!'—'True enough! He is not my son, but that of my brother.'—'What hath become of thy brother?'—'He died while his wife was still pregnant with my nephew.'—'Thou dost speak the truth. Mark then my words: lose no time in returning to thy country with thy brother's son and watch over him with constant vigilance. Above all, beware of Jews! If they saw him and learnt what I have just learnt about him, by Allah! they would do him harm, for this son of thy brother is chosen to play a great part in the world!'

Abu Talib, much impressed by the warnings of a man whose scientific reputation was universally recognised, made haste to finish his business at Busra in Syria, and started back home to Makkah with his nephew, where they arrived safe and sound.

Protected by Allah and guided by his uncle, who watched over him with true paternal care, Mohammad grew up and became an accomplished young man. He was extremely chaste. Abu Talib being busily engaged in executing some repairs in the Zamzam well, several Quraish striplings, among them being Mohammad, fetched and carried big stones fitted to the work. So as to be more at their ease, they lifted up their *izars* (a kind of tunic) in front, passing them over their head and rolling them round their neck, thus protected from the sharp edges of the stones carried on the shoulders; and all this was done without troubling about the fact that they were showing their nakedness. Mohammad was obliged to imitate them; but so soon as he felt his nakedness exposed to every eye, he was seized with a fit of atrocious anguish; great drops of sweat stood out on his brow; a shudder of shame shook his entire frame and he fainted away.

THE SECOND SYRIAN VOYAGE *(A.D. 594)*

Such innate modesty, and the protection granted by Allah to his Elect, safeguarded the young man from the excesses in which lads often fall at the period of puberty. Among all the youths of the same age, he was the best-looking; the most generous; the most easygoing; the most truth-telling; the most

The Night of the "Mouled", the anniversary of the Birth of the Prophet, Muslims leaving a village Mosque.

devoted friend; and the most devoid of debauchery, to such an extent that his fellow-citizens called him "Al-Amin," which means: "The Reliable Man."

Like Abu Talib, most of the men of Makkah were obliged, to eke out a living, to traffic with Syria and the Yaman.

Their town, situated in one of the most frightfully barren countries of the world, offered no resources and its citizens only made both ends meet by dint of trading with these two countries between which it served as a link.

Its caravans crawled to the Yaman to procure raw materials from that region, known as Arabia Felix; and also products brought from overseas, imported from Ethiopia, India and even far China. The camels came laden with fragrant spices, sweet-smelling incense, ivory, gold dust, silks and many other articles of luxury. Arriving in the Hijaz, they added dates from Yasrib or Taif. Then they wended their way into Syria, to exchange these goods for agricultural produce, such as grain, wheat, barley, rice, figs and raisins, as well as for imports of Greek and Roman civilization.

Even women carried on this kind of trade, confiding their goods to those who organised caravans. These female traffickers sold the merchandise in return for a share of the profits.

Khadijah bint Khuaild, a rich and noble widow, at the head of a thriving enterprise of this kind, hearing that everybody was unanimous in extolling Mohammad's well-merited reputation for prudence and probity, thought it would be well to entrust him with the direction of her commerce. She sent for him and, as a beginning, proposed that he should take charge of a caravan she was despatching to Syria and offered a salary twice as large as she was generally in the habit of paying.

Mohammad accepted; but Abu Talib, calling to mind what the monk Bahira had told him, grew uneasy when the camels were ready to start. He spoke privately to each of the caravaneers, urging them to watch over his nephew, and making them responsible for any harm that might come to him. It was with Maisarah, a slave, Khadijah's right-hand man, that Abu Talib was most solemn in his warnings. About to travel with Mohammad, Maisarah, a good servant, simple-minded and devoted, already greatly impressed by the confidential observations of such a prominent citizen as Abu Talib, fell under the sway of the charm and influence exercised by his young master over all who approached him. Maisarah felt great liking and boundless admiration for Mohammad.

In every incident of the journey, Maisarah noted miraculous tokens, proving the superhuman disposition of the man he served, and indeed, certain events showed that the slave guessed aright. The road he had so often travelled, knowing all its fatigue and danger; the interminable tracks where the inexorable orb of day dried up the water-skins and gave the mortals who went that way a foretaste of the flames of Jahannam; the paths, marked out by the bones of men and animals that had succumbed to pitiless thirst, were passed as easily as if they been enchanted.

Every day, at the hour when the sun, rising high over the heads of the travellers, threatened them with its deadly, blazing rays, light clouds, like the feathers of a bird, floated in the azure sky. They increased and met; then they were stretched out in long lines resembling the beam-feathers of enormous wings, opened to protect Mohammad beneath their shade. When the sun, losing its formidable power, began to sink gradually below the horizon, the feathers of these clouds dropped away one by one, vanishing in the last golden rays that the incandescent orb threw out through space before disappearing. The protecting wings, now useless, closed, making room for the stars which sparkle nowhere in the world so brilliantly as over deserts. Even the camels seemed overjoyed; they doubled the stride of their great long legs and the path seems to fold itself backwards as they advance. No dead body of any of them was added to the sinister skeletons left behind by previous caravans.

CHAPTER THE SECOND

Once only during the whole journey, a couple of Khadijah's camels showed signs of exhaustion and lagged behind the convoy. Despite the insults and blows showered on them, Maisarah failed to bring them in line with the others. The two wretched beasts were completely bathed in sweat, a certain sign that they would soon fall, never to rise again. Maisarah, devoted to his mistress's interests, was extremely perplexed. He did not want to forsake his tired camels; but on the other hand, he had not forgotten Abu Talib's pressing recommendations concerning the young man then leading the caravan, so the slave ran to apprise him of what was taking place.

Mohammad halted and came back with Maisarah to see the pair of camels who were lying down, uttering painful, pitiful groans each time an effort was made to make them get up. He leant over them and, with his blessed hands, touched their feet hacked by the sharp pebbles of the Hammadah, and the poor beasts that had not even stirred under the lash, suddenly rose to their feet and with enormous strides, grunting joyously caught up with the leaders of the caravan.

Good luck lasted when the caravan reached Busra, in Syria. Mohammad sold out all the goods he brought with unexpected profit, and found, at extraordinarily advantageous rates, what he had come to get, without even having to undergo the horrors of never-ending haggling, according to Oriental custom.

He awakened the sympathy and interest of everyone by his winning ways, frankness and honesty; but above all, by that mysterious radiance emanating from Predestinated Beings; which the old masters interpreted by a golden aureola, called magnetism by the scientists of the present day, because they lack the power of explaining its nature.

In this region, where enthusiasm for questions of religion ran high; where every hill is topped by a monastery and where every stone calls up the remembrance of a Prophet, (Peace be on him) this young traveller, before whom Nature itself seemed to bow down, excited in the highest degree the curiosity of all these monks. They were renowned for researches in sacred texts and lived in hopes of the coming of a new Apostle of Allah. All flocked to put questions to Maisarah, known to many among them during previous journeys. They soon divined that he was Mohammad's confidential slave; and a Nestorian monk, named Jordis, predicted great things to the devoted serving-man, making the same kind of recommendations as Bahira had made to Abu Talib.

All transactions being terminated, the caravan turned homewards, and immediately the mysterious cloud, that seemed to be awaiting the travellers, took its place over Mohammad's head and never ceased to accompany him until the journey's end. On the outskirts of Makkah, at the spot called Bathen Mou, Maisarah prevailed on Mohammad to go on ahead of the convoy, so as to carry to Khadijah, without the least delay, the good news of their return.

The widow was in the habit of going up with her servants to the top of her house whence she could see the road to Syria, dipping, in a north easterly direction, into the ravine overlooked by the Jabal Quayqwan. She certainly felt no anxiety concerning her goods, but without confessing as much to herself as yet, she was fearful lest anything harmful should happen to the man to whom she had confided them; young Mohammad who, by his noble bearing and upright disposition, had so deeply impressed her that his absence weighed her down. It seemed to be never-ending.

One day, among all these weary weeks of waiting, when the sun at its zenith was setting the town in a blaze, preventing the inhabitants from stirring out in the streets, Khadijah lingered at her usual observatory. Her beautiful eyes, their lids scorched by dint of staring searchingly into the depths of the white-hot horizon, had just reluctantly closed, in despair at not seeing the caravan so impatiently desired . . . All of a sudden, the house became filled with delicious cool air, while the blinding reverberation of sunlight on the white terraces and calcined rocks was softened by a gauzy veil of sheltering violet shade . . . Just then, the door opened and Mohammad entered Khadijah's dwelling.

Doing his duty like a scrupulous manager, he turned in all the accounts of his expedition, and enumerated the magnificent results thereof. She thanked and complimented him warmly, but without being very much astonished at his success, for she began to think he was predestinated.

The coincidence of his arrival with that of the cloud which granted such beneficent shade had not failed to strike her, and she divined the obvious connection of the circumstances. 'Where is Maisarah?' quoth she. 'With the caravan over which he watches.' 'Go back at once and fetch him; increase the camels' speed, for great is my haste to admire the riches thou dost bring me.'

Mohammad heard and obeyed; and the cloud flying away from the house, followed and accompanied him on the Syrian road. Henceforward, Khadijah's doubts were dispelled, and her faithful slave Maisarah, who soon arrived, confirmed her opinion. 'The cloud thou didst remark,' he told her, 'accompanied us unceasingly from the day we left Makkah until we returned. Ever since we went out of Busra, and enlightened by the predictions of the learned monks of the Hauran; I am forced to acknowledge that it was formed by the wings of two angels whose mission was to protect my master from the sun's ardent rays.'

He then narrated all those incidents of the journey in which he could make out miraculous tokens and Khadijah never grew tired of questioning him.

MARRIAGE OF MOHAMMAD AND KHADIJAH *(A.D. 595)*

This noble, generous woman rewarded Mohammad by giving him double the salary she had promised and thenceforward had but one idea: to get him to take care of her entire wealth. The best way was to marry him, and the dictates of her heart urged her to carry out her plan. There was but one objection: the difference in their ages. Mohammad had only just attained his twenty-fifth year, while she was close upon forty. Nevertheless, Khadijah's age did not prevent her from being the most marriageable lady in all the town, not, as might be rightly thought, on account of her riches (according to Arab customs, the husband brings the dowry and has no right to his wife's property), but because of her personal qualities, charming ways, distinguished manners, chastity and aristocratic descent, Khadijah being the daughter of Khuaild bin Asad, bin Abdul Ozza, bin Qusaiy, bin Kilab, bin Morra, bin Kab, bin Lawaiy, bin Ghalib . . .

She was therefore the queen of a court of suitors trying to dazzle her, some by the purity of their pedigrees; others by the extent of their riches. But all in vain. Since the death of her second husband, Abu Hala, it seemed as if she had made up her mind to end her days without contracting a third alliance. When she met Mohammad and began to appreciate his moral qualities, all her resolutions soon weakened and the feelings that drew her towards him increased each day in intensity. She determined to sound him.

Maisarah has said: "Two months and twenty days after our return from Syria, my mistress sent me to my master and I questioned him thus: 'O Mohammad! hast thou any reason for remaining a bachelor?'—'My hands are empty. I do not possess the wherewithal to furnish the dowry of a betrothed bride.'—'But if the small amount thou hast should be considered enough by a rich, worthy and noble lady—what then?'—'To whom dost thou allude?'—'I mean Khadijah!''Why joke with me? How, with the trifle I could offer as a dowry, should I dare to seek her presence and offer her in marriage?'—'Rest easy on that score. I'll see to it.' My master's accounts and looks sufficed for me to become aware of his feelings towards my mistress. Without further delay, I sought her out and told her what I thought. Beaming with joy, she made all her arrangements for speedy nuptials."

CHAPTER THE SECOND

At first, Khadijah had to obtain the consent of Khuaild, her father, who so far had inexorably repulsed all suitors, as he never found any rich or noble enough for his daughter. To gain her ends, she resorted to trickery.

Coached by her, Mohammad made arrangements for a big feast, inviting his uncles, Khuaild and a group of Quraish tribesmen of the highest rank. Khuaild's weak point was a love of fermented beverages and, as was his wont, he drank a little more than was reasonable. His daughter seized the opportunity to speak to him thus: 'O my father? Mohammad ben Abdullah asks me to marry him and I beg thee to bring about our union.'

Khuaild, giddy with the fumes of wine, and seeing everything tinted with a rosy hue, gave his consent without reflecting, and Khadijah, immediately, following the custom prevailing at that epoch, bedewed her betrothed with perfumes and threw a sumptuous mantle over his shoulders.

Khuaild woke up out of his fit of drunkenness and interrogated his daughter: 'What doth all this signify?'—'Thou knowest full well, O my father! Thou hast just settled my betrothal with Mohammad, son of Abdullah.'—'Could I have done this thing: marry thee to the orphan adopted by Abu Talib? Ah no! Never will I consent while I live!'—'Dost desire then to dishonour thyself in the eyes of the Quraish chiefs here this day, by confessing thou wert drunk just now?'

She continued in this strain, until at last Khuaild, finding nothing to say in response, was obliged to give his definite consent. Thereupon Abu Talib made the following speech: 'Praise be to Allah who created us, the Bani Hashem, descendants of Ibrahim (Abraham) and of the seed of Ishmael, who did appoint us to be custodians of His House, the Holy Ka'bah, and Administrators of His Sacred Territory; and who made us as Lords over the Arabs. Here before ye standeth my brother's son, Mohammad bin Abdullah; no man can be weighed in the balance with him, for he is far above all others as regards nobility, merit, generosity and wisdom. If he be not favoured by fortune, remember that wealth is naught else than a passing, inconstant shadow; a loan to be repaid eventually. Now the soul of Mohammad bin Abdullah leaneth towards the noble dame Khadijah, whose soul also leaneth towards him; and he doth beg at this hour that thou, O Khuaild! in thy generosity, should give her to him to be his wife. As dowry, he bringeth twenty young female camels, and I call upon ye to be my witness, O my Quraish brethren!'

The marriage took place, and so as to celebrate it duly Khadijah had her young and graceful slaves to dance to the sound of tabors, before the company assembled; all unanimously overjoyed at this alliance between two such noble families.

Khadijah was Mohammad's first wife. She never had a rival in her husband's heart, and, until the day of her death, she was his sole, beloved spouse. She gave him seven children; three sons: al-Qasim, at-Tahir and four daughters: Ruqaiyah, Fatimah, Zainab and Ummu Kulsum.

After the birth of Al-Qasim, the eldest boy, a familiar surname, "Abul Qasim," that is to say, the Father of Qasim, was bestowed on Mohammad, full of joy at the coming of a scion of his house. Unfortunately, the poor child, greatly cherished by his father, was destined to die in infancy. The same fate overtook his brothers, at-Tahir and at-Taiyib, who passed away in like fashion in "The Days of Ignorance." Only Mohammad's daughters witnessed the advent of Islam and were counted among its first and most faithful servants.

WHEN THE TEMPLE OF THE KA'BAH WAS REBUILT *(A.D. 605)*

After partial destruction by fire, the Ka'bah had been badly restored. The roof fell in, and thieves took

E. DINET

The herds.

advantage of the breach to get into the Sanctuary and carry off part of the treasure, constituted by pilgrims' offerings.

Fresh repairs were urgently needed; but as bad luck would have it, the walls were so dilapidated that they could no longer bear the least weight. There was nothing to be done but to raze them to the ground. If, however, the idea of rebuilding such a revered monument met with no objection, its demolition seemed to be the most dangerous sacrilege imaginable.

After much hesitation, finally dispelled by a series of obvious miracles, the Quraish men came to the resolution of tearing down the old walls of which the remains were in heaps on the ground. Then, as the ancient foundations were formed of blocks of stone admirably fitting one into the other, each clan of the Quraish tribe undertook part of the task of rebuilding.

The workers, actuated by the zeal that always arises from rivality, soon built up the walls to the height at which the famous Black Stone, "al-Hajaru'l-Aswad," should be fixed. Who was to have the honour of putting the precious relic back in its place? There was not the slightest chance of coming to an agreement on this point, and, in consequence of each party pleading the precedence of the purest noble descent or the greatest merit, the discussion grew so heated that the most tragical results were to be feared. Under the influence of jealousy, groups were formed and stood face to face. The Bani Abed-Dar, joining the Bani Adiyy bin Kab, brought forth a bowl filled with blood, plunging their hands therein, and swearing they would die sooner than relinquish the privilege in anyone else's favour, because they thought it devolved upon them by right.

For four days and four nights, the adversaries with threatening mien, remained on the look-out, absorbed in the task of vigilantly watching each other. At last, Abu Ummayh, their senior, spoke out, saying: 'There will come a time when all this must finish and this what I propose: name as umpire, the first man who cometh into our midst, and let him settle the dispute that destroyeth our union.'

The advice given was not displeasing to the stubborn rivals and they finally agreed to follow it. It happened then, at that very moment, that they saw coming towards them a young man about thirty years of age. They recognised him as "Al-Amin" (The Reliable); in other words: Mohammad. Nothing could have been more fortunate, and all being as of one mind on this point, they accepted him as arbitrator at once, submitting the cause of their conflict to his judgement. When they terminated explaining the case, Mohammad, instead of hearkening to their respective claims, only said: 'Bring a mantle and spread it out on the ground.'

When they had obeyed his behest, he took the Black Stone in his hands and placing it in the middle of the cloak, he went on: 'Let the most influential person of each party take hold of the mantle by the corner that is in front of him.' All did as they were told, and then he turned towards those who held the corners of the mantle. 'Now, lift the cloak,' he continued; 'all together, up to the height of the wall which is being built.'

They obeyed and when the lifted cloak was level with the spot where the Black Stone was to be built in, Mohammad took the Relic and with his own hands, put it in its place.

Thanks to his presence of mind, all cause of discord disappeared. He had given satisfaction to each of the rival groups, without favouring one more than the other; and caused the proud Arabs to be reconciled without bloodshed, for the first time in all their history; in short, there was honour due to him which no one contested.

High above the Black Stone, the walls rose rapidly, carried up by the workers toiling as friends. The ribs of a ship wrecked on the Jeddah coast furnished a flat terrace roof, and when the monument was finished, it was entirely draped with a veil of the finest lawn, woven by the Copts.

In later years, the veil consisted of striped Yaman cloth; and still later, the Ka'bah was covered by Hajaj bin Yusef with the "Kiswah," or garment of black silk, such as is still thrown over it at the present day, being renewed yearly.

وَتَزَوَّدُوا فَإِنَّ خَيْرَ الزَّادِ التَّقْوَى

CHAPTER THREE — *Decorative plate.*

إنا أنزلناه في ليلة القدر

CHAPTER THE THIRD

DESERT RETIREMENT

To him they called "Al-Amin," (the Reliable), his fellow-citizens were ready to grant the highest and most coveted honours, with a post of preponderance in their city.

But being of a disposition equally devoid of vanity or ambition, he disdainfully refused to reply to their flattering advances, and his fortuitous intervention in the dispute arising from the rebuilding of the Ka'bah was the only time he was mixed up with public affairs during a period of fifteen years, dating from his wedding-day.

How did he pass his time? Allah had inspired him with the love of solitude, and Mohammad loved more than anything to wander all alone on great empty plains stretching away farther than the eye could reach.

What were the causes of this liking? Doubtless, in the gloomy desert surrounding Makkah, he conjured up over and over again the delightful memories of his childhood, passed in the Badya; but his highly-gifted soul found satisfaction of a more exalted kind. In the first place, he was spared the sight of the moral and religious errors of the Arabs at that period.

The Arabs were, in the highest degree, aristocratic, proud, independent and courageous. Their generosity towards their guests was exemplified in a refined manner that has never been surpassed; and among them, a certain Hatim Tay may be looked upon as the Prince of Generous Hosts.

By their natural gifts of eloquence and poetry, they can bear comparison with the most brilliant orators or magnificent poets of the universe. Their poetry, above all, allowing them to celebrate heroic exploits; and their open-minded generosity by which they were led to sing love's joy and sadness, became, for such hot-blooded men, the object of passionate adoration, marvellously well served by the most enchanting language ever known.

Their public fairs, particularly that held at Okaz, furnished an opportunity for real poetical contests, where the winner heard his poem applauded by a madly delighted throng, and then it was written out fully in letters of gold, and hung up in the Temple of the Ka'bah. Of these poetical triumphs, called "Al-Muaalaquate", ("The Suspended"), seven have been handed down to us and prove what great heights were attained by the genius of the Bedouin primitive poets.

But, at the same time as we admire such brilliant qualities innate in the Arabs, we have to deplore great errors. The monotheistic religion of their great ancestors Ibrahim (Abraham) was entirely forgotten, despite their continued veneration of the Temple built with their own hands. They had become Mushrikun, "Mushrikun", ("Associates"). To Allah, the Only One, partners were adjoined in the shape of idols, who were generally preferred. Every tribe and family possessed a favourite idol; and, at that epoch three hundred and sixty false gods, of wood or stone dishonoured the Holy Ka'bah.

The most gross superstition flourished in addition to idolatory. Games of chance, divining by arrows, drunkenness and sorcery debased the brains of these men, all otherwise remarkably gifted. Fretting under all restraint, lacking all ideas of decency, they married as many women as they could afford to feed; and as widows were considered to belong to their husbands' estate, revolting unions took place between step-mothers and step-sons.

Still more abominable was the custom of the "Wadul-Binat", (Burying Girls Alive). By some strange morbid decay of the feeling of honour, and also through fear that the debauchery of daughters or their capture by an enemy might one day bring opprobrium on their families, many unnatural fathers preferred to get rid of their female offspring, by burying them alive as soon as they were born.

To sum up: the Arabs' leaning towards ostentation, their aristocratic prejudice and overweening pride caused them to rebel against all discipline or authority. Consequently, union and progress becoming impossible, incessant warfare and pitiless vendettas between tribes and families submerged all Arabia in a sea of blood.

Such were the errors that saddened Mohammad. He could no longer bring himself to look upon them, and as he saw no cure for such deep-rooted and general evil, which he thought was infallibly destined to draw down on his people the terrible punishment of Heaven, such as annihilated the inhabitants of Thamud and Ad, he hid himself away in the most deserted spots he could find. Far from the contact of human beings, he was able to drive out of his memory the odious remembrance of their iniquity.

It was then that he gave way entirely to the imperious need of meditation and religious worship that mastered his soul. He wandered in sandy ravines, following capricious meandering watercourses, or climbing up the steep sides of rocky mountains, to recline at their summits and let his glance and imagination be lost in the depths of the arid expanse that stretched away at his feet as far as the most unattainable horizon.

During many long hours, stock-still in the midst of such impressive empty space; in this ocean of light where deathly silence reigned, he would be engrossed in mute and ecstatic contemplation of the sight-incomparably grand and varied-offered to him by the elements of heaven and earth obeying a mysterious, unknown, inconceivable, universal and unique Power. . .

He gazed on dunes and rocks, veiled at first by the dawn's rosy gauze, studded with humble pebbles that became sparkling precious stones when the early rays of the sun broke forth. Next came the shroud of dazzling light which the orb of day, at its zenith, spread over the tired earth that was as still as a corpse. Then followed a golden flood that the sun, as it declined, let loose in great waves all over the world, as if wishing that its departure should give rise to even greater regret. At last was seen the moon's scarf, opalescent like a pigeon's breast, splashing the sky with its sparks that changed into myriads of stars.

And there arose proud columns that in still weather the sand erected joyously, as if trying to reach the blue vault above; or furious spout which, on stormy days, gushed from the bottom of ravines, to attack dark, lightning-loaded mists. Caravans of cloud sometimes careered, shaped like flocks of white sheep, driven by the wind away from the high peaks where they were formed; forced to depart before they could bedew their birthplace with rainy tears. On other days, diluvian storms broke in cascades over bare mountains, vomiting forth impetuous, torrents, thundering in the valleys.

In comparison with these formidable elements, which, never dared to rebel against the law imposed upon them by Supreme Power, how weak and arrogant Humanity seemed to be! It relied upon the strength of mundane institutions, and now such feeble trifles were liquified by the mirage viewed by Mohammad in the mirrored waves of seething ether, as if to proffer the image of the absolute vanity of the things of this world.

The Desert Retirement was the main source of Mohammad's education. It cleansed his heart of all wordly thoughts. That is why tradition has named it "Safat as Safa", – "The Purity of Purity".

Little by little, the soul of the boundless Desert penetrated his soul, bringing him the intuition of the unlimited grandeur of the Lord of All the Worlds. The most imperceptible secrets of Nature communed in the uttermost hidden depths of his being, impregnating his mind so violently that these ethereal truths were on the point of escaping from his lips. Carlyle, the great thinker, cannot restrain his admiration in this connection. "The word of such a man is a Voice direct from Nature's own heart. Men do and must listen to that as "to nothing else is wind in comparison." (*The Hero as Prophet*, London, 1840).

How is it that some Orientalists of the West have put forward the theory that Mohammad profited by this retirement to arrange and elaborate his future task in its most minute details? Some of these scholars have even gone so far as to insinuate that, during his seclusion, he composed the Qur'an in its entirety. Have they noticed that, in this Divine Book, there is no preconceived plan according to human methods; and that each of the Surahs, taken alone, is applicable to events that happened later, extending over a period of more than two decades and which it was impossible for Mohammad to foresee?

That they could find no other explanation of his long meditation is due to their ignorance of the Arab mind. If these learned men had lived among the Bedouins long enough to understand that the contemplation in which the denizens of the desert are often seen engrossed, squatting on a hilltop, staring into vacancy, is not that state of empty headed idiocy described by a few travellers, possessed of more humour than observation. If, above all, they themselves had the opportunity of revelling in the unutterable charm of the ecstasy, which can only arise from viewing the immensity of the desert, they would have acknowledged that thereby surprising advantage accrues to the intuitive faculties of the intellect, and therefore they could never have been so clumsily mistaken.

This contemplation is as a crucible in which melt nascent emotive feelings and thoughts, issuing therefrom in a state of extraordinary purity. It may be also compared to an accumulator storing up supernatural force, although hidden and unknowing, such as the latent power of fire lurking in the core of a tree-trunk. The forces accumulated by contemplation remain unsuspected by all, even by those in whom they reside. But let the tiniest spark fly out and a flashing flame will immediately rise heaven-wards to dazzle the universe.

At that epoch, it is certain that Mohammad had none of the intentions with which Orientalists have credited him. He had not even made a plan of any kind. In his "Khilwah" there was meditation, but no pre-meditation. Mohammad, at last, enjoyed luminous visions and heard mysterious calls, at the moment fixed by Providence to manifest His bounty by the intervention of the man He had chosen to be His Prophet.

Mohammad has said: "For ten months before the first Revelation, my sleep was disturbed by dazzling dreams like to the rays of early dawn, and when I could no longer be seen from the houses, I heard voices calling: 'O Mohammad! O Mohammad!'. I turned round and looked behind me first to the right, then to the left, but I could only see shrubs and stone. It was then that I was overwhelmed with frightful anguish. Hating sorcerers and diviners I feared lest I had become like them, unknowingly and against my will. These voices that seemed to spring from inanimate objects, might have been those of the Jinn in hiding – the Jinn that gave information to wizards and fortune tellers concerning celestial matters

Scripture lesson in a village Koranic school.

and so help them to carry on their nefarious trade".

Hollowed out of a block of red granite on the Jabal An-Noor, or Mountain of Light, about three miles from Makkah, to the left of the Arfa road, is the grotto of Hira, chosen by Mohammad to seek seclusion there yearly for one whole month, living day and night in absolute retirement.

He would take some provisions, consisting mainly of "Kaak" (a kind of biscuit cooked in oil and which possessed the advantage of remaining indefinitely in good state of preservation), so as not to be forced to return to the town. If, by any chance, his stock of food became exhausted and he was obliged to go and fetch other eatables, he went back to his cave, for any interruption of his ecstatic meditations made him suffer greatly.

He was now forty, and, for the last fifteen years, by dint of anxious Adoration, he tried to rid the Hanif religion, that is to say the monotheistic creed of his ancestor Abraham, of the vulgar modifications from which it had suffered at the hands of the citizens of Makkah, when one night, the twenty-fifth, twenty-seventh or twenty-ninth of the month of Ramadhan (January 15-17, of 19, AD. 611), the unforgettable Event occurred by which the Merciful One proved His generosity to His creature, by sending His Revelation on earth in the first verses of the Qur'an, by the lips of His Messenger.

The Prophet (Peace be on him) has said: "I had fallen asleep in the grotto of Hira, when the angel Jibra'il appeared to me, and unfolding before my eyes a long strip of silken stuff embroidered with written letters: 'Read!' said he. – 'I am not one of those who read', I replied. He caught hold of me at once, tightening the silken folds round my limbs, mouth and nostrils with such violence that I could not breathe. I thought the hour of my death had arrived.

Letting me go, he repeated: 'Read!' – 'I am not one of those who read,' I answered as before. Again he clutched me and I felt my last breath about to escape from my breast. Finally he loosened his hold and repeated for the third time: 'Read!' – 'What am I to read?' I asked, in my affright lest he tighten the silk around me anew and this time I felt certain that my lungs would not have held out.

It was then that he said to me: *"Read! in the name of thy Lord who created Created man from clots of blood Read! For thy Lord is the most beneficent Who hath taught the use of the pen Hath taught Man that which he know not."* (the Qur'an, xcvi, 1-5).

I recited these words after him. He vanished. Starting out of my sleep, I had the impression that the whole of a Book had just been engraved on my heart.

I went out of the cave to collect my thoughts, when halfway down the mountain, I heard a voice that came from Heaven, crying out to me: 'O Mohammad, thou art the Prophet of Allah and I am Jibra'il!' I raised my glance to the sky. It was filled with Jibra'il's presence. Despite all I could do to turn my eyes, wellnigh blinded, in the direction of other parts of the horizon, the angel's dazzling apparition was always before me. And I stood rooted to the spot, unable to go backwards or forwards. I was petrified.

For the second time, Jibra'il said to me: 'O Mohammad, thou art the Prophet of Allah and I am Jibra'il!' He then disappeared like a vision in a dream. It was then that in great haste, my heart beating in the most terrible anguish, I ran towards my dwelling. . ."

"When the Prophet (Peace be on him) crossed the threshold of his house, he rushed to Khadijah, hiding his face in her lap and trembling as if in a fit of ague, as he cried: 'Cover me up! Cover me up!' His servants flocked busily round him, keeping him enwrapped until his emotion had subsided. Khadijah, much upset, questioned him: 'O Father of Qasim, where wert thou? By Allah, what befell thee? I sent some of my servants to meet thee, but they came back without having met thee either at Hira, or on the outskirts of the city."

The Prophet (Peace be on him) told her what had happened to him. 'I thought I should have died!' he added. 'That could not be,' answered Khadijah, regaining her composure. 'Surely Allah sought not to do thee harm, for thou art kind to thy family, merciful to the weak and helpful towards the victims of injustice. O son of my uncle! thou dost bring me excellent tidings and that I do affirm. I swear, by the name of Him who heldest in His hands the soul of Khadijah, that I hoped for this news. There is no doubt about it – thou wilt be the Prophet (Peace be on him) of our nation.'

Ever since she had heard the miraculous reports that Maisarah, her slave, brought her, and which confirmed what she had remarked herself, Khadijah was convinced that the highest destiny was in store for her husband, and she was not at all astonished at such a Revelation. She quickly gathered her flowing robes about her, and hastened to the house of her cousin Waraqah ibn Naufal to apprise him of what had just come to her ears.

No man in Makkah was more conversant with Holy Writ than Waraqah, a convert to Christianity; and, like the Syrian monks, he lived in hopes of the advent of a Prophet to be born in Arab-land. Therefore, he had no sooner heard his cousin's story than he cried out, while tears of joy welled up in his eyes: 'Most Holy God! If what thou sayest is exact, O Khadijah, He who manifested His presence to thy husband is the great Namus, Allah's confidant: the Angel who appeared to Our Lord Moses! Mohammad will be the Prophet of our Nation! Doubt it not and repeat my words to him that he be convinced thereof.'

What time the Prophet, (Peace be on him) according to his wont after each term of retirement, was performing the ritual circuits round the Ka'bah, Waraqah, despite weakness due to his great age and blindness caused by too much reading, had himself led at once into Mohammad's presence, so as to listen to the story of his adventure from his own lips. When the sightless old man was satisfied that Mohammad told the truth and had repeated to him the same predictions, he exclaimed: 'Ah, I should like to be still in the land of the living when your fellow-men will send thee into exile!' – 'How so?' cried the Prophet (Peace be on him). 'Shall I be banished?' – 'Of a surety, they will send thee into exile', Waraqah went on, 'for never hath mortal man brought what thou bringest without falling a victim to the most dastardly persecution. Ah! if God deigned to lengthen my days until then, I would devote all my energies to helping thee triumph over thy enemies!' Death, however, prevented Waraqah from seeing his wishes fulfilled.

All Mohammad's doubt vanished. The fulgurating Revelation set all his unknowing aspirations in a blaze and fanned the flame of the latent forces stored in his soul during fifteen years of contemplation. It had opened his eyes and taught him the formidable, superhuman part he had to play and which was now forced upon him. In reality, all this was quite unexpected, despite the monks' predictions that he had forgotten long ago, even if he had ever paid the slightest attention to them. His anguish and his fear lest he should have fallen a victim to diabolical hallucinations furnishes us with indisputable proof of his state of mind.

He who had fled from his fellows and had never aspired to fill any post of public utility, such as his citizen-comrades would have been glad to grant, was ready now, with resolute faith and courage, to fulfil the most overwhelming mission that can be confided to a human being, and he cared not a jot for the terrible ordeals that he knew were inevitable.

During that night, for ever memorable, known by the name of "Leilat-al-Qada" or "Night of Destiny", the Qur'an came down in its entirety from the highest Heaven where it was kept, as far as the inferior Heaven, situated immediately above the earth. And there it had been deposited in the "Baital-Izza", or "House of Glory", underneath which was erected the "Baitu'l-Lah", or "House of Allah", which signifies the Holy Ka'bah.

"Verily, we have caused It (the Qur'an) to descend on the night of Power And that shall teach thee what the Night of Power is. The Night of Power is better than a thousand months! Therein descend the angels and the Spirit by permission of their Lord for every matter. All is peace until the breaking of the morn." (the Qur'an, xcvii, 1-5.)

Then from this lower Heaven, after the first verses were revealed to Mohammad, together with a general comprehension of his Mission, the words of Allah, comprising the Qur'an, came down now from between his lips, Surah following Surah, for a period of twenty-three years so as to guide all his actions, establish the laws of religion and organise the triumph of Islam.

For the benefit of our European readers, we consider it needful to add the following commentary to this story of the Revelation, according to Arab historians:

The angel Jibra'il, who sought out the Prophet (Peace be on him) at Hira is none other than the angel Gabriel who appeared to Daniel, and to Mary, the mother of Jesus; but real Moslems say that Jibra'il is totally unlike the pink-cheeked, fair haired youth, with wings of varied hues, as seen in cheap, religious saintly images of the Europeans. The angel Jibra'il is "ar-Ruh", the "Pure Spirit", (the Qur'an, xcvii, 6); and also "An Namus", or "The Invisible Adviser". Sometimes he manifested his presence to Mohammad by stray sounds resembling tinkling bells or the hum of bees, by which he caused Allah's Messenger to suffer more than anything. His brow would be bathed in sweat, even during cold, wintry days, and it was only when the noise died away that he understood what the angel had revealed to him. At other times, when Jibra'il taught Mohammad ritual movements, the angel made his presence manifest by assuming the appearance of a mortal resembling Dihyah ibn Khalifah, one of the Prophet's (Peace be on him) companions.

The Revelation, of which the angel is the symbolic intermediary, is a divine Irradiation and should be looked upon as the highest degree of the mysterious Force, evidently surrounding mortals, since it is totally independent of a man's will-power, and which we call Inspiration.

THE FIRST MOSLEM

Prayer, preceded by ablutions, was the first duty taught to the Prophet (Peace be on him) by the celestial envoy. Mohammad, having returned to the place where he had first heard the Revelation, Jibra'il appeared again, in the shape of a human being. 'O Prophet!' he said, 'You must lead men to proclaim that there is no God but Allah.'

He drove him towards a watercourse where Jibra'il stamped on the ground with his foot. A spring immediately gushed forth, and setting the example, the angel taught Mohammad the rites of Purification by means of ablutions preceding all prayers. He then went through the prayers, with the bowing, prostrations and sentences of which they should be comprised; and the Prophet (Peace be on him) prayed with him, guided by the angel's movements and words.

Mohammad felt his body relieved from a weighty burden by the purification, and his soul brightened by the benefits of these prayers. Then it was that, thrilling with the faith of belief, Mohammad was about to return home to his wife when Jibra'il appearing once more, said to him: "Teach Khadijah salvation by Islam!" That is to say, by voluntary resignation to all the Creator's commands. He obeyed and spoke thus: 'O Khadijah! Jibra'il ordereth me to teach thee salvation by Islam.' And Khadijah answered: 'Allah is Salvation: from Him cometh Salvation, and let Salvation be on Jibra'il.'

Thus it came about that of all living beings Khadijah was Islam's first convert. The Prophet (Peace be on him) took her at once to the miraculous spring, where he taught her what he had just learnt. Copying her husband, she purified herself by the ablutions and recited the prayers. Ever since that day, Allah made use of this admirable woman to mitigate the sorrows and pains of His Prophet in all the ordeals he had to undergo. Khadijah's devotion endowed Mohammad with deep contempt for mortals' wickedness, and his wife's firm faith served to comfort him when he was looked upon as an impostor.

One of the first of the Prophet's (Peace be on him) companions to believe in his mission was Ali, son of Abu Talib, only about ten years old just then, and who Mohammad had adopted during a period of famine, so as to relieve his uncle, at the head of a very large family.

Noticing that Mohammad and Khadijah kept aloof and became absorbed in prayer, he marvelled greatly at seeing no object of worship set up in front of them and he put this question to the Prophet: (Peace be on him) 'What rites were ye both performing just now?' – 'We were saying the prayers of the pure religion that Allah hath chosen for Himself and for which He hath chosen me to be the Prophet,' (Peace be on him) he replied. 'O Ali! I do invite thee to join with me. I invite thee to worship with the Only Allah that hath no partners and I call upon thee to renounce the idols Lat and Uzza who can neither benefit nor harm their worshippers.'

Say then: *"He is one Allah: Allah the everlasting! He begetteth not, and He is not begotten; And there is none like unto him. He is Allah whom there is no god. He knoweth things visible and invisible. He is the Compassionate, the Merciful! And when He decreeth a thing, He only saith to it, "Be", and it is. There is no Allah but He; the Living, the Self-subsisting. Neither slumber seizeth Him, nor sleep. No vision taketh in Him, but He taketh in all vision: and He is the Subtile, the All-informed! It is He who causeth to laugh and to weep. He causeth to die and maketh alive. He bringeth forth the living out of the dead and the dead out of the living. He quickeneth the earth after its death; thus it is that ye too shall be brought forth. The East and the West is Allah's: therefore, whichever way ye turn, there is the Face of Allah: truly Allah is Omnipresent and Omniscient. . .This is Allah, your Lord. All power is His, But gods whom ye call on beside Him have no power over the husk of a date stone!"* (the Qur'an, cxii I, 4. lix, 22, ii, iii, 256. vi, 103 liii, 44, 45. xxx, 18. ii, 109. xxxv, 14.)

'Never until this day', Ali replied, 'have I hearkened unto such words and I wish to consult Abu Talib, my father.' – 'Do nothing of the sort!' the Prophet (Peace be on him) hastened to tell him, for Mohammad feared lest the news of his Mission should be noised abroad before the hour arrived to divulge it in open day. 'If thou dost come to Islam, O Ali! thou must keep the secret.'

Greatly troubled in his mind by all he had just heard, Ali passed a sleepless night, but Allah (Glory be to Him!) guided him on the Road to Salvation. Early in the morning, he went to Mohammad and professed the religion of Islam with all his heart. From that day onwards, when came the hour of prayer, Ali followed Mohammad to the ravine to pray with him, unbeknown to the boy's father and uncles.

But one day, when they were both praying at the place called, "Nakhlat-al-Mahal", Abu Talib caught them unawares and questioned the Prophet, (Peace be on him) saying: 'O son of my brother, what is this religion of which thou dost follow the rites in thy prayers?' – 'It is the religion of Allah, of his Angels and His Prophets – the religion of our ancestor Ibrahim. Allah hath sent me to preach it to all men; and thou, the most worthy and the nearest of my relatives, I invite thee to tread the Road to Salvation.' – 'I cannot give up the religion and tradition of my fathers,' Abu Talib declared; 'and yet I hold thee to be so sincere that I believe in the truth of what thou sayest. Continue, however, to fulfill thy Mission without anxiety, for no harm shall come to thee so long as I live.' Turning towards his son, he added: 'Thou mayest harken to Mohammad, and follow him as obediently as thou canst, for he will never guide thy footsteps except in the path of righteousness.'

Zayd ibn Harith, a captive, freed and adopted by Mohammad, and who had so much affection for his liberator that he refused to go away with his father when he came to pay the ransom, soon followed

Muslims at prayer on the terraces of their houses.

Ali's example and became a convert to Islam. Next followed one of the most noted men of Makkah, Abdul-Ka'bah, son of Abu Quhafah, who we shall call henceforward Abu Bakr, being the name he assumed later and caused to become celebrated.

He happened one day to be at the house of Hakim ibn Hazam, when a slave of the household came and spoke to his master as follows: 'Khadijah, thy aunt maintaineth that her husband is a Prophet sent by the Most High, like Moses!' Hearing this, Abu Bakr, who had great faith in Mohammad's sincerity, and had heard some of Waraqah's predictions, jumped up hurriedly, much moved, and sought out the Prophet (Peace be on him) to interrogate him. No soon had Abu Bakr hearkened to Mohammad's utterances giving details of the Revelation, than he was overtaken by enthusiasm and cried out: 'By my father and my mother and by all the friends of truth, I believe what thou hast told me and I bear witness that there is no God but Allah and that thou are His Prophet!' Hearing his speech, Khadijah, draped in a crimson veil, came out of a near-by room and said to Abu Bakr: 'Praised be Allah who hath guided thee, O son of Abu Quhafah!'

This conversion was a source of great joy for the Prophet (Peace be on him). Abu Bakr held high rank in the city. He was very rich, remarkably well favoured, with fine features and aristocratic bearing; conversant with the sciences of genealogy and the meaning of dreams. Truthful in his speech; affable in neighbourly intercourse, he had been chosen by his fellow citizens for the extremely delicate post of the umpire whose duty it was to judge cases of homicide and fix the amount of the "Qisas", or money compensation for wilful murder.

A fervent Believer, Abu Bakr's entire efforts were now devoted to leading his friends and the people of his party to the Prophet, so that he might invite them to Islam. Abu Bakr's activities were successful; the confidence he inspired induced his partisans to hearken with favour to Mohammad's discourse. The enunciation of this religion, so simple and withal so great, in such conformity with the inward longings of the soul of mortals, led them gradually to look with open horror upon the state of gross idolatry in which they had hitherto wallowed. Besides, this religion was that of Abraham, their ancestor, and as his creed was still dormant in their hearts, despite themselves, it was easy for them to acknowledge it. Last of all, the superhuman accents of the man who preached this new belief and his radiant, expressive looks, stirred up their whole being and they hastened to be converted by him.

About fifteen of the leading men of the Quraish tribe came to the Prophet (Peace be on him) in the same way and became ennobled by Islam. We may mention Usman ibn Affan, Abd ar Ralman ibn Auf, Sad ibn Abi Waqqs, Subayr ibn al-Auwam, Talha Ubaydullah, Ubayda ibn Harith, Jafar ibn Abdlu Muttalib, and many others.

At the same time as these conversions, so important by reason of the proselytes ranking highly, we must not forget one more humble, most touching: that of Mohammad's nurse. As soon as the call of her foster-son came to her ears, good Halimah, who had always believed that the boy she had reared would make his mark in life, hastened with Haris, her husband, to be counted among the Faithful. Every person, too, belonging to Mohammad's household, had become a convert from the onset, and among them, his daughters still very young, without forgetting a negress, Umm al Ayman. This little group of Believers now led a life filled with everchanging emotion. What could be more charming than their secret meetings when they prayed and adored Allah in perfect union? But they had to take unheard-of precautions so as not to awaken the hostile suspicions of idolaters. Even in his own house, the Prophet (Peace be on him) was forced to beware of his neighbours, and when he proclaimed the "Takbir", he spoke into a pitcher buried in the ground, so as to deaden the sound of his voice. In these circumstances, only clandestine propaganda was possible, and during the first three years, the progress of Islam was excessively slow and timid.

On the other hand, Revelation had suddenly stopped; and Mohammad, no longer feeling himself upheld by the inspiration of the Almighty, began to doubt and despair.

He was wandering to and fro, anxious and alone, in a wide valley, when he heard a celestial voice causing him to look up. In the vivid brightness of great light, he recognised the Angel that had appeared to him at Hira. He could not support the brilliancy of this formidable apparition and, blinded, rushed to his dwelling where he had himself wrapped up in his mantle, so as to calm the tremor of his frame and shade his dazzled eyes. It was then that Allah sent down the following verses: *"O thou enwrapped in thy mantle! Arise and warn! Warn thy relatives of nearer kin And lower thy wing over the Faithful who follow thee. And if they disobey thee, then say: 'I verily am clear of your doings'; And put thy trust in the Mighty, the Merciful."* (the Qur'an, lxxvi, 1, 2, xxvi, 214-220).

The Prophet (Peace be on him) rose up, his eyes sparkling with sublime energy. Until that day, he had never dared to proclaim his Mission publicly, for he foresaw the hatred it would foment among his idolatrous fellow-citizens. But having been ordered by his Supreme Master to preach the doctrines of Islam, which was Mohammad's most earnest wish, he threw off the restraint that crushed him, and resolved to have recourse to strong measures. He ordered Ali to prepare a meal composed of a leg of lamb, hot corn and a Jar of milk. He then invited his relatives to partake of it.

Not one refused, and there came forty persons all told; among them his uncles on his father's side: Abu Talib, Hamzh, Abbas and Abu Eahab. When the guests had eaten fill, much to their great surprise, for this modest repast could have been easily swallowed up by any one man among them, Mohammad made as if to address the meeting. But Abu Lahab, having some suspicions respecting his nephew's ideas which did not meet with his approval, took the words out of his mouth: 'What kind of spell does our host seek to cast over us?' he cried. In superstitious fear of being bewitched, the proof of such a dire fate being furnished by the fact that their hunger had been appeased by a most meagre banquet, the guests scattered away in great haste.

Affronted by their lack of courtesy, the Prophet (Peace be on him) said to Ali: 'Didst thou give heed to my uncle when he cared not how impolitely he behaved in preventing me from speaking? But no matter! Get another meal ready for tomorrow, and go round and invite all the same people.'

Next day, in the presence of the guests once more gathered together, Mohammad hastened to make himself heard and succeeded in so doing. 'No one living hath ever brought to the Arabs what I bring,' he declared; 'that is to say, glorious good fortune in this world and supreme felicity in the next. Allah the Most High hath commanded me to summon all men to Him. Who among ye wisheth to share my work and help me to accomplish my mission? Such a man shall be my proxy and my lieutenant – nay, my brother!'

At this unexpected declaration, all the people present stared at each other in stupefaction; and knowing not what to reply, their features betrayed naught else but fierce enmity and showed what their answer would have been. Faithful Ali, expecting an outburst of joy, at such great, good news, coupled with ardent competition in hopes of the honour of becoming Mohammad's henchman, forgot that his youth demanded his silence in the midst of such a gathering of noble folks; and standing up erect, carried away by his enthusiasm, he cried out: 'O Prophet of Allah! I will be thy lieutenant!'

Instead of smiling at the pretensions of the lad, the Prophet (Peace be on him) patted Ali's neck affectionately while proclaiming: 'Here is my proxy and my lieutenant! Here standeth my brother! Listen to him and obey!'

By this time the stupefaction of the guests was boundless, but they suppressed their rage and received the declaration with great bursts of merriment. Abu Lahab turned to Abu Talib and shouted ironically. 'Hast heard thy nephew's speech? He ordered thee to listen to his son and obey him!'

With the exception of Abu Talib saddened by this scandalous scene, all went away, jeering sarcastically and exasperated.

It is certain that this utter defeat grieved the Prophet (Peace be on him) without discouraging him in the least, for, from that day, the Revelation gave him support, instruction and guidance unceasingly.

And Mohammad began to preach. He was hurried along by the Revelations which came to him quickly, one after the other, all terrible; and announcing "The Frightful Blow, being the End of the World and the Day of Judgement".

"The Blow! what is the Blow! And what shall teach thee what the Blow is? The Day when men shall be like scattered moths, And the mountains shall be like flocks of carded wool." (the Qur'an, ci, 1,4.)

Mohammad thought this disaster, destined to punish mankind for its perversity, was imminent. So he increased his reproofs among his fellow men, in order to deliver them from the sway of their passions and guide them into the Path of salvation before the Blow fell. But they answered him, saying: *"The Hour will not come upon us!"* (the Qur'an, xxxiv, 3.)

Obeying the orders of Allah, he reiterated his adjurations: *"Verily, the Hour will surely arrive: there is no doubt with regard to it. O Men, fear your Lord! Verily, the earthquake of the Hour will be a tremendous thing! When the Earth is shaken with its shaking, and when the Earth hath cast forth the burdens of buried dead, And man shall say: What aileth her? On that day shall she tell out her tidings, Because thy Lord hath inspired her. On that day shall men come forward in bands to behold their works. And whosoever shall have wrought an atom's weight of goods shall behold it. And whosoever shall have wrought an atom's weight of evil shall behold it."* (the Qur'an, xl, 61. xxii, l. xcix, 1-6.)

As a result of these gruesome prophecies, given out with accents of firm conviction, unbelievers felt a shudder of anguish convulsing their being; but as they saw nothing take place as time went on, not even precursory signs, they soon regained their equanimity and fell back again into their erring ways.

The Prophet (Peace be on him) could not tell for what time the hour was fixed: *"The knowledge of it is only with my Lord".* (the Qur'an, vii, 186.) But Mohammad knew punishment was inevitable in this world or the next, and he was in despair at having to think that his infidel fellowmen would meet with a fate even sadder than that of the peoples of Thamud and Ad.

THE FIRST HOSTILITIES

Following the Prophet's (Peace be on him) first sermons, the Faithful sought no longer to hide their belief; but, to avoid useless disputes, they held clandestine meetings in a desert ravine where they said their prayers.

A group of idolaters dogged their footsteps and having succeeded in discovering their retreat, lavished foul epithets on them. The Believers, unable to put up with the insults offered to their religion, grew furious and a fight took place, during which Sad ibn Abi Waqqes picked up the jawbone of a camel's skeleton in the sand and dashed it violently in the face of one of the Associates, causing the vital fluid to flow. These were the first drops of blood shed in the struggle now beginning between Islam and idolatry.

Wishing to prevent a renewal of these incidents, the Prophet (Peace be on him) resolved to retreat to pray in peace with his disciples in the house of Arqam, situated on the Sufah hill. Nevertheless, fury increased among the idol-worshippers. So long as Mohammad had gone no further than to summon them to salvation, even blaming them and threatening them with the punishment of divine wrath, his adversaries merely shrugged their shoulders and laughed at him; but when he retaliated by turning their wooden or stone images into ridicule, pointing out that they were dumb, deaf, blind and powerless, the rage of the idolaters was unbounded. Not only did he sting them to the quick through attacking their beliefs, but he did them great harm commercially, for in the hands of leading citizens, the idols were a source of considerable revenue, and constituted efficacious means of domination over the superstitious common people.

Alone, among the men of his party who had refused to embrace the Islamic faith, his uncle, Abu Talib still gave him proofs of affection, thus greatly scandalising the other members of the Quraish tribe, who sent him a deputation of the most influential among them: Utbah ibn Rabiyah, Abu Sufyan ibn Harib, Abu Jahal and several chieftains of equal note.

'O Abu Talib!' said these delegates, 'your brother's son insulteth our gods and our beliefs. He mocketh at the religion and traditions of our forefathers. Shall we not rid ourselves of him? Or wilt thou not remain neutral and thus let us be free to act towards him as we think fit? For we know that thou dost not share his convictions any more than we do.' Abu Talib dismissed them with a polite and conciliatory reply.

Mohammad, as may well be surmised, continued his sermons with unfailing ardour. The enmity of the Quaraish tribesmen assumed a more serious aspect; their representatives returning to see Abu Talib, to make the following declaration: 'We have the greatest respect for thine age, nobility and rank, but we asked thee to rid us of thy brother's son and thou didst not do so. Now, we can no longer put up with the affronts with which he overwhelmeth our beliefs and traditions, so deprive him of thy protection and leave us free to treat him as we choose. In case of refusal on thy part, we must reckon thee as being against us in the war we declare on him, and which will last until one of the two parties are exterminated!' They then departed, leaving Abu Talib in despair at being cut off from his partisans and, on the other hand, firmly resolving never to throw over his nephew.

In that state of mind, he sent for Mohammad. 'O son of my brother!' quoth he, 'our fellow citizens of the Quaraish have returned and made solemn declarations to me.' Reflect; take compassion on me; have pity for thyself, and do not put upon me a burden too heavy to bear.'

'O my uncle!' replied the Prophet; (Peace be on him) 'if in order to make me renounce my Mission, they placed the Sun on my left and the Moon on my right, I swear that, by Allah, I would not yield before I fulfilled my task triumphantly or perished in the attempt!'

Thinking that Abu Talib had spoken as he did as a hint that he would have to cast him adrift, by reason of his inability to protect him, his nephew burst into tears and went away. Abu Talib, much moved, called him back at once and said to him affectionately: 'Go, O son of my brother! Go forth and preach as thou will. By God, I'll never turn away from thee!'

Finding that no threats succeeded in estranging uncle and nephew, the delegates went back to Abu Talib for the third time, taking with them Ammarah ibn Walid, and then the deputation made the following proposal:

'O Abu Talib! here is Ammarah ibn Walid, one of the most accomplished and handsome young men among all the youths of Makkah. We bring him to thee. Adopt him for thy son. He belongeth to thee: in exchange, hand over to us thy brother's son thou didst adopt, so that we put him to death, for he hath stirred up strife in our tribe.' – 'By god!' replied Abu Talib, 'what's this fine bargain ye now put forward? You would fain give me your son, so that I feed and clothe him and I should have to let you take mine to be killed with you! That could not be! No, by God! – never.'

With rage in their hearts, the delegates left him. The Mausam – the time for the pilgrimage – drawing night, the Quaraish idolaters held a meeting at the dwelling of Walid ibn Moghayrah so as to consult

"El Tekbir", or the Glorification.

together with regard to the way in which they ought to behave to the Prophet. (Peace be on him). Walid was spokesman, and he said: 'O assembly of Quaraish men! the Mausaum will soon bring innumerable pilgrims to Makkah. Of a surety, they have heard about Mohammad, and they will question you concerning him. How will ye answer? Ye must be all of one mind, so as not to contradict each other, which would nullify the effect of your utterances'. – 'It is for thee to advise us, O Walid!' – 'It is for you to speak first. I will listen and discuss your opinions.' – 'Well then! we shall say that Mohammad is a diviner.' – 'No! We know the diviners! He hath none of their mutterings or rhyming emphasis.' – 'We'll say that he is possessed.' – 'No! We have seen men possessed; and unlike them, he is not subject to fits of suffocations and convulsions.' – 'We'll say he is a poet.' – 'No! He is no poet. We know all the styles of versification as used by the poets, and his speech does not resemble that of any of them.' – 'We'll say he is a sorcerer.' – 'No! for we have fallen across sorcerers, and he performeth none of their magical operations. Of a truth, his success is due to the charm and beauty of his discourse.'

Arraigned before the tribunal of their own conscience, the citizens assembled were forced to acknowledge the rigorous truth of this last remark. All of them more or less had felt the words springing from the ecstatic soul of Allah's Apostle go home to them. All of them had ofttimes been about to give way to the fascination caused by his accents, ringing with the inspiration of superhuman faith. The Quaraish men were only restrained by the importance of their material interests and the violence of their earthly passions, thus seriously threatened by his pure doctrine.

Nevertheless, they were bound to come to a decision at once, so as to prevent, at all costs, the Arabs belonging to distant tribes from undergoing the same ordeal. Therefore, they agreed to say that Mohammad possessed potent spells by which he stirred up strife in families, estranging a brother from his brother, a son from his father, and a husband from a wife.

When the pilgrime began to pour in, Walid and his accomplices were on the watch, posted on all the roads leading to Makkah. Not a single Arab passed along these highways without being warned against Mohammad by the conspirators in ambush. But although a few pilgrims were alarmed at these warnings and feared the spells that they were informed were threatening them, the majority felt their curiosity increasing with regard to this extraordinary man, whose utterances gave rise to such great apprehension among the lords of the city. Thus it came to pass that when the travellers returned to their tribes, they told what they had seen; so that it plainly resulted that the campaign, organised against Mohammad by his enemies, only achieved the purpose of spreading his renown all over Arabia.

In order to add fresh fuel to the fire of their rage, increasing as the Prophet's (Peace be on him) reputation became established – a result partly due to their involuntary efforts – the idol-worshippers sought every opportunity to heap insults on him. Being all together, one day in the precincts of the Temple, they worked each other up. 'No! never have we endured from anybody what this man hath made us endure', they cried out in chorus. At that very moment, Mohammad came on the scene and began to perform the ritual circuits round the Ka'bah. They rushed at him, all at one bound. 'Art thou the man who dareth to insult the gods of our fathers?' they shouted. 'Aye, I am that man!' he replied, undisturbed.

One of the enraged citizens caught hold of the collar of his mantle, and twisting it roughly, tried to strangle him. Abu Bakr, who chanced to be standing near, interfered. 'How now? Would ye kill a man who proclaimeth that Allah is his God?' he said sadly, and freed the Prophet, (Peace be on him) not without suffering ill-treatment himself, for a portion of his beard was plucked out by Mohammad's assailant.

The danger he had risked in these circumstances did not prevent the Prophet (Peace be on him) from returning to the Ka'bah to perform his devotions, without letting the furious glances of his assembled adversaries trouble him. Acting under the orders of Abu Jahal a man fetched some sheeps' entrails from the slaughterhouse. He chose those of an animal that had been killed several days before, and while the Prophet (Peace be on him) was prostrate as he prayed, the rascal covered the nape of his neck and shoulders with the offal. All those present were seized with such outrageous fits of mirth that they fell seated on the ground, rolling one against the other. As for Allah's Elect, he seemed not even to have noticed the affront offered to him, and continued to pray. It was his daughter Fatimah who, arriving a few moments later, threw the filth far from her father, and railed at the wretches who had belittled themselves by the infliction of such a repulsive insult.

On a par with Abu Jahal, ranking with those who are branded eternally in history's pages on account of their atrocious treatment of the Prophet, (Peace be on him) was one of his uncles, a son of Abu Muttalib, surnamed Abu Lahab, "The Man Vowed to Hell-Fire". Mohammad was preaching one day on the hill of Safa, in the midst of a crowd of inhabitants of that region, when Abu Lahab interrupted him rudely. 'Mayst thout be annihilated!' he bawled, 'thou who has called us together to listen to such nonsense!' To this insult the following Surah of the Qur'an (cxi) replies: *"Let the hands of Abu Lahab perish and let himself perish. His wealth and his gains shall avail him not. Burned shall he be at the fiery flame, And his wife laden with the fire-wood, On her neck a rope of twisted palm fibre."*

This Surah, quickly becoming renowned, increased Abu Lahab's resentment and probably had even more effect on that of his wife, Umm Jemil, who found herself attacked therein in a way that was as annoying as it was deserved. To be nicknamed "carrier of fire-wood" was past endurance; but had she not, on one occasion, strewn the path of Mohammad with thorny branches; had not her tongue lit up the fires of hatred with the faggots of calumny that she hawked about everywhere? The odious couple resorted shamelessly to the vilest acts, daily throwing heaps of filth on the terrace of Mohammad's house or in front of his door, for he was their neighbour.

Worked up or terrorised by these fanatics, most of the dwellers in Makkah repulsed the Prophet (Peace be on him) or avoided him. Children and wastrels pursued him with their jibes in the street. He was perfectly indifferent to such provocations. What was it all to him? Nothing more than a passing breeze. He never seemed to notice the persons who acted thus; he only looked at those he hoped to convert.

THE INCIDENT OF THE BLIND MAN

It happened one day when Mohammad had taken in hand some of the most noted townsmen who were beginning to be moved by his arguments, that a blind pauper, Ibn Umm Maktum, came forward and humbly begged to be granted a small share of the knowledge vouchsafed to the Prophet (Peace be on him) by Allah. Engrossed in his discussion with the citizens whose conversions he so ardently desired; fearing, too, to miss an opportunity which might never occur again, Mohammad was seized with a fit of momentary vexation and replied curtly to the blind man, who stumbled away sorrowfully without having been enlightened.

Immediately afterwards, the Prophet (Peace be on him) fell a prey to remorse. Might not that blind man, enlightened by faith, have been able to open the eyes of other human beings imprisoned in the darkness of ignorance? And the Revelation increased Mohammad's remorse by confirming his error: *"He frowned, and he turned his back. Because the blind man came to him. . .As to him who hath become wealthy. Him therefore thou didst receive with honour Yet it is not thy concern that he endeavours not to be pure; But as to him who cometh to thee in earnest, And full of fears, Him dost thou neglect. Do not so. Verily this surah is a warning."* (the Qur'an, lxxx' 1-11.)

Ever since that day, the Prophet (Peace be on him) took great care to treat rich and poor, slaves and nobles alike, with the same consideration. The exasperation of the idolaters reached the highest pitch when they saw their own slaves drawn towards Mohammad by his levelling doctrines; and when the town rang with the Revelation of Surahs threatening the rich and the sweaters of the people. *"The desire of increasing riches occupieth you, Till ye come to the grave. Nay! but in the end ye shall know. Nay! once more; in the end ye shall know your folly. Nay! would that ye knew it with knowledge of Certainty; Then shall ye surely on that day be taken to task concerning the pleasures of this life."* (the Qur'an, ch, 1-8.)

Abu Jahal, meeting the Prophet (Peace be on him) at Safa, could not contain himself, and forgetting the self-control befitting a man of his high social position, he blurted out such a vulgar insult that the pen refuses to write it. The Prophet (Peace be on him) answered not a word, as was his wont, but a freed female slave of Abdullah ibn Jedhan had witnessed the scene, while looking out of the back of her dwelling that was just on the spot. Al Hamzah, Mohammad's uncle, came by a few moments later, she told him what she heard.

Hamzah's disposition was haughty and choleric. He felt his blood boiling with rage when he heard of the affront offered to his nephew. When returning from the chase – his favourite pastime – he generally stopped to gossip with the folk he met on the road, but this time he never halted, hurrying as fast as his legs would carry him towards the Temple. When he caught sight of Abu Jahal, seated in a group of his partisans, he went straight up to him, and brandishing his bow above his head, he slashed the face of Mohammad's uncle by a stinging blow. 'So! thou dost insult my nephew', he cried. 'Learn that I profess the same religion as he. All he proclaimeth, do I proclaim likewise, stop me from doing so, if thou dost believe thou canst!'

All the assistants, belonging to the Banu Makhzum tribe of whom Abu Jahal was a chieftain, rose up to avenge him. But Abu Jahal, ashamed at having done a thing unworthy of a high-born lord, under the influence of profound hatred, bid them stand back. 'Let Hamah go in peace,' he said to them, 'for verily, I did grievously offend my brother's son.'

As for Hamzah, the blessing of Allah was upon him in his outburst of rage and ennobled him by Islam of which he became one of the most devoted and formidable defenders.

Utbah ibn Rabiyah, one of the most noted idol-worshippers, was greatly shocked when his young son, Huzdifah, became a convert to Islam and drew away from his father. Hoping to put an end to the discord established by Mohammad's doctrines, not only in the Quraish tribe, but even in the bosom of families, he planned to come forward as mediator. Seeing Allah's Apostle seated, quite alone, near the Temple, Utbah said to his partisans: 'Will ye authorise me to speak to him, and discuss one or two proposals in your name? Perhaps he may accept them and so leave us in peace.'

Under the influence of the consternation they felt at the conversion of such an important personage as Hamzha – a conversion that had led others to follow suit – and well knowing that it would be best to come to some agreement, they replied: 'Aye, go to him and speak in our name.' Thereupon, Utbah left them and went to sit by the side of the Prophet. (Peace be on him) 'O son of my friend!' said Utbah in most affectionate tones; thou dost belong to us, although by insulting our religion and the traditions of our fathers, thou hast embroiled us. Therefore I come to thee to put an end to this great misfortune. Give an ear to my proposals. Maybe they will find grace in thy sight.' – 'Speak! I am listening.' – 'O son of my friend! If thou dost hope that any undertaking will make thee wealthy, each of us is willing to sacrifice a part of his fortune, in order that thou shalt become the richest man among us. If thou seekest honours, we will set thee up as a lord over us all and come to no decision without consulting thee. Dost dream of royal privileges? We will make thee our king. If, on the contrary, the thoughts that inspire thee arise from some malady which thou art powerless to resist, we will have fetched at any cost and from any country the most celebrated doctors, so that thou mayst be cured. Choose therefore!'

The Prophet (Peace be on him) had listened unmoved. 'Hast thou no more to say?' he answered Utbah. 'Now 'tis thy time to hearken to my words!' He then recited the Surah of "The Made Plaid", in which Unbelievers are menaced with the eternal torments of hell, and Believers comforted by the promise of the inconceivable felicity of Paradise (the Qur'an, xli). Utbah, his hands clasped behind his back, stood hearkening to the sentences, now imperative and then compassionate, that fell upon his ears in rhythm and cadence totally new to him. Stupefied, he remained stockstill, his attitude unchanged, although the Prophet (Peace be on him) had ceased speaking some little time. Mohammad, after having prostrated himself, his brow touching the earth, rose up and turned to Utbah, saying "Thou hast heard me, O Utbah? Now, 'tis for thee to choose".

Utbah, bewildered, went back to his companions. They all noticed his troubled face, so different on his return from what it had been before he left them. 'Come now, O Utbah! what aileth thee?' they queried. – 'I have just listened to extraordinary words,' he answered. 'By our Gods! I've never heard anything like it before. 'Tis neither poetry, nor sorcery, nor magic. O Quraish men assembled! Believe me and let this man fulfil his Mission among the Arabs, for his words are full of surprising prophecies. If harm cometh to him by the Arabs fault, ye will be freed from all anxiety. If, on the other hand, he suceedeth and shall conquer the Arabs, his empire will be thy empire, seeing that he is one of us, and thanks to him, ye will attain the highest pinnacle of power.'

But what availed such prudent conclusions in the face of jealousy and hatred? 'With his tongue he hath cast a spell over thee, as he hath done to others,' his hearers replied; and Utbah, shrugging his shoulders, went away, declaring: 'Such is my advice. Now do as ye please.'

Nevertheless, Utbah's opinion impressed the idolaters. Next day, after sunset, they foregathered, according to custom, in the precincts of the Temple, and decided to speak to Mohammad in person. They sent for him, and he came hoping that their eyes were open to the light. But they only wanted to renew the proposals of the day before. He refused just as scornfully. 'Since thou dost set thyself up as Prophet,' they said, changing their arguments, 'take pity on thy country. There is no land more hemmed-in by mountains, or more poor in its water-supply; more difficult to live in. Therefore, ask Allah to put aside the girdle of mountains, make the soil easier to till, and give us rivers resembling those of Syria and Iraq. Or else, ask him to resuscitate one of our ancestors, Qusaiyy ibn Kilab, for instance, who was a wise and truthful man, so that we may consult him concerning thy pretensions and let us know if they are veracious or false. If he giveth thee right and thou dost satisfy our demands, then will we believe thee and have faith in thy mission as Allah's Apostle.'

'I have not been sent to thee for this,' was all the Prophet (Peace be on him) cared to reply. 'I have told you what I was charged to do; and I tell you once more that if you accept, your happiness is assured in this life and the next. Should ye refuse, then I bow down to the decrees of Allah who shall judge between us.' – 'Since thou wilt ask nothing for us,' they returned; 'crave a favour for thyself: Ask Allah to send one of his angels to convince us; ask Him to lavish on thee all the pleasures of this world that thy heart can desire, such as delicious gardens, marvellous palaces, or treasures of gold and silver. Instead of which, we see thee as one who *"eateth food and walketh the marts"* (the Qur'an, xxv, 8), exactly the same as the most humble among us! If thou art really a Prophet, let Allah give us proofs of the power with which He hath endowed thee, and of the dignity to which He hath raised thee'. – 'I am not one of those who make such demands of Allah, and to you I renew my adjuration.' – 'Ask Allah to *"make the*

E. DINET

SCENES FROM THE BADIS OR NOMADIC LIFE. *The encampment.*

Heaven to fall in pieces on us, as thou hast given out," (the Qur'an, xii, 94), if He hath power to do so, according to what thou dost maintain. If not thy word deserveth no credit'. – 'Nothing could be easier for the Almighty. If He shall decide to act as ye say, He will accomplish the task. Ye ask Him for miracles? The miracles are to be found in all He hath created and ye do not understand! See how death springeth from life and life from death! Of a surety, He can, by a miracle, undo the prodigies of the order of Nature he hath created. Thus did He for my predecessors, but in vain. Therefore, admire His unceasing miracles in Nature and crave no others.'

Unable to catch the Prophet (Peace be on him) tripping, the idol worshippers, to check him, brought forward Nazir ibn Haris who, having been a great traveller, had garnered many fine stories. As soon as Mohammad began to preach, Nazir took his stand quite near him, trying to get his hearers away by reciting the wonderful exploits of Rustam and Isfandyar. 'See now, I lavish on my audiences fine tales,' Nazir was bold enough to add, 'that will bear comparison with those sent down by Allah to His Prophet.'

The Quraish man also sent a delegation to the learned Jews of Yasrib and to the Prince Halib ibn Malik, illustrious above all men by reason of his wisdom, science and power, in order to ask that some means should be found to prove that Mohammad was an impostor. But all these efforts were useless, and there was no need to believe in the end of a miracle based on these words of the Qur'an: *"The hour hath approached and the moon hath been cleft"* (liv, 1).

Some writers assert that Habib, having asked the Prophet (Peace be on him) to perform a miracle, in order to prove the veracity of his mission, Mohammad gave an order to the moon which incontinently split into two equal parts; one ascending towards the East and the other to the West. According to the opinion of the most trustworthy doctors of Islam, such as A Baidawi and Zamakhshri, this verse really means: 'The hour (of the Day of Resurrection) approacheth and (to announce it) the moon will be cleft.' The truth of this assertion is proved by the verses that follow almost immediately: *"Turn away then from (The Unbelievers)! On the day when the summoner shall summon to a horrible affair, With downcast eyes shall they come forth from their graves, as if they were scattered locusts."* (the Qur'an, liv, 6 and 7.)

Besides, this supposed miracle is so flagrantly contradicted by numerous verses of the Qur'an that it is not possible to admit it. *"Nothing hindered Us from sending thee (Mohammad) with the power of working miracles, except that the people of old treated them as lies,"* (the Qur'an xvi 61.).

There was such slight efficacity in miracles! The Israelites bowed down to the Golden Calf immediately after the miracle wrought by Moses to save them from the waves of the Red Sea and Pharaoh's hosts. The idolaters of Makkah would not have been more greatly impressed by the sight of the most astonishing miracle. *"With their most binding oath have they sworn by Allah, that if a sign came unto them, they will certainly believe it; Say: Signs are in the power of Allah alone: And what shall make ye to understand that if they were wrought these men would not believe it And though We had sent down the Angels to them, and the dead had spoken to them, and We had gathered all things about them in hosts, they had not believed, unless Allah willed it."* (the Qur'an, vi, 10, 111.)

THE MIRACLE OF THE QUR'AN

Nevertheless there was one miracle, the only one placed to Mohammad's credit, and which was the cause of great anxiety among the Quraish idolaters: the miracle of the "Ayates", a word generally rendered by "Verses", but really meaning: "miraculous signs" of the Qur'an.

The miracles wrought by earlier Prophets had been transient, so to say, and for that very reason, rapidly forgotten, while that of the Verses may be called "The Permanent Miracle". It activity was unceasing. Everywhere and at all hours, each Believer, by reciting the Verses, helped to realise the miracle, and in this can be found the explanation of many sudden conversions, incomprehensible for the European who knows nothing of the Qur'an, or judges it by cold and inaccurate translations.

The wonderful charm of this Book, resembling no other masterpiece of the literature of mankind, needs not to be explained to us Moslems, because we consider it emanates from the words of Allah Himself, sent down through the mouth of His Prophet. In this connection, we think it will be interesting to quote the opinion of two Orientalists, justly celebrated.

This is the conception of Savary, the first to translate the Qur'an into French: "Mohammad was learned in the study of his language, the richest and most harmonious in the world, and which, by the composition of its verses, permits thoughts as they soar to be correctly described. By the harmony of its sounds, it imitates the cries of animals, murmuring waters, thunder and the breeze. Mohammad, I repeat, being past master of a language that so many poets have embellished and which exists since the beginning of the world, took great pains to add every charm of elocution to his precepts of morality. Poets were greatly looked up to in Arabia. Libid ibn Rabyah, an illustrious poet, nailed one of his poems on the door of the Temple of Makkah. His reputation and the value of his works kept all competitors away. None came forward to compete for the prize . . . The second chapter of the Qur'an – some writers say the 55th – was then placed by the side of the poem. Labid, although a worshipper of graven images, was seized with a fit of admiration after reading the first verses and confessed himself vanquished."

He became a convert very soon after and one day, his admirers being desirous of gathering together his complete works, questioned him on this subject. 'I have no recollection of any of my poetry,' he replied, 'for my entire memory hath been absorbed by the verses of the Book of Revelation.'

We will now give the opinion of Stanley Lane Poole. "The style (of the Surahs) is haughty in every part and full of passion. The words are those of a man who tries with all his heart to convince his readers. Even nowadays, they given an impression of the vehemence and fire with which they were originally hurled forth at Mohammad's hearers surrounding him. These are the broken utterances of a human heart totally incapable of hypocrisy; the heart of a man who has exercised extraordinary influence over mankind."

If the magic of the style and the thoughts of the Qur'an produced this effect on learned men, who were neither Arabs nor Moslems, how great then was the enthusiasm created among the Arabs of the Hijaz, especially as the verses were couched in their own poetical language? You only, travellers who had have an opportunity of seeing the emotion that overcomes the audience of an Imam reciting the Sacred Verses, can have a slight idea of this feeling. You may have seen poor caravaneers, still powdered all over by the sand of their desert, where they have just endured the greatest fatigue, running towards the Mosque, instead of seeking refreshing repose; drawn thither, as if hypnotised by the Imam's voice. Sometimes even, in the time of Ramadhan, Moslems, after having fasted all day, pass the whole of the night in ecstasy, as they listen to the Divine Word.

It is certain that the illiterate Bedouins of our day do not always understand the real meaning of the words recited by the Imam, but the rhythm, the cadence, the harmony of the assonances animating the wonderful verses, echoing in their breasts to the beatings of their hearts, convey to them an explanation, vague perhaps, but truly in accordance with the spirit of the text, and above all, full of incomparable suggestion. On the other hand, how vapid would seem to them the explanation, more literal but less emotional, of a "Tlib" pendant or a frigid grammarian.

As for the Arab of the Hijaz, comprehending the most subtle hints of the language of the Qur'an his own language and who welcomed the Surahs as they issued from the lips of his fellow countryman: the genial, inspired messenger of Allah, that listener was overwhelmed by such sudden surprise that he remained as if petrified. Could this supernatural language come from Mohammad, known to be completely illiterate and possessing no other knowledge than that due to nature and intuition? This seemed perfectly impossible. The Arab was therefore forced to admit that Mohammad's words were dictated by the Almighty. Besides, it was following no ingenious falsehood that the Prophet (Peace be on him) attributed the verses of the Qur'an to Allah. He was absolutely convinced of their divine origin. The terrible crises by which the Revelation manifested itself, bringing him the solution of unknown problems in language so new to his; so different to his own; even upbraiding him when he made mistakes and commanding him to recite these verses, despite any resistance he might make, left him without the slightest doubt on that head.

Consequently, it was with the most perfect faith that he felt boundless admiration for the Qur'an; that is to say for the Words of Allah. Not not Allah revealed to him these verses: *"Say: Then bring ten Surahs like it of your devising, and call whom ye can to your aid beside Allah, if ye are men of truth"* (the Qur'an, xi, 16). Convinced of their powerlessness, "The Unlettered Prophet", (the Qur'an, 'vii, 156), challenged the most celebrated poets, giving them the right to call him a cheat, if they could compose ten Surah resembling his.

To doubt the absolute and strangely moving sincerity of Mohammad and picture him as a vulgar, but clever, ambitious man, as some modern historians have done, one must be blinded by preconceived ideas, worthy of the days of the Inquisition. Carlyle, in his book, "On Heroes", treated such fanaticism or stupidity as it deserved: "A false man found a religion?" he exclaims, speaking of Mohammad. "Why a false man cannot build a brick house! If he do not know and follow truly the properties of mortar, burnt clay and what else he works in, it is no house that he makes, but a rubbish-heap. It will not stand for twelve centuries, to lodge a hundred and eighty millions; it will fall straightway."

HOW IT WAS FORBIDDEN TO LISTEN TO THE QUR'AN

Being powerless to struggle against the irresistible effect produced by the recitation of the Qur'an, the Quraish idol worshippers resolved to forbid people to listen to it.

By threats, the tribesmen frightened those who tried to approach the Prophet, (Peace be on him), when as was his wont, he recited, on the threshold of the Ka'bah, a few passages of the Revealed Book. So as not to hear him, they put their fingers in their ears; or else, to drown his voice, they whistled, clapped their hands, or bawled, as loudly as they could, scraps of doggerel composed by idolatrous poets. The unexpected result was that the very men who had made it a crime to listen to the celebrated verses, were moved by that unconquerable curiosity which attracts weak mortals towards forbidden things.

One night, Abu Safyan, Abu Jahal and Al-Akhnas went out of their houses, bending their steps, each unknown to the other, towards the dwelling of the Prophet, (Peace be on him). Once there, their ears glued to the wall, they tried to overhear the recital of some of the Divine Surahs. In the darkness of the night, they did not see one another.

But when day dawned, they came face to face on their homeward road, and blamed each other mutually: 'What would our partisans think, if they had caught us doing this thing?' And they took a solemn oath never to be so imprudent again.

But the next night and the night after that, the same thing occurred, followed by the same exchange of reproaches.

يا أيها المدثر قم فأنذر وربك فكبر

CHAPTER FOUR — Decorative plate.

لتبلون في أموالكم وأنفسكم

CHAPTER THE FOURTH

PERSECUTION

Quoth the Prophet: (Peace be on him) 'Allah created Paradise for the man who obeyeth Him, even if only a black Abyssinian slave; and Hell for the man rebelling against Him, even if he be a nobleman of the Quraish.'

Islam, tending towards the perfect equality of castes and races, naturally attracts all the poor and downtrodden of the city. With increasing vexation, the idolatrous masters saw their slaves, in eager crowds, converted to the new faith. But as these wretched folks were in the tyrants' power they glutted their vengeance on them, not daring to attack disciples of the Prophet (Peace be on him) occupying higher rank.

Oummayatah ibn Khalaf, having become aware of the conversion of his black slave, Bilal ibn Hammah, was engrossed with but a single thought: that of torturing him with the most dastardly refinements. Placing his neck in a noose made from a rough rope of palm fibre, he gave him into the hands of boys knowing no pity. They dragged him along behind them, like a beast of burden, just for amusement. The rope, pulled this way and that by the juvenile wrongdoers, ploughed a sanguinary furrow in Bilah's flesh. Nevertheless, he seemed insensible to pain. Thereupon his master deprived him of food and drink, and led him from the town at noonday, in the middle of summer, throwing him out in the "Ramada", a sandy plain, so torrid that a slice of meat, thrown on the ground, cooked itself immediately. He made his slave lie down, stretched out on his back, an enormous stone on his breast. 'Thou shalt stop there', he ordered, 'until thou dost abjure Mohammad's doctrines, and worship Lat and Uzza.'

But the stoical Moslem did nothing more than lift the forefinger of his right hand, saying again and again: 'Ahad! Ahad! 'Allah is one! Allah is one!' thus testifying the scorn he felt for his master who dared to couple wooden or stone associates with the Master of the Worlds. The affirmation of the slave produced insensibility to pain, because the ineffable joy of the sacrifice for his faith mingled with and mastered the bitterness of torture.

Passing one day near the Ramada, Abu Bakr witnessed his cruel sight. 'Fearest thou not the justice of Allah, the Most High, O Ommayatah! when thou dost inflict such torment on that wretched man?' he cried indignantly.—'Thou didst corrupt him; therefore tis thy duty to save him,' was the cynical reply.— 'Willingly! I posses a young black slave, stronger and a better worker than thine. Moreover, he is entirely devoted to thy idols. I offer him to thee in exchange.' Oummayatah accepted and turned Bilal over to Abu Bakr who granted him his freedom straightaway. Besides, this generous man (may Allah make him welcome in His Grace!) purchased six other slaves, Islamic converts, merely to set them free, and deliver them out of the hands of their idolatrous masters.

These persecutions continued notwithstanding, becoming more and more barbarous. The Banu Makhzum tribe took Ammar, the Yaser, his father, and Summayy, his mother, out on the Ramada, in order to make them suffer all the tortures prompted by diabolical ferocity. Ammar was enclosed in an iron breastplate that held him down on the ground, exposed to the blazing rays of the sun at its zenith. His flesh crackled as if in contact with molten metal. But the same thing happened as with Bilal; the idolaters were unable to drag from Ammar or his parents, tortured in like fashion, one blasphemous word. It was then that, blinded by rage, Abu Jahal drove his spear through Summayy's heart, mocking the dying woman by telling her: 'If thou dost believe in Mohammad, tis because thou art in love with his beauty!'

Summayy was the first martyr to Islam, but such constancy was not to be found in all. A few Believers, enfeebled by privation and torture to such an extent that they could not stand upright, finished by letting fall from their lips, despite themselves, the blasphemous utterances ensuring release. For such as these, crushed by shame and shedding tears of repentance, the following Surah of consolation has come down: *"Whoso after he hath believed in God, denieth Him, if he were forced to it and if his heart remain steadfast in the faith (shall be guiltless:) But whoso openeth his breast to infidelity—on them in that case shall be wrath from God, and a severe punishment awaiteth them."* (the Qur'an, xvi, 108).

When the Prophet (Peace be on him) saw what tortures were inflicted on his disciples and that he was powerless to protect them, he was overwhelmed with intense sadness. The martyrs' courage proved to him how deeply the roots of faith were planted in their hearts; nevertheless he considered that such sacrifices should be avoided. So he advised all who were weak, or even as were not forced by imperious necessity to remain to Makkah, to emigrate to Abyssinia, a land inhabited by Christians, whose Chieftain, the Najashi (Negus) was celebrated for his tolerance and justice.

THE EMIGRATION TO ABYSSINIA *(A.D. 615)*

Sixteen Moslem were the first to depart. Among them was Usman ibn Affan and his wife Ruqaiyah, one of the Prophet's (Peace be on him) (AD. 615) daughters. They went out from Makkah secretly and on foot. Reaching the shore of the Red Sea, they chartered a *felucca* which carried them over to the opposite bank, from whence they journeyed to the Court of the Najashi who welcomed them kindly. Another caravan soon joined them, and the little Mussulman colony, having taken refuge in Abyssinian territory, was made up of eighty-three men and eighteen women.

Exasperated at seeing their victims escape from their clutches; and still more furious to have include among the emigrants members of their own families, such as Umm-i-Habbibah, daughter of Abu Sufyan, the idolaters despatched to the Najashi two ambassadors, Uman ibn al As and Abdullah, son of Abu Rabiyah, bearing rich presents, with a view to claiming the fugitives, described as being dangerous agitators, capable of causing a revolution in his kingdom.

The Najashi had already seen that the contrary was the case. By their honesty and virtue, the fugitives had gained the esteem and sympathy of his subjects, so that he did not feel inclined to favour the request of the ambassadors, despite their valuable gifts. They then thought it would be as well to touch upon the religious susceptibilities of the Christian monarch, and put him on his guard against the danger of Islam. 'Know then what these imposters seek to attain,' said they to him. 'They have set foot in thine empire in order to turn thy subjects away from the religion of Jesus, even as they sought to lead the

Quraish astray from the religion of their ancestors. Shouldst thou wish to put our veracity to the test, question them concerning their opinions with regard to Jesus, thy God.'

The Najashi followed this piece of advice. He interrogated the most learned among the emigrants and elicited the following reply from Jafar, Mohammad's cousin, son of Abu Talib: 'These are the Verses revealed to the Prophet: (Peace be on him) *"The Messiah Isa (Jesus), son of Maryam- (Mary), is only an apostle of Allah, and His Word which He conveyed into Maryam. . .* (the Qur'an, iv, 169.)

This answer was not at all displeasing to the Najashi. If it did not acknowledge the divinity of Jesus, it showed, at least, the deep veneration in which He was held by the Moslems, and the Abyssinian monarch was fully reassured as to the fugitives' intentions. He sent the ambassadors away, without accepting any of their presents or giving them the slightest satisfaction.

THE CONVERSION OF UMAR, SON OF AL KHATTAB

The Unbelievers had succeeded in making fierce Umar think that he would save his country by ridding it of Mohammad. So Umar, having buckled on his sword, and his eyes flashing fire, bent his steps in the direction of the Safa district, where he fancied he might fall across the Prophet. Umar, on his way, met Na'im, who had gone over to Islam unbeknown to his fellow-tribesmen. 'Wither goest thou, O Umar?'queried the convert.—'To seek out this fellow Mohammad who hath stirred up strife in the midst of the Quraish. Oh, by our Gods! I must kill him!'—'By Allah! the soul leadeth thee to do a mad act, O Umar! Dost thou think that the Abd-i-Maaf will leave thee in peace on the face of the earth, if thou dost put to death their relative, Mohammad?' he added, trying to deter him from carrying out his abominable plan. 'Would it not be far better to get certain members of thine own household to explain their doings?'—'Who are these persons under my roof?'—'Thy sister Fatimah and thy brother-in-law Said ibn Zayd. They, too, are Moslems.'

At these words, Umar stopped dead, the direction of his fury changing, and in great haste, he hurried to the dwelling of Fatimah, his sister. Just as he got there, Khubah, a fervent disciple, was reading the "Surah Ta-Ha" written out on a piece of parchment. At the sound of Umar's furious knocking, Khubab fled into an adjoining room, and Fatimah hid the parchment in the folds of her attire.

But Khubab's voice had been overheard by Umar who asked in imperative accents: 'What is this recitation in an undertone that I heard, and which ye cut short when I arrived?'—'There was nothing to hear. Thou art mistaken,' his brother-in-law and sister protested in chorus. 'No, no! There is no mistake; neither do I err when I tell you I have learnt that ye follow Mohammad's religion!' Without waiting for any further explanation, he rushed at his brother-in-law, knocked him down, sat on his chest and seized him by the beard.

Fatimah threw herself on her brother and made desperate efforts to free her husband. 'Thou speakest the truth! We are Moslem!' Umar lost his wits at this confession and by a brutal blow in the face, he dashed courageous Fatimah to the ground. 'Yea, we are Moslems, O enemy of Allah!' she repeated, staring boldly at him, her blood flowing freely. 'Yea, we believe in Allah and His Prophet! Now do with us as thou wilt!'

When Umar saw his sisters blood, the indomitable courage of the weak women impressed him greatly and he was ashamed of what he had done. 'Give me the parchment that I heard you reading,' he asked his sister in softer accents, 'I wish to get some idea of that which hath been revealed to Mohammad.'—'We fear thou mayest destroy the writing.'—'Be not afraid! By Allah! ye shall have it back as soon as I shall have read it.'

Despite her wish to try and convert her brother, Fatimah raised objections. 'O my brother! I cannot

"El Rekaa" or the Inclination.

confide it to thee, for thou art unclean. Only pure hands are allowed to touch the Book in which are inscribed the words of Allah.'

Umar rose with docility and performed his ablutions. Then did Fatimah hand over the parchment on which was written the Surah, "Ta'Ha", which begins with these words: *"Not to sadden thee have We sent down this Qur'an to thee But as a warning for him who feareth."* (xx, 1 and 2.)

Immediately after reading of the first verses, Umar, who was remarkably well learnt, could not refrain from uttering a cry of admiration: 'How beautiful! What sublime language!'—'O Umar!' exclaimed Khubab, coming out of his hiding-place, 'I had great hopes that the Almighty would fulfil, in thy favour, the wish I heard the Prophet (Peace be on him) make but yesterday: 'O Allah!' said he, 'strengthen Islam by the conversion of either one or the other of those women: Abu Jahal or Umar.'—'Lead me at once to Mohammad', replied Umar, 'so that I may become a convert to Islam in his presence. Where is he?' Khubah, in triumph, sent him to the dwelling of Arqam in the Safa district.

In that house, the disciples, clustering in union round the Prophet, (Peace be on him) were drinking in his words, when imperative knocks a shook the door. One of the comrades rose up and, by a crack in the wood, caught sight of the terrible warrior, his sword dangling from his belt. Thunderstruck at this apparition, he came back to warn the Prophet (Peace be on him) who calmly told him: 'Bring him in here. If he cometh with good intentions, we will grant him generous welcome, but if evil designs guide his footsteps, we will kill him with his own sword'.

The companions having obeyed, Umar entered. Mohammad went to meet him, and coming face to face with him in the entrance-hall, he caught him by the collar and, with a sudden pull, dragged him into the midst of the company assembled. 'What is thy motive in coming here, O son of Al Khattab?' he asked. Dost thou still mean to remain wallowing in impiety until the wrath of the Almighty crusheth thee?'—'O Prophet!' answered Umar with unaccustomed humility, 'I come to declare my faith in Allah, His Messenger, and His Revelation.'—'Praise to be Allah! Glory to Him! Mohammad'. When his companions were informed of Umar's sudden conversion, they went their different ways, full of gratitude towards Him who had decreed it.

Umar was not a man to remain patient and conceal his convictions. In the street, he stopped the first passer-by he met, one Jamil ibn Mamar, of the Jumah tribe, and said to him: 'Dost know, O Jamil that I have become a Mussulman?' The words were hardly out of his mouth, before Jamil, an incorrigible gossip, tucked his mantle tightly round him and ran to the Temple. 'O Assembly of the Quraish men!' shouted he to the idolaters who were there in groups. 'An astounding piece of news! The son of Al Khattab hath lost his reason!'—'Thou liest!' interrupted Umar who had followed him. 'On the contrary, I have set out on the Road to Salvation. I bear witness that there is no other God but Allah and that Mohammad is His Prophet!'

On hearing these words, amounting to insulting aggression, the Quraish bounded forward, as one man, to throw themselves on Umar, who steadfastly awaited their attack and a fearful struggle took place. The sun, darting its flaming rays on the fighters, forced them to desist for a short space of time. During the truce, Umar sat down on the ground, surrounded by his enemies whose threatening hands were stretched over his head. 'Do with me as ye will', he told them in tones of the most scornful indifference, 'but by Allah! if I were only at the head of three hundred Mussulmans, we shall not be long before we wrested this Temple from you, and never would ye be able to retake it!'

At this Juncture, a respected old man, attired in a striped mantle and a sumptuously embroided tunic, draw nigh, brought there by the tumult of which he asked the cause. 'Umar is demented,' was the answer.—'How so?' said the old man to the idolaters. 'If this man hath voluntarily chosen some religion different to yours, hath he not a right to do so? What want ye of him? Moreover, think ye that his relatives will not feel inclined to interfere on his behalf?' Struck more by the fear of reprisals than by the wisdom of his words, Umar's assailants clustering round him, dropped back and dispersed. It seemed as if a heavy cloak had been lifted from his shoulders.

No one, except Mohammad, deared to pray in public. Umar, caring naught for the fury he might cause, made up his mind to follow the Prophet's (Peace be on him) example, and every day, the sturdy warrior turned like Mohammad in the direction of the Bait-ul-Muquaddas (The Holy Temple of Jerusalem). Doing exactly the same as the Prophet, (Peace be on him) Umar took his stand between the angle of the Ka'bah where the Black Stone is enframed and the angle looking towards the Yaman; and there publicly said his prayers. Encouraged by this audacity, numerous were the Moslems who came to pray in public by his side, despite the angry glances of the Unbelievers, only restrained by the reputation of Umar who had earned the surname of "Al Faruq," (The Cleaver), because he had once cleft in twain an Arab who refused to bow down to a decision given out by the Prophet (Peace be on him) .

THE TEXTILE OF THE BANUHA SHAM
(A.D. 616)

Despite the superiority of numbers, the idol-worshippers of the Quraish were obliged to acknowledge the critical state of their party. Unless they could put an end to the irresistible movement that daily brought new conversions, their domination over the Arabs would soon become a thing of the past.

They called a meeting, and, after consulting resolved a break off all relations with the Banu Hasham and the Banu Muttalib who were to be banished from Makkah until they consented to hand over Mohammad, their relative. In order to prevent themselves being tempted to break their word, the Quraish leaders wrote out the conditions of this compact on a sheet of parchment which they hung up inside the Ka'bah.

Their plan was most cunning. Among the Banu Hasham and the Banu Muttalib were a large number of idolaters who the Quraish thought would refuse to identify themselves with Mohammad and suffer for his cause. Therefore, strife would be stirred up in the bosom of the Prophet's (Peace be on him) family. But, contrary to the idol-worshippers' example, Abu Talib, Mohammad's uncle, carried away all the members of his family—with the exception of irreducible Abu Lahab—actuated by feelings of unanimous solidarity.

This fact enables us to divine one of the reasons that prevented Abu Talib from adopting the Islamic religions, although he worked hard and successfully, helping it to triumph. He did not forget Abu Lahab's ironical remark: 'Thou has naught else to do than to obey thy son Ali, now that Mohammad hath chosen him to be his lieutenant.' Abu Talib's pride caused him to dread mockery. 'I would willingly become a convert, to Islam,' said he, one day, 'were it not that I fear to become the laughing stock of the men of Makkah when they would see me saying my prayers'. Nevertheless, these motives would not have held him back, if he had not considered that the protection he granted to his nephew, threatened on all sides, would lose all its power following the day when the uncle also should have abjured the religion of his forefathers.

Directly after the proclamation of the decree of expulsion, the members of the Prophet's (Peace be on Him) family, Mussulmans or idolaters, left their houses, scattered here and there in different districts of the town, and assembled in the neighbouring ravine where Abu Talib possessed a stronghold.

During a period of two years, the exiles endured the greatest privations. Their provisions were quickly exhausted and it was impossible to renew them. They were forbidden to show themselves in the markets, and if one among them, having succeeded in getting to follow a caravan, tried to procure a few articles of food, the dealers, watched by Abu Jahal or fearing to be denounced, asked such high prices that the luckless one was obliged to give up all ideas of purchase, and return empty-handed to his starving family.

The outlaws were sometimes secretly revictualled by compassionate folks, such as Hisham ibn Umar who had recourse to the following stratagem. At nightfall, he led a camel, laden with provisions, to the entrance of the ravine, and gave him a violent cut with a whip, in such a way that the animal bolted in the direction of the starving fugitives and was captured by them. But such a godsend was not an everyday occurrence, and Mohammad and his family were driven to feed on the leaves of the thorny bushes growing in the valley.

THE DECREE OF EXPULSION DESTROYED BY A WORM

Meanwhile, the Prophet (Peace be on him) was apprised by a vision that, in order to destroy the impious document, written by the Quraish, Allah had sent a gnawing worm and only the Holy Name had been respected.

Abu Talib, hearing about this, and having faith in his nephew's vision, went with his brothers and sought out the Unbelievers. They exulted on seeing his approach, his features distorted by the pangs of hunger. Conquered by famine, was Abu Talib about to throw over his nephew? They were so sure that this was the case, that they accepted his proposals without hesitation. 'Let us go and look at the parchment,' he said, 'If Mohammad speaketh truly, the act is abolished. Should that be, ye must swear to cancel your ruling of outlawry that oppresseth us. For my part, I swear to give Mohammad up to you if he hath lied.'

The act was sealed with three seals. Since it had been deposited in the Ka'bah, it had neither been seen nor touched by anyone. Therefore Allah's enemies thought it impossible that the Prophet's (Peace be on him) vision could be authentic and, anticipating victory, they went to the Temple with Abu Talib, to see the state of the parchment. The Prophet's (Peace be on him) words had come true. In the act in question, the gnawing maggot had destroyed every unjust and impious sentence. Naught remained intact except a narrow strip of parchment on which could be read those words: "In Thy name, Allah!"

This verification plunged the idolaters into a state of unspeakable stupor. Abu Jahal was the first to leave the Temple and he tried to retract the promise given by the Quraish. Thereupon, many among them—Hisham ibn Umar, Zohair ibn Abi Ommayah, Moutam ibn Adiyy, etc., whose interests and intercourse suffered on account of the odious decree, having only signed it under duress, protested one after the other. 'We supported this iniquitous law against our will. Now it no longer exists. Therefore the impious pact set forth therein should be annulled.'

Abu Jahal was forced to bow down in the face of the prodigy and these vehement protestations. The compact was cancelled. The Banu Hasham and the Banu Mattalib returned without let or hindrance to their dwellings.

THE DEATH OF ABU TALIB AND KHADIJAH

It seemed as if Islam was henceforward to soar aloft safely, when two events suddenly caused its wings to be clipped.

We have already mentioned that, despite all his sympathy for Islam, Abu Talib had never consented to profess it. Abu Talib, in his dying moments having advised all present to obey Mohammad in everything, for he was sure to lead them into the Prophet (Peace be on him) of Righteousness, the Prophet (Peace be on him) risked a supreme effort. 'O my uncle!', said Mohammad, 'thou dost soothe their souls with wise counsel, but wilt thou do nothing for thine own?'—'What wouldst have me do?'—'Bear witness simply that there is no Allah but Allah!'—'O son of my brother! I know that thou dost speak truly, but I fear to be accused of only testifying in affright at the approach of death. Were it not for this fear, be assured that I would follow thy advice, in order to freshen thine eyes in which I read the high degree of thy affection.'

Some writers maintain that Abbas, seeing the dying man's lips move, and having placed his ear close to them, made the following declaration to the Prophet (Peace be on him), 'Be not uneasy, O son of my brother! thy uncle hath just uttered words thou didst wish him to say.' But the most accredited traditions refuse to accept this version. Where is the truth? Allah only knows!

Three days after this bereavement, fraught with fatal consequences the Prophet (Peace be on him) had to put up with a still more grievous loss.

Khadijah, his admirable companion, who gave herself to him when he was poor and had believed in him when he was called an imposter; Khadijah, to whom he confided all his hopes; Khadijah, the sweet consoling creature when he was crushed by the weight of despair; Khadijah, the first female Moslem, the "Mother of the Believers", was taken from him by the Fates at the age of sixty-five. (May Allah welcome her in his Grace!)

Khadijah's ascendancy over him was so great and yet so tender that while she lived, he had never been unfaithful. Never, although he was then in the prime of his life, would he consent to have other wives or concubines, as permitted by the customs of his country, in spite of being invited on all sides to do so. And never, when Khadijah was no more, did he forget her.

Ayishah, who later on became Mohammad's favourite spouse, was keenly jealous of the remembrance of his first wife, daily evoked by him. "Never was I so jealous of any wife of the Prophet (Peace be on him) as of Khadijah," Ayishah is known to have said, "although I never met her and notwithstanding that her death took place long before my marriage. But the Prophet (Peace be on him) was always talking about her, and when he slaughtered a sheep, he always kept back a liberal share to be given to Khadijah's female friends.

I said to him once, 'It seems as if Khadijah was the only woman in the whole world!' Thereupon he began to enumerate her incomparable qualities and declared that she would have a palace built of pearls in Paradise, with no noise or household cares to trouble her.

Hala bint Khuaild, Khadijah's sister, was taken to see Allah's Messenger. He noticed that she spoke in the same way as his dead wife, and was so stirred that, overcome by jealousy, I could not help showing temper and I exclaimed: 'What meanest thou by continually conjuring up the remembrances of these old Quraish females, with their toothless red gums and faces betraying the ravages of age? Hath not Allah given thee better women in their stead?'

But despite these scenes, despite the beauty and intelligence of Ayishah and his other wives, the Prophet (Peace be on him) always preferred Khadijah. He included her among the four most perfect women that ever came to earth. The three others were Asiya, Pharoah's wife who saved Moses; Maryam (Mary), mother of Isa (Jesus); and Fatimah-tuz-Zahra, one of the Mohammad's daughters by Khadijah.

THE JOURNEY TO TAIF

Stricken by his double mourning, threatened by the Unbelievers who no longer concealed their intentions, now that his noble protector was no more, the Prophet resolved to preach outside Makkah. If he succeeded in gaining over some of the neighbouring Arab peoples, these reinforcements, increasing the number of citizens of Makkah already converted, and which was far from inconsiderable, would

Muslims visiting the cemetery on Friday.

make up a party sufficiently strong to hold his detractors in respect.

His first attempt was made at Taif, a small town about seventy-two miles to the east of Makkah, renowned for its grapes, figs, pomegranates and the roses of its enchanting gardens. Accompanied by Zayd ibn Haris, the Prophet (Peace be on him) arrived in the market place where he found many noted Saqifs assembled. He sat by their side and stated the reasons of his journey: his Divine Mission and the hostility of his party.

Most of those present were beginning to fall under the influence of the wonted charm of his words, when three brothers, ranking among them the most noble and predominant of the Saqifs, interrupted him abruptly. 'This man hath doubtless stolen or torn the veil of the Ka'bah!' exclaimed the first of the brothers', 'and now, having taken to his heels, he tells you a story about being Allah's Messenger!'—'Hath Allah not been able to find anyone but thee?' jeered the second.—'By Allah! I'll never have anything to do with thee!' declared the third. 'If thou art truly the Prophet (Peace be on him) of Allah as thou dost assert, thou art so far above that I dare not argue with thee; and if thou art merely any impostor, it would not be fitting that I belittle myself by replying.'

These remarks broke the charm, and the crowd, veering round, showed its hostility by shouting insults. The Prophet (Peace be on him) saw that there was no hope for him in that town for the moment, and rose up to depart.

So as to make it impossible for him to renew his attempt, his contradictors stirred up the lowest dregs of the populace against him. Slaves and vagabonds, arrayed in a double row, awaited him on each side of the road he was bound to take. They found amusement in stoning his bare legs. When exhausted by his sufferings, he sat down in the middle of the road, trying to shield his bleeding feet, his tormentors lifted him up by the arms and continued their barbarous fun. In vain, devoted Zayd tried to protect him by getting in front of him; the faithful henchman was struck down by a stone that cut his face. Staggering, falling, rising and dragging themselves along in the midst of sneering jibes, Mohammad and his companion at last reached a garden wall, behind which they took refuge and dropped exhausted in the shade of a tree covered with vine branches, leaves and grapes.

'O Allah!' cried the Prophet,' (Peace be on him) 'To thee I complain of my puny strength and the failure of my zeal with regard to these men. O Thou! most Compassionate and Merciful, Thou art the Lord of the weak and Thou art my Lord! I have none but Thee on whom to lean! But if Thou be not angry with me because I am powerless to ensure love and respect for Thy Word I care nothing for all the ordeals I undergo!'

The villainous mob did not dare to trespass in the garden in order to follow up their victims. The owners of the property, charitable folks, indignant at the scene they had just witnessed, ordered Adas, their gardener, to gather bunches of grapes and carry a basketful to their momentary guests.

When the inflammation of their limbs had subsided by reason of repose in the beneficial shade; and their thirst being quenched by the honeyed juice of the celebrated grapes of Taif, the Prophet (Peace be on him) and his companion set out again on the road to Makkah.

Foreseeing the welcome in store for him, Mohammad could not do otherwise than claim the assistance of some influential citizen. Halting at the cave of Mount Hira, he sent Zayd to find a protector. After two rebuffs at the hands of Al Akhnas and Sohail, who excused themselves, Zayd approached Muta'm bin Adiyy who, consenting to take the responsibility on himself, armed his serving-men and posted them in the precincts of the Ka'bah.

Brought back by Zayd, Mohammad was then enabled, thanks to the escort of this little army, to make the seven ritual circuits before returning to his dwelling.

CHAPTER THE FOURTH

THE NOCTURNAL JOURNEY AND ASCENSION

"Al-Isra", the Nocturnal Journey, and "Al-Miraj," the Prophet's (Peace be on him) Ascension, have given rise to innumerable debates between the doctors of Islam. Some think that his miraculous journey was really, physically accomplished; whilst others, relying on the most accredited traditions—among which is that of Ayishah, Abu Bakr's daughter and Mohammad's favourite wife—maintain that Mohammad's soul alone undertook the journey, and that it should only be looked upon as a veracious vision such as frequently came to the Prophet (Peace be on him) in his sleep.

One night, the twenty-seventh of the month of Rabi'-ul-Awwal, the angel Jibra'il, upon whom devolved the duty of directing the heavenly bodies, was ordered by the Almighty to increase the moon's brilliancy by adding a part of the sun's radiance; and that of the stars by a share of the moon's brightness, so that the firmament that night should be resplendent with light. The Angel was then to descend to where Mohammad was sleeping, and carry him up to Allah through the seven zones of Heaven.

Quoth the Prophet: (Peace be on him) "I was in a deep sleep when Jibra'il appeared to me, bringing Al-Buraq's, the Prophet's (Peace be on him) usual mount. This animal resembled none to be found on earth. His size was greater than that of an ass; less than that of a mule. His coat was more dazzlingly white than snow; he had the face of a man, but was dumb. Great wings like those of a bird allowed him to rise in the air and career through space. His mane, tail, feathers and breast-piece were studded with priceless precious stones that sparkled like myriads of stars.

I got on his back and, in a twinkling, he carried me from the "Masjidu'l-Haram" to the "Masjidu'l-Aqsa" (*i.e.* the Sacred Makkan Temple to the faraway Temple of Jerusalem). I alighted and fastened his bridle to the ring used by the Prophets. A man appeared in front of me, offering a cup of milk and a cup of wine. I drank the milk and refused the wine. Jibra'il who had accompanied me without outstripping me or allowing me to outrun him, approved what I had done. "If thou hadst preferred wine to milk," he told me, "thy people would have preferred Error to Truth".

After visiting the Temple, the Prophet (Peace be on him) climbed up the "Sakhrah," the Sacred Rock (on which now stands the marvellous dome of the Mosque of Umar) which bowed down in his honour and also so as to enable him to remount Al-Buraq. Still led by his celestial guide, he continued his journey by ascending through the Heavens.

We need not copy the descriptions of this Ascension, or "Miraj," in every detail. Writers, particularly the Persians, have given a free rein to their imagination in this connection, whilst others, more serious, such as Ibn-i-Hisham, Ibn-i-Sad and Abul Fida, are content to set forth an extremely simple narrative. We shall only mention Mohammad's meeting with the Prophets known before him: Abraham, Moses and Jesus; then his visit to the Paradise of Believers, where the gardens honoured him by giving out sweet odours and his halt in Hell, destined to receive Unbelievers, where the flames congealed when he went along.

After having passed through the seven zones of the Heavens, it was not long before he heard the scratching of pens writing in the "Book of Fate," and the thanksgivings of angels glorifying the Almighty. Finally, he reached the "Sldratu'l-Muntaha," the "Lote-tree of the Extremity." At this spot, Jibra'il left him, saying: "Here is the boundary of Knowledge, where I am forced to halt. As for thee, O Prince of Messengers! O friend of the Master of the Worlds! Continue thy glorious Ascension and progress in the city of thy Lights."

And the Chosen One continued to pass through the veils covering that which is hidden, until he reached the veil of Unity and looked upon that which eyes cannot see, nor minds imagine. The eyes of his body would not have been able to support the brilliancy of this sight which must have brought on blindness. Therefore, Allah opened the eyes of Mohammad's heart, thus permitting him to contemplate the Infinite Splendour.

Allah had him draw near to His throne, *"at the distance of two hows, or even closer"* (the Qur'an, liii, i), and after having confirmed the choice He had made in charging Mohammad to be the carrier of Good Tidings to His servants, He fixed the number of prayers-fifty in all-that each Believer should offer up daily to the Creator, in gratitude for His bounty.

When the Chosen One went down, Moses met him again and questioned him. 'O Prophet of Allah! what hath our Master ordered thee with regard to the number of prayers which His disciples should offer up?' 'Fifty prayers during the day and night.'—'O thou, the best created being!' Moses rejoined, 'go back to our Master, and beg Him to lighten this burden, too heavy for the weakness and laziness of mankind.' So Mohammad went back several times into the presence of the Master of the Worlds, until he prevailed upon Him to reduce the number of prayers to five only.

This parable, which serves to decide definitively the number of daily prayers, also demonstrates admirably that an excess of devotion, in the Islamic creed, is considered to be an error. *"Allah desireth to make your burden light to you: for man hath been created weak"*. (the Qur'an, iv, 32). Why should the Almighty be in need of the prayers of mankind? *"We ask not of Thee to make provision for Thyself We will provide for Thee"*. (the Qur'an, xx, 132).

Allah has sent prayer to His servants as one of His most salutary favours. Five times daily, devotion brings absolute rest to Believers; that is to say, complete interruption of the feelings that stir them, whether an excess of joy leading to ruin in the aberrations of debauchery, or an excess of sadness causing them to perish in the madness of despair. Five times daily, prayer forces them by its accompanying ablutions to call to mind the cleanliness of the body, at the same time as the purity of the soul.

The day after his vision, the Prophet (Peace be on him) beaming with delight, was met by his mortal enemy, Abu Jahal, who addressed him ironically: 'O Mohammad! thou has not one of those marvellous tales which we are used to hear from thee to tell us this morning?'—'Indeed I have!' replies Prophet. (Peace be on him) Between yesternight and this morning I have been to Jerusalem and back.'—'Gather round quickly, O Quraish! Hasten and hearken to the wonderful adventure of the nocturnal journey undertaken by Mohammad!' shouted Abu Jahal.

The crowd soon grew, and the Prophet (Peace be on him) gave out the narrative we have just set forth. Most of his hearers, belonging to the clan of the idol-worshippers, followed the example of their chieftain and received it with outbursts of the coarsest merriment. Some clapped their hands; others held their heads in their hands as if to stop their brains from bursting. As for the Believers, one party was undecided whether to put faith in the story or not; and the remainder, unsettled by the attitude of the public, dare not manifest their confidence openly.

Profiting by the confusion, Abu Jahal hastened to speak to Abu Bakr. 'Maybe thou dost know the last extraordinary adventure of thy Prophet? He pretends to have accomplished in the night the journey from the "Holy Temple" of Makkah to the "Faraway Temple" of Jerusalem there and back! 'Abu Jahal was full of glee, in anticipation, at the thought of the vexation and bewilderment which were sure to be seen in the face of his fellow citizen.

Contrary to Abu Jahal's expectations, however, Abu Bakr replied without uneasiness: 'Whatever Mohammad asserts is true and I believe it. If he maintains that he went up to the seventh Heaven in an hour and came back in the same space of time, I should still have faith in his declarations.'

Such dependable testimony caused the Faithful to take heart. Thus it turned out that Abu Jahal, by trying to put incredulity in men's minds, only succeeded in strengthening their beliefs. Desirous of catching the Prophet (Peace be on him) red-handed as a cheat, Abu Jahal interrogated him concerning the Temple of Jerusalem, calling on him for a description thereof. But he was utterly routed when Mohammad, whom his foe thought had never set foot in Jerusalem, except during his nocturnal vision, described the city in all its peculiarities and with great accuracy, endorsed by all among those assembled who had ever undertaken that journey.

Therefore the Believers, their faith reviven, hastened to put on the five "Garments of Purity", which means they offer up the five prayers brought down to them from Heaven by the Prophet (Peace be on him) .

HOW SIX INHABITANTS OF YASRIB WERE CONVERTED *(A.D. 620)*

Towards the end of the year, Usman ibn Affan and his wife Ruqaiyah returned from Abyssinia, accompanied by a few emigrants, among whom, one of them, called Sukran, died on arrival. The Prophet (Peace be on him) married his widow, Sauda, daughter of Zoma, thus rewarding the zeal of one of the first female converts to Islam, who had so valiantly undergone the ordeals of persecution and exile.

Wishing, in the same way, to show his appreciation of the unchanging devotion of Abu Bakr, the Veracious, and to bind him still closer by a matrimonial alliance, the Prophet (Peace be on him) at the same epoch, espoused his daughter Ayishah, although she had barely reached the age of ten. But, in her case, the marriage was not consummated until many years later, at Al Madinah, after the Hegira.

Despite Abu Bakr's energetic affirmations; despite the strengthening of the Believers' zeal by the rule of the five prayers, the story of the Nocturnal Ascension was far from being advantageous to the cause of Islam. The narrative, on the contrary, furnished its enemies with an opportunity of petty triumph, enabling them to pile up fresh mockery and institute greater persecution.

The case would have seemed hopeless to any other but Mohammad. He knew not what it meant to be discouraged, feeling certain that the Almighty would never abandon His Apostle to whom He had revealed the following verses: *"Say: I betake me for refuge to the Lord of Men, The King of Men, Allah of Men Against the mischief of the stealthily withdrawing whisper (Satan) Who hides himself at the Name of Allah, Who whispereth in man's breast against Jinn and men."* (Qur'an, cxiv, 16.)

Postponing for the time being the conversion of the Makkans, the Prophet (Peace be on him) turned his attention towards Arab strangers in the town attracted in great crowds by the ceremonies of the pilgrimage to the Kabah and the ritual circuits. During the fair that was held at that time, he went untiringly from group to group. But, just as indefatigable, close behind, was his uncle, Abu Lahab, who, as soon as he saw the Prophet (Peace be on him) in the centre of a ring of men, would call out loudly to them: 'Hearken not to that man! His sole thought is to tear the cult of Lat and Uzza from out of your hearts; and trick ye all with the insane doctrines that he pretends it is his Mission to preach'.

These words aroused the Arabs' suspicious, and they turned away from Mohammad with remarks after this fashion: 'Thy fellow-citizens know thee better than we,so begin by convincing them!' Or else: 'If Allah should cause thee to triumph, thy glory will not profit us, but only thy party. Therefore, it is not to our advantage to ally ourselves to thee.'

These rebuffs had no effect on the Prophet (Peace be on him). No sooner did any noteworthy person arrive in Makkah than Mohammad sought his presence at once.

One, day on the hill of Aqabah, he went up to a group of six men, fresh arrivals, and with his usual politeness, he addressed them thus: 'What are you, O my good Lords?'—'We are of the Khazraj tribe.'—'Masters over the Jews settled in Yasrib, methinks?'—'We are indeed their masters.'—'Will ye not sit down here awhile so that I may speak with you?'—'Willingly.'

E. DINET.

SCENES FROM THE BADIA OR NOMADIC LIFE. *The Exodus*

They sat by his side, and he tried to gather them into the fold of Islam by reciting verses of the Qur'an. Charmed by his eloquence and the novelty of his words, the Khazraj men listened attentively and paused to reflect.

The Jews, inhabiting their land and bent beneath their yoke, were folks well versed in the knowledge of Holy Writ. Thus it was that whenever disagreement arose between them and their masters, these children of Israel were wont to murmur: 'We await the coming of the Prophet. When his hour arrives, we shall all follow him and thanks to his assistance, we shall triumph over you and become your masters in our turn.' Whilst Mohammad spoke unto the tribesmen, they exchanged glances and came to this conclusion: 'Evidently this is the Prophet (Peace be on him) whose advent is threatened by the Jews. We must not let them forestall us with him.'

So they replied to his appeal, saying: 'Our land is made desolate by perpetual war waged between us and our Arab bothers, the Aus tribe. We will go to them, call their attention to thy cause and thy religion. If through thee Allah should reconcile and unite us, there will not be in all Arabia a man more powerful than thee!'

THE TWO OATHS OF THE ARABAH *(A.D. 621)*

The new converts kept their word and spread Mohammad's doctrines in their region. The following year, twelve Mussulmans from Yasrib, ten being of the Khazraj and two belonging to the Aus, arrived in Makkah for the Mausam rejoicings. They met the Prophet (Peace be on him) on the Aqabah and took an oath of fidelity towards him. With a view to completing their religious education and making fresh converts, Mohammad delegated Musab ibn Umr, one of his most learned disciples, who went away with them.

In Yasrib, the Islamic creed did not meet with the difficulties that hampered its progress in Makkah, where it was harmful to the interests of the exploiters of the idols. Musab's task turned out to be particularly easy, and the "Permanent Miracle" of the Surahs of the Qur'an, recited by him, produced its effect with lightning-like rapidity. Resembling a beneficial rainstorm which might have broke, in a few minutes, over every part of a country suffering from drought, restoring life and fertility, Islam had diffused its wholesome dew over every district of the town, calming dissensions and causing the virtues necessary for its triumph to take root and flourish in the citizens' hearts.

Soon there was not a single family among the Aus or the Khazraj which did not count several Believers among its members. Musab, who had good reasons to be proud of the results of his mission, returned to Makkah to report progress to Mohammad. When the data of the pilgrimage came due, seventy-five Mussulmans, two being women, joined the caravan of their fellow-citizens who were still idolaters. The converts, full of zeal, arranged to meet the Prophet (Peace be on him) on the Aqabah, during the night proceeding the second day of Tashriq, in order to offer a safe place of refuge in their city, for him and his disciples.

Ka'bibn Malik, one of the pilgrims, has said: 'We made up our minds to keep our moments secret from our idolatrous fellow-citizens, among them we slept until one third of the night was passed. We then went out, one after another, stealthily, making our way, slowly and silently, towards a pass on the slopes of the Aqabah, where we all met together to await the Prophet (Peace be on him). He soon arrived, accompanied by his uncle Abbas ibn Abdul-Muttalib.

He had not yet abjured the religion of his ancestors, but had great affection for his nephew from whom he wished to ward off all misfortune, following the example of his brother, Abu Talib. Having been informed of the plans of the people of Yasrib, Abbasa wanted to see for himself, what amount of confidence Mohammad could have in their proposals. Abbas was the first to address the meeting and spoke as follows: 'O Assembly of the Khazraj and the Aus! My brother's son as ye know, holds high rank among us, and although we do not share his convictions, we have hitherto protected him against his follow-citizens. In our "qawm" he finds honour and safety. Nevertheless, at the present hour, he turns towards you, and desires to settle in your midst. Reflect! If ye decide to remain faithful to your promises and shield him from all dangers whatsoever, it will be well. But should ye fear to be forced one day to throw him over, and give him, into the hands of his enemies, it would be better now at once, to confess that your purpose is not steadfast by withdrawing your proposals and leaving him with his own party.'

Without the slightest hesitation, we answered Abbas: 'Thou hast heard what we proposed. Thou canst rely on us absolutely!' Then we turned to Mohammad: 'Speak, O Prophet! What dost thou want of us, for thy Lord and for thyself?'

After having recited a few Surahs and recapitulated the fundamental principles of Islam, the Prophet (Peace be on him) added: 'Swear that ye will fight to defend me and my desciples, as ye would fight to defend your wives and children.'

We took the required oath with unanimous enthusiasm: 'By Allah! We are war-children, and our fathers have taught us how to manufacture all weapons!' 'O Prophet!' broke in Abul Hasham, 'there exists a compact, between the Jews and Yasrib and us, which we shall have to break, perhaps, in order to uphold thy cause. What would be our position, in our land, if, after being victorious thanks to us, thou didst go back to thy "qawm"?'

The Prophet (Peace be on him) smiled and protested: 'Rest easy on that score! Your blood hath become my blood and your honour, my honour. He who wrongeth you, wrongeth me. I'll fight the enemies you fight, and support whom ye support; ye are mine and I am yours! Choose then twelve Najibs among you as leaders.'

After having consulted together, we chose nine Khazru and three Aus. When we brought the twelve men to him, he said: 'Ye shall be my delegates in your "qawm," as were the apostles of Jesus, son of Mary, among their people.'

The Najibs pledged their words; but, just as the solemn oath was about to be sworn, Ibn-i-Ubadah rose and said: 'O Assembly of Khazraj and Aus! Have ye reflected seriously about the consequences of the compact ye intend to make with this man? For his sake ye swear to go to war with white, swarthy and black men. But if, in days to come, seeing your property pillaged and your nobles massacred, ye were to forsake him, shame would be brought upon you in this world and the next.'—'We are resigned in anticipation of the loss of our property and to the death of our best men, if such a sacrifice is useful for the cause of Islam,' we replied unhesitatingly, 'but may we ask the Prophet (Peace be on him) what we shall receive in exchange?' He replied: 'Paradise!'

"Who, from desire to behold the face of their Lord, are constant amid trials, and observe prayer, and give alms in secret and openly out of what We have bestowed upon them and turn aside evil by good: for these is the recompense of the abode, Gardens of Eden—into which they shall enter together with the just of their wives, and their descendents: and the angels shall go in unto them at every portal: Peace be upon you! say they, because ye have patiently endured! And charming is the recompense of the Abode!"

So oft as they are fed therefrom with fruit for sustenance, they shall say, "This same was our sustenance of old!' But they will only resemble those of earth, being infinitely more delicious . . . And theirs shall be the Houris with large black eyes like close-kept pearls . . . No vain discourse shall they hear therein, nor charge of sin We will remove whatever rancour was in their hearts . . . and shall say 'Praise to be Allah who hath guided us hither.'

And other things which ye desire will He bestow: Help from Allah and greedy conquest! . . . O ye who believe! be ansars of Allah (i.e. helpers, soldiers.)" (the Qur'an, xiii, 22, 23, 24. ii, 23. lvi, 22, 24. vii, 41. lxi, 13, 14.)

When they heaped these promises of inconceivable bliss in Paradise, announced by such tokens as are understood by mortals' weak brains, the Faithful felt their souls filled with hope and said to the Prophet (Peace be on him) 'Stretch out thine hand!' Mohammad offered his hand, opened out, the palm turned upwards; and Asad ibn Zarara came and struck it with his right hand, followed by Abul Hisham and Al Bara; and one after the other, all the Yasrib pilgrims, who from that day fourth called themselves, "Ansars".

We were getting ready to return furtively to our encampment, our heart brimming over with joy and hope, when, in the silence of the night, on the summit of the Aqabah, a voice resounded, the most shrill I had heard. 'O Assembly of Quraish!' it shouted, 'be on your guard! The sons of the Khazraj and Aus have sworn to fall upon you with the sword!'

We shuddered, but the Prophet (Peace be on him) removed our fears by saying: 'That is the voice of the demon of the Aqabah which means that Iblis (Satan) is shrieking. He is Allah's enemy, and his cry has not been heard by any of our adversaries.' We returned to our tents, where we found our fellow-citizens sleeping soundly, suspecting naught of that which had taken place.

Nevertheless, upon awaking, next day, a deputation of Quraish nobles arrived, warned either by the voice of Iblis, or by reports of spies dogging the Prophet's (Peace be on him) footsteps. 'O Assembly of the Khazraj and Aus!' said these delegates, 'it hath come to our ears that ye have allured one of our men, Mohammad ibn Abdullah and taken an oath with him to wage war upon us.'

The idolaters of our party, knowing nothing about the events of the nights, swore with most evident sincerity that the Quraish were mistaken. 'This business is improbable!' exclaimed one of their chieftains, Abu Salul by name, 'My "qawm" would not have hidden it from me and I have heard naught about it.'

The Quraish tribesmen went away, more or less tranquilised, but they met on their road some Bedouins who had been witnesses of the strange gathering in the Aqabah ravine and who imparted their suspicions. The Quraish, convinced of the treachery of the Khazraj and the Aus, turned back in great haste to the encampment. But the tents were struck; the birds had flown and were far off by that time, out of danger.

THE PLOT AGAINST THE PROPHET

Henceforward the Prophet (Peace be on him) could reckon on safety and shelter in the town of Yasrib and he gave orders to all his disciples to take refuge within its walls.

The idolaters could not help feeling great apprehension, by reason of their victims meeting with the inhabitants of a rival city. The worshippers of images impeded the union by means of great violence, and it was only one by one, or in small, successive groups that the Believers were able to reach their place of safety. From that day onwards, they took the name of "Muhajirun," or emigrants.

As for the Prophet, (Peace be on him) relieved of all anxiety concerning them, he stopped in Makkah with Ali and Abu Bakr only. They knew full well the risk they ran, but despite Abu Bakr's adjurations, Mohammad wished to make a supreme effort, and not resort to force before leaving his native town. He still hoped to rescue some of his fellow-countrymen from idolatry, especially as he now had a shelter to offer them; and besides, he did not like to leave his post without authorisation from the Lord.

The emigration of the Believers carried the fury of the Quraish idolaters to the highest pitch as well as causing them great anxiety. They resolved a strike a decisive blow.

They called a meeting in the "Dar-un-Nadwa," "House of Counsel," built by the ancestor, Qusayy ibn Kilab. The most important resolutions were taken in this "Dar-un-Nadwa," where only the descendants of Qusayy were admitted, but not until they reached the age of forty.

Just as representatives of every division of the Quraish were entering the "House of Counsel," a tall, old man of haughty bearing, attired in woollen garments, appeared on the threshold. In reply to questions as to who he was and what he wanted, he replied: 'I am a Shaikh of the Najd. Attracted by your noble gait and the sweetness of your favourite scents, I feel great desire to hear you speak. If ye consent to admit me to your noble assembly, perchance my advice may not be entirely useless.'

The inhabitants of the Najd lived too far away to be suspected of acting in complicity with Mohammad, therefore the Committee of the Elders found that nothing prevented them from authorising the noble stranger to be present during their meeting, and he followed them into the hall of debate. The Head Committee started the discussion at once. 'We all know,' they said to each other, 'about the intrigues of this man Mohammad and the danger with which he threatens our country. We will talk over the best means of defence. Let each of us give his opinion freely.'

The first to speak was Abul Bukhtari who made this proposal: 'Let us cast our enemy into a dungeon, load him with chains, and bolt the door upon him until he dies.'—'Such a proceeding would be fraught with fatal consequences,' the Shaikh of the Najd objected, 'if you carry it out. The news of your act of violence would filter through the prison gates and reach the ears of Mohammad's companions who, ye may be sure, would quickly attack you in order to free him. Thanks to assistance of the Yasrib Mussulmans, they would be victorious. Let us hear someone else's proposition.'

Asad ibn Rabiya rose and said: 'Why cannot we expulse him from among us and banish him from our country? When he is gone, little we reck where he taketh refuge or what becometh of him. We shall be well rid of him.'—'Truly, a fine piece of advice!' exclaimed the Shaikh of the Najd. 'Know ye nothing about the beauty of your adversary's speech, the charm of his voice and the strength of his arguments? Scarcely will he have set foot among the neighbouring Arab tribes, when he will dominate by his eloquence, cause them to follow in his wake, and come back from exile at their head, to have his own way with you all! Try and find a more reasonable plan to crush him.'

Then it was the turn of Abu Jahal. 'By our gods!' said he, 'I have a project which, I am certain will satisfy you entirely.'—'Speak! What is thy plan?' exclaimed his audience.—'This is it. In each subdivision of our tribe we'll choose a young, vigorous warrior belonging to a family equally noble and respected, and we'll place in his hand a well-sharpened sword. These young warriors, banded together, shall throw themselves on Mohammad at the same instant; all striking him at once. By acting in this way, the responsibility of shedding his blood will be shared among all the subdivisions to which the murderers belong, and the Abd Manaf, relatives of the dead man, unable to declare war upon every subdivision of our tribe, will be obliged to content themselves with receiving the "Diyah" (blood ransom) that we may be good enough to offer.'—'These are words of intelligence!' exclaimed the Shaikh of the Najd, who was no other than Iblis (Satan) disguised in human shape. 'That man's motion points to the only way out of your difficulty.'

This perfidious counsel met with the unanimous approval of the assembly. The Unbelievers flattered themselves that their enemy was already got rid of, but they had reckoned without the will of the Almighty. The angel Jibra'il, sent by Him, warned the Prophet of the conspiracy to take his life, and brought him orders to emigrate in his turn, at the same time warning him as follows: 'Sleep not this night upon thy wonted couch.'

In Mohammad's house were several sums of money deposited with him by Unbelievers, and he did not care to go away before having given back what was due to each rightful owner. He charged his faithful Ali to carry this out, after having told him what he had just heard and saying: 'Sleep in my stead, on my habitual couch, and wrap thyself in this—my green mantle of the Hazramaut. Fear naught; no harm can come to thee from my enemies.'

When the first four hours of the night had gone by, the conspirators, among whom was Abu Jahal who had come to excite their zeal, were posted in ambush close to the door of the house, to prevent Mohammad from escaping. They did not wish to consummate their crime in darkness, for people might then have denied the participation of the Quraish. They preferred to await daybreak, so that it might be plainly visible that each and every one had an equal share in the murder. But He who never sleeps watched over His Prophet surrounded by foes.

"Verily on their necks, We have placed chains which reach the chin, and forced up their heads, And before them have We set a barrier and behind them a barrier, and We have shrouded them in a veil, so that they shall not see." the Qur'an, xxxvi, 7–8).

Confiding in the protection of his Lord, Mohammad crept quietly out of his dwelling, picking up some loose earth and throwing a handful or two on the head of each conspirator. He then went away. The eyes of the miscreants, beneath lids heavy with tedious waiting and blinded by the bandage of sleep that Allah had placed thereon, saw nothing.

'For whom are ye watching here?' quoth a passer-by, coming on the scene.—'For Mohammad.'—'Allah hath saved him and he hath tricked you all. He hath departed right under your noses and after covering your pates with dust, he strode away gaily.'

Each startled man swiftly clapped his hand to his head and, withdrawing his fingers dirty with dust, gave signs of stupefaction. But, peering through a crack in the door, they saw Ali asleep on the Prophet's (Peace be on him) couch and wrapped in his green mantle. This sight set the villains' minds at rest and they all stood sentinel till drawn.

Actuated by the same impulse, when the sun rose, they battered down the door and with swords unsheathed threw themselves on Ali. He sat up facing them. They recognised him and called out: 'How now! Can it be thee, O Ali? Where is thy companion?'—'I know not.'

In their fury at having been so finely tricked, they seize up Ali and imprisoned him in the Temple; but quickly recognising what a grave mistake they would make by being revenged on the son of Abu Talib, they set him free.

وَجَعَلْنَا مِن بَيْنِ أَيْدِيهِمْ سَدًّا وَمِنْ خَلْفِهِمْ
سَدًّا فَأَغْشَيْنَاهُمْ فَهُمْ لَا يُبْصِرُونَ

Old traditional scribe from the Desert.

CHAPTER FIVE — *Decorative plate.*

وَقَاتِلُوا فِي سَبِيلِ اللَّهِ الَّذِينَ يُقَاتِلُونَكُمْ

CHAPTER THE FIFTH

THE HEGIRA, OR THE EMIGRATION OF THE PROPHET TO MADINAH

At the moment when the Mohammedans were emigrating to Yasrib, Abu Bakr begged the Prophet (Peace be on him) to let him join them, but was answered thus: 'It is needless to hurry. Maybe Allah may give thee the companion thou dost prefer to undertake the journey in thy company.'

Hoping that this companion would turn out to be the Prophet (Peace be on him) in person, Abu Bakr purchased two swift she-camels, which he stabled in the courtyard of his house, feeding them liberally, and keeping them in readiness to take to the road.

Ayishah has said: "The Prophet, (Peace be on him) who never let a day go by, without coming to see my father, morning or evening, arrived suddenly at an unwonted hour. Abu Bakr guessed that some serious matter brought his son-in-law to our dwelling, and told him: 'Allah authoriseth me to depart from Makkah with my "qawm." My turn hath come to emigrate.'—'With me, O Prophet! in company with me?' supplicated Abu Bakr, plying him with questions. 'Yea in thy company.'—'At this answer, tears of joy such as I had never seen before, welled up in my father's eyes, and he apprised Mohammad of his preparations for travel."

The she-camels, in rare fettle, were handed over to Ibn-i-Arqs, idolater, but in whom, nevertheless, Abu Bakr placed great confidence. Ibn-i-Aqrs was to take them to graze, and three days later, lead them to a meeting-place appointed at the mouth of a cave in the Jabal Saur, about an hour and half's walk from Makkah, on the road leading to the sea. Ibn-i-Arqs would then serve as a guide as far as Yasrib.

By a small door at the back of the house, the two fugitives went off secretly, stepping softly, and making their way to the Saur cave. The Prophet's (Peace be on him) naked feet were soon bleeding, cut by the sharp, loose stones of the mountain paths. Abu Bakr, in despair at seeing the blood of God's Chosen One flowing, carried him on his back the rest of the way, and put him down in front of the entrance to the grot in which he entered first. He explored every hole and corner to make sure that it did not serve as a refuge for wild beasts or reptiles. He picked up all the stones which he piled in his cloak and threw down the side of the mountain. Then, with torn fragments of his apparel, he stopped up any holes which might have been places of concealment for scorpions or other venomous insects. Then only did he admit Mohammad who fell asleep, his head resting on his companion's thigh.

But under the sand carpeting the cave, was hidden a viper which had thus escaped Abu Bakr's vigilant, searching glances. By an involuntary movement, the devoted disciple stamped on the reptile which, furious, turned with a hiss, and drove its dart into Abu Bakr's heel. The pain was atrocious, but, fearing to awaken the Prophet (Peace be on him) whose head was pillowed on his companion's thigh, Abu Bakr made not the slightest movement, nor did he let a cry escape his lips.

Shortly afterwards, the venom began its malignant course through his veins and the intensity of the pain drew tears from his eyes. A few burning drops fell on Mohammad's cheek. Waking up with a start, the Prophet (Peace be on him) asked, 'What ails thee, O sincere friend?'—'I have been stung by a viper.'

The sacrifice of his being, made by Abu Bakr, had overwelmed him with joy bringing warmth to his heart, and triumphed over the evil effects of the poison that had begun to freeze his limbs, so that directly the Prophet (Peace be on him) rubbed the poisonous wound with a little of his saliva, all pain and swelling disappeared.

The Quraish, disturbed and maddened by the flight of Mohammad and Abu Bakr, despatched two town-criers, one on each side of the city of Makkah, charging them to offer a reward of a hundred she-camels for anyone who should overtake the fugitives. The most cunning trackers set out in all directions.

Abu Jabal lost no time in rushing to Abu Bakr's dwelling, and knocked furiously at the door. Asma, Ayishah's daughter came out to him. 'Where is thy father?' he asked.—'By God! I know not,' she replied. He lifted his hand and slapped her face so brutally that he tore out one of her earrings. He then rejoined a group of young men who were following a clue that took them to the Jabal Saur.

Scarcely had His Apostle sought shelter in the grot, than Allah ordered a shrub, grown to about a man's height, and known as "Umm-ul-Ghilan," a little way off from the cave, to leave the spot where it flourished and block up the entrance. Then He sent a spider to spin its web between the branches of the shrub and the jagged edges of the cavern's mouth; and also a pair of wild pigeons that built a nest and laid eggs in the narrow entrance.

At that juncture, the trackers began to arrive from all parts, enticed by the bait of the reward; but they were brought to a standstill by the fragile barrier built by the most humble among insects: a web that the slightest breath of a breeze sufficed to destroy.

'There is nothing to be done in this cave,' declared one of the Unbelievers, Ummayyata ibn Khalaf, just as they were getting ready to enter. 'See this cobweb. It dates, without a doubt, from before the birth of the man we are pursuing. How could Mohammad have entered the cave without tearing these slender threads? And look at those pigeons' eggs. Would he not have broken them as well?'

All found these deductions well-grounded and gave up the search that seemed futile. Abu Jahal was the only one who guessed they were on the right track. 'Nevertheless, I feel that our enemy is not far off,' he said. 'He is looking at us now, but magic spells cloud our eyes!' They went away, never thinking about searching on the ground for the tell-tale traces of the fugitives' footsteps.

While this scene was being enacted, Abu Bakr trembled greatly; not for his own life, but for that of his companion, to whom he said: 'My death means nothing more than a man dying; but thine means all the lives of thy disciples!'

They remained in their hiding-place three days and three nights. Abdullah, son of Abu Bakr, passed the whole of the day among the Unbelievers of Makkah; and at night, brought all the news he could gather. Ibn-i-Fuhairah, one of Abu Bakr's shepherds, led his flock to graze among those of the Quraish. At night, he drove his sheep in front of the cave, thus bringing food to the fugitives: milk and the flesh of the lambs. The following day, he went away with his flock, leading it over Abdullah's tracks so as to efface them.

On the third day, the vigilance of the Quraish being somewhat relaxed, Ibn-i-Aeqas kept his appointment punctually, bringing Abu Bakr's two she-camels, and a third belonging to him. Asma, too, had not been idle. She brought bags filled with provisions. All being in readiness, Abu Bakr made the best camel kneel down in front of the Prophet (Peace be on him) whom he asked to mount on her back. 'I cannot ride a camel that doth not belong to me', replied Mohammad.—'By my father and mother, she's thine! I give her to thee,'—'I cannot accept the gift. Tell me what she cost thee. I'll buy her for the same price.'

The bargain concluded, the Prophet (Peace be on him) bestrode that she-camel. Abu Bakr rode the other, taking up behind him, Ibn-i-Fulairah, his faithful servingman. Ibn-i-Arqas, on his own camel, guided the little caravan on the western road to Yasrib which runs, now and again, along the seashore.

SURAQA'S MISHAP

Quoth Suraqa ibn Malik: 'I was in a group of Makkans gossiping over recent events and the price set upon Mohammad's head, when a man of the nomadic tribes, coming from the Badya-land, told us the following story: On the road leading to the sea, I passed a small caravan comprising three she-camels. I seemed to recognise the riders. They were Mohammad and his companions.'

I winked to him to be silent and said out loud, in an indifferent sort of tone: 'Thou art mistaken. The folks thou didst meet were Bedouins that I sent out to search for straying camels belonging to me.'

I remained a little longer in the midst of the citizens, before returning to my dwelling, where I ordered my serving-maid to lead my horse to a secluded spot in the valley. I also ordered one of my slaves, a negro gifted with prodigious strength and indomitable courage, to drive one of my camels to the same place and there await my coming. I left my house by a back-door, bending down, trailing my spear low, on a level with the ground, so as to prevent the glistening of steel in the sunlight. I took all these precautions so as not to call the attention of those who, allured by the promised reward, might have followed and forced me to share with them, were I successful.

Arrived at the place of meeting, I mounted my camel and, accompanied by my slave who ran behind, holding my horse by the bridle, I diligently followed the track of the fugitives. When I thought I was sufficiently near to them, I mounted my horse, and left my camel to the care of my slave, giving him orders to rejoin me as quickly as possible.

My steed was fresh, not having been ridden for some days and he was renowned for his speed. I put him at a gallop. But after a few strides, he stuck his toes in the ground and fell, his nostrils in the sand, snorting and trembling. I was thrown off. Impressed by this evil omen, I pulled some "azlams" (divining arrows) out of my quiver to consult the decrees of fate. The signs pointed to bad luck, but the reward excited my greed, so I stuck to my plan and continued in pursuit.

Shortly afterwards I caught sight of the fugitives and, urging on my steed, I got so near that I could hear the voice of the Prophet (Peace be on him) reciting the Qur'an; but to my great astonishment, the noise of my galloping horse's hooves did not cause him the least uneasiness. He did not even deign to turn his head. On the other hand, Abu Bakr kept on looking round, and seemed to be in a state of the liveliest anxiety.

Just another effort and I was right up with them, when suddenly my horse's legs sank up to his knees into the earth, although it seemed very hard and firm in that spot. I was thrown over his head. I got up, exasperated, swearing at him and lashing him to make him get a foothold. But all in vain. His struggles and efforts only succeeded in making him sink more deeply down, as far as his belly, whilst a dust-cloud resembling a pillar of smoke, issued from the hole where he was swallowed up. I was overcome by sudden fear.

Once more I tried my luck by the arrows. The forebodings of evil fortune were just as plainly shown.

Interior of a Mosque. El Mihrab, or the Niche indicating the direction of Mecca.

Feeling sure, therefore, that some great calamity was in store to punish me for my projects, I cried out: 'O Mohammad, I plead for mercy at thy hands! In exchange, I'll bring thee useful tidings and beguile all those who are following me; but pray to thy God that He set my horse free.'

Mohammad threw up his hands, saying: 'O Allah! if Suraqa is sincere, deliver his steed.' The words were no sooner out of his mouth than the soil lessened its grip and getting up on my horse whose legs were now at liberty, I rejoined the fugitives with whom I offered to share my arms, and provisions. They refused, not wishing to accept anything from an unbeliever and they commanded me to leave them in peace.

From what I had witnessed, I became convinced that Mohammad would conquer in the end, and I persisted in demanding a safe-conduct, proving that he granted me his pardon and that there no longer existed any cause for enmity between him and me. Obeying his orders, Abu Bakr made out on a piece of leather, the document I claimed. It saved my life during the Taif expedition. I then turned back. Once more in Makkah I told my black slave and all my fellow citizens who had guessed the motives governing my journey that I had seen nothing, and I cursed the information that had led me to set out on such a useless and fatiguing expedition.

THE PROPHET'S ARRIVAL AT QUBA *(June 28th A.D. 622)*

Thanks to the inconceivable rapidity with which news travels in Arabian countries, the Mussulmans of Yasrib had already heard of the Prophet's (Peace be on him) departure and that he intended to rejoin them.

Quoth one among them. "Every day after the morning prayer we go to the Hira, a burning plain, covered with scattered black pebbles and which stretches out south-west of the town. There, our hands shading our eyes from the dazzling sun, we gaze as far as our sight permits, hoping to catch sight of Allah's Apostle. We turn not back in the direction of our dwellings until high noon, doubly defeated by the blaze of the perpendicular rays of the sun and their reverberation on white sand and calcined stones."

One day, among all these days of overwhelming heat, we had just returned, when a Jew, noted for the extraordinary acuity of his sight, made out, from the top of one of the towers on the ramparts, a caravan consisting of a few men in white garb, mounted on camels. They seemed to be rising and falling, driven to and fro by the eddying mirage.

Guessing that he saw the Prophet (Peace be on him) and his companions, the Jew turned round in the direction of the city. 'O Assembly of the Arabs!' he shouted in resounding assents, 'the good luck ye did expect hath come at last!'

Awakened from our siesta, we rushed in the direction of the caravan. It was encamped at the foot of a solitary palm-tree, a few paces off the Quba oasis. With Abu Bakr, the Prophet (Peace be on him) was resting in the shade of this tree. As both appeared to be about the same age, and considering that the majority had never met Allah's Apostle, we hesitated, not knowing to whom of the couple we should pay homage.

Just then, the palm's scanty shade having changed its direction, the sunlight fell on the face of one of the travellers. Thereupon, we noticed the other rise to his feet and stretch his mantle over the head of his companion, to protect him from the rays of the orb of day. Thus an end was put to our hesitation."

The Baun Amir ibn Auf to whom the hamlet of Quba belonged, now arrived, transported with joy, to invite to sojourn in their midst the illustrious guest sent to them by Allah. The Prophet (Peace be on him) lodged with Kulsum ibn Hidmi; Abu Bakr with Khubib ibn Saf, while the other Muhajirun took up their quarters with Sad ibn Khazinah, one of the Najibs.

This happy ending of Mohammad's journey took place on a Monday, at noon, the twelfth day of the month Rabiu'l-Awwal. The year of this emigration, renowned under the name of "Hijrah" (called "Hegira" by the Europeans), has been adopted by Musulmans for the beginning of their era. It corresponds to A.D. 622.

At first, such a choice creates surprise, and yet no other event in the Prophet's (Peace be on him) existence exercised more decisive influence over the world-wide success of his cause. Had he remained in Makkah, granting even his final triumph, Islam would have remained there with him. The Arabs of all Arabia, fearing the power with which Islam endowed the Quraish alone, would have formed a coalition to prevent it spreading out of the Sacred City. Whereas, after having begun, despite all malice, to plant the roots of his religion firmly in his native town, it was easy for the Prophet (Peace be on him) to return there when he had won over the rest of the Arabs to his cause.

This proves how impenetrable are the designs of Providence, and how frequently the misfortunes which God afflicts us, burdening us with suffering, determine the cause of our successes. If the Prophet (Peace be on him) had not been persecuted and banished by his own people, he would never have been able to fulfil his universal missions, and the world would never have been enlightened by Islam.

The Prophet (Peace be on him) sojourned at Quba on Tuesday, Wednesday and Thursday. All rejoined him there. His faithful henchman, after having restituted all the deposits confided to his care to their rightful owners, arrived at Quba, his feet badly lacerated, having tramped night and day. Mohammad embraced him warmly, bandaged his wounds with his blessed hands, and made him rest by his side in Kulsum's dwelling.

Mohammad also busied himself with laying the first brick of a Mosque—the first place of public prayer in Islam—and left to Ammar ibn Yasar the care of finishing it. This Mosque was called "At Taqwa." *i.e.* the Mosque of "The Fear of God." Reference is made to it in these verses: *"There is indeed a Mosque founded from its first day upon the fear of God; More right it is that thou take thy stand therein; therein are men who aspire to keep themselves pure and Allah loveth who purify themselves."* (the Qu'ran, ix, 109.)

Despite the persistence of the Banu Amir who wished him to remain in their hamlet, the Prophet (Peace be on him) departed on Friday, at daybreak, riding the she-camel he had bought of Abu Bakr, and which became celebrated under the name of "al-Qaswa," *i.e.* "She that hath split ears and nostrils." A great throng of horsemen and people on foot followed him, and his companions fought for the honour of holding his bridle.

ARRIVAL OF THE PROPHET AT YASRIB

The hour of prayer arrived when he was passing through the territory of the Banu Salin ibn Auf. He alighted and recited, for the first time, the Friday prayer, leading a numerous band of Believers in pious array behind him. At the termination of the prayer, he turned towards the Faithful to preach them a sermon. Then he once more bestrode his she-camel, and escorted by a corwd animated by the most ardent enthusiasm, made a triumphal entry into Yasrib. On every terrace-roof, the "Zawat-ul-Kh'dar" those who are generally hidden inside houses—women and young girls—were grouped together, resembling, in their bright-hued draperies, pretty birds of vividly-tinted plumage perched on the edges of cliffs. With melodious voices, quavering by reason of emotion, they sang in chorus:

"The full moon hath risen above our heads—Emerging from the Sanniyat-ul-Wida (the Farwell Mountain Pass)!—Numerous are the thanksgivings we must offer up to Allah,—With the purest fervour of our supplications!—O thou, His Messenger among us,—The orders thou dost bring us shall be piously executed!"

In every district through which the Prophet (Peace be on him) passed, that of the Banu Baid, Banu Saida, Banu Haris, Banu Adyy, etc., a deputation of leading men caught his camel by the bridle and stopped it, to be able to say: 'Remain with us, O Prophet! Here wilt thou find riches, power and safety.' But he replied: 'Let my she-camel go, for she hath received orders from on High.' And smiling kindly, he added: "The blessing of Allah be upon you!"

He let the reins hang loose on the neck of the animal he was riding, and she, stretching her long neck far above the escort of Believers, turned her head first to the right and then to the left, as if searching, with her great black eyes shaded by lengthy lashes, for the halting-place assigned to her by Providence. After a thousand windings and turnings, she stopped in the middle of a wide expanse of waste ground, and knelt down; but as the Prophet (Peace be on him) did not alight, she rose and took a few more strides, hesitatingly. Finally, and decisively, she went back to the spot where she had stopped at first, and knelt down again. She stretched the entire length of her neck on the ground and uttered low grunts.

So then Mohammad alighted, saying: 'Allah causeth me to set foot on the ground in a blessed spot. Here will be the finest place in which to dwell.' This piece of property was a "marbad," *i.e.* a barn-floor, where dates were laid out to dry. It was situated in the district of the Banu Nijar, not far from the house of Abu Ayyub Ansari who offered hospitality to the Prophet, (Peace be on him) and took his saddle and saddle-bags to his dwelling. Whilst the Apostle, momentarily freed from the veneration of the populace, was settling under that friendly roof, young people and slaves dispersed in all directions, singing: 'Mohammad hath come! The Prophet (Peace be on him) of Allah hath come to our town!' Ever since that day, eternally memorable, the city of Yasrib was called, "Madinatu'n-Nabi," the City of the prophet; and by abbreviation, "Al-Madinah." (Medinah).

HOW THE MOSQUE OF AL-MADINAH WAS BUILT

At Al-Madinah, Mohammad's first care was to erect a Mosque.

He sought for the owners of the ground where his she-camel had knelt, and they turned out to be two orphans, named Sahil and Sohail, whose guardian was Muaz ibn Afra. The Prophet (Peace be on him) asked them how much they wanted for their pice of property. 'Allah's reward is the only price we ask,' was their reply. Mohammad, however, refused the gift. The purchase-money, fixed at ten dinars, was advanced by Abu Bakr, who had transferred all his wealth from Makkah to Al-Madinah.

Acting under the Prophet's (Peace be on him) orders, the Believers lost no time in getting to work. They cleared up the "Marbad," where there were ruined walls, a palm-tree and a few neglected tombs. They levelled the ground and, as soon as the foundations were dug, Mohammad lifted a big stone to place in the cavity, and his noble breast became covered in dust. Seeing this, his companions tried to prevent him from doing manual labour, but he said to Abu Bakr: 'Say no more, but follow my example. Put a stone next to mine.' He then commanded Umar to place another at the side of the one set down by Abu Bakr; and each of the leading Moslems contributed in succession his stone to the structure.

When the stone foundations reached up to a third of the eventual height of the walls, the Believers began to knead clay with water, making unbaked bricks, with which they intended to finish the building. The Prophet, (Peace be on him) as before, continued to encourage his followers by his example, and he carried bricks in his mantle. Seeing one of the workers with a double load on his back, Mohammad wiped his disciple's hair and neck, soiled with clay, and said: 'The reward of the labourer awaits him in heaven, but thou wilt find a double reward.'

All the Believers toiled in high spirits, and to quicken their task by working in measure, the masons sang in chorus, and the verses of their chants related to their exalted hopes. When the walls were seven cubits high, the Faithful covered the building with a flat roof, made of palm-tree trunks, thatched with lathes and palm-leaves. On this, they spread a layer of beaten earth, thick enough to prevent rain filtering through. The ceiling was supported inside by columns of date-tree trunks, and the floor was sprinkled with gravel.

The building was one hundred cubits in length; its breadth being a little less. It could be entered by three doors; of which the principal was called "Bab-ur-Rahrra" or "Door of Mercy." The "Minbar" or pulpit, was fashioned out of a single palm-tree trunk on which the Prophet (Peace be on him) mounted when he preached his sermons.

It can thus be seen that this first Mosque, identical with those of the poorest villages of the Sahara, was far from resembling the marvellous edifices which were to be constructed later for the Islamic religion.

At the same time as the Mosque was being finished, Mohammad had caused two little hovels to be built with clods of earth—"Hujrah"—leaning against the walls of the temple. The Prophet (Peace be on him) proposed to live there with his family and he sent Zayd, his adopted son, to Makkah to fetch them. When the houses were finished, he left the dwelling of Abu Ayyub and settled down with his people who lost no time in arriving.

As for the Muhajirun, they had all been generously and hospitably welcomed by the Ansars, proud and joyful to receive beneath their roof-trees those of the strangers who fell to them by lot.

Mohammad was especially moved by the cordial welcome extended to his fellow-countrymen by his new disciples. But, with his great insight concerning the souls of mortals, he resolved to tighten the bonds of such touching friendship, so that it should be proof against all insinuations dictated by the rivalry, inevitable in the future, between the Muhajirun who had forsaken their country, families and wealth to follow him, and the Ansars who had offered the safe shelter and material assistance to which his triumph was due. Would not each party have some little reason to claim for it alone first rank in the Prophet's affection and the annals of Islam?

In order to avoid such dangers and create real family ties for the exiles Mohammad, profited by the cloudless exaltation uniting Muhajirun and Ansars just then, decided to issue a decree of perfect brotherhood between them. He ordained that they should pair off in couples consisting of a man of the Mohajirun and an Ansar. 'Fraternise in Allah!' he told them. 'Ye are brothers!' Henceforward, every Mussulman of Al-Madinah had for brother a Mussulman of Makkah.

It would be sheer madness to try and find words to express the degree of devotion attained by this brotherhood of religion, stronger than ties of blood, for it was supernatural. All these men's hearts, united in the love of Allah, were now nothing more than a single heart, palpitating in different breasts. Each man loved his brother better than himself, and during the first years of the Hegra, when one died, the other inherited his property, to the exclusion of his natural heirs. Among the fraternal unions thus constituted, we may note those of Abu Bakr with Khahrijah ibn Zayd; Ummar with Usman ibn Malik; Abu Ubaidah with Sad ibn Muaz; and Usman ibn Affan with Aus ibn Najar. The prophet had been the first to choose Ali for his brother, thus sealing the bond of fraternity that he had signed when beginning his mission. But as Ali belonged to the Muhajirun, the Ansars might have been vexed because the Apostle did not choose a brother in their ranks. That was why, at the death of one of their Najiba, Asad ibn Zararah, Mohammad took his place as Najib, pretexting that he was one of them, because his uncle on his mother's side had formerly dwelt in their city.

In this way, thanks to his sense of psychology and diplomatic skill, Mohammad achieved a wonderful result: the wars between the Kajraz and the Aus which, for centuries past, had deluged Yasrib with blood, ceased as by magic, soon after his arrival. He metamorphosed the inhabitants of Al-Madinah into the brothers of the Makkah emigrants, formerly their rivals.

THE QUIBLAH OF MAKKAH

In the beginning, the Prophet (Peace be on him) allowed the Believers full liberty to turn in any direction they pleased when saying their prayers, for: *"The East and the West is Allah's; therefore, whichever way ye turn, there is the face of Allah, Truly Allah is Omnipresent, Omniscient."* (the Qur'an, ii, 109).

While terminating the building of the first Mosque, the Prophet (Peace be on him) divined that prayerful impulsiveness diverted in one direction would be more thrilling, because of the feeling of union in the same ideals that was bound to result. By means of a cube of masonry, composed of stone and clay and placed against the wall of the building looking south, he primitively established the Qiblah, or direction of prayer, towards the Temple of Jerusalem.

But he was ordered by a verse to change the direction towards Malkkah: *"We have formerly seen thee turning thy face towards every part of the Heaven; but We will assuredly have thee turn to a Qiblah which shall please thee. Turn then thy face towards the Sacred Mosque, and wherever ye be, turn your faces in that direction."* (the Qur'an ii, 139).

And ever since that day, the Qiblah remains definitively fixed for all the Musulmans of the world, in the direction of the Temple of Makkah.

INSTITUTION OF THE AZAN, OR CALL OF THE MU'EZZIN

Prayer in common is incontestably the most profitable; the fervour of each Believer communicating with the soul of his neighbour. "It is worth twenty-seven times more than isolated prayer," says the Prophet. (Peace be on him). It was therefore necessary to summon all Believers together every day, at the same hour fixed for the five prayers.

How was the exact time of meeting to be determined? Scattered over the different districts of the city, some came too early; others too late. A consultation of the leading Moslems took place. Some were for the use of a beacon, to be lit on a commanding eminence; other suggested the blowing of a horn; and the rest proposed bell-ringing. But all these methods were rejected, because they were borrowed, from Persians, Jews or Christians.

Meanwhile, Abdullah ibn Zayd arrived, and he told of a dream he had had the night before. 'A man attired all in green passed close to me, carrying a hand-bell. I stopped him and begged him to sell me his bell.'—'What dost thou want it for?'—'To summon Believers to prayer.'—'A much better way', he replied, 'would be to proclaim the profession of faith of Islam with all the strength of thy lungs'.

The Prophet, (Peace be on him) alive to the fact that the resonance of the human voice is more capable of communicating emotion than the most perfect metal instrument of music, declared at once: 'In thy dream was truth. Go and find Bilal, His voice is powerful and harmonious. I charge thee to order him to mount to the roof of the Mosque and summon the Believers to prayers'. So Bilal, the freed negro, told to call all the Believers together of all ranks and races, uttered from the terrace of the Mosque the cry of the Islamic soul: *"Allah is great! There is no God but Allah, and Mohammad is the Prophet (Peace be on him) of Allah! Come to Salvation!"*

Like exquisite perfume wafted from a priceless flask, these words in the melodious voice of Bilal and issuing from his strong lungs, resounded through the city. Echoing in all dwellings, they caused every citizen to inhale with delight the refreshing scent of prayer.

Ever since, in every Mosque all the world over, it is the duty of a crier called a "muezzin" to give this summons to prayer five time daily which he does from the top of a slender minaret for that purpose.

THE FAST OF RAMADHAN

After having decided that the human voice should be used for the call to prayer, Mohammad, when first he dwelt in Al-Madinah, continued to set forth the formal obligations of the Islamic religion.

He was in the habit of fasting three days every month when he received this Revelation: *"As the month Ramanhan, in which the Qur'an was sent down to be man's guidance . . . as soon as anyone of you observeth the moon, let him set about the fast . . . You are allowed on the night of the fast to approach your wives: they are your garment and ye are their garment . . . Eat and drink until ye can discern a white thread from a black thread by the daybreak: afterwards fast strictly till night, and go not in unto them, but pass time in the Mosques."* (the Qur'an, ii, 181, 183).

By these verses was the fast of the month of Ramadhan established, and numerous were the advantages accruing therefrom: man, full of self-love, runs after everything bringing material gratification, and flees from all that falls to the lot of the poor and the weak. To rid him of this fatal propensity, nothing is more salutary than the pangs of hunger and thirst. The Faithful, their bodies no longer burdened by their aliments, forgathered all day long, and the nourishment that prayer provided for their souls was more impatiently expected than the nourishment of their stomachs.

In the torrid climate of Al-Madinah, nevertheless, their thirst, unquenched during never-ending summer days, became real torture. With dry throats, gasping, many among them were on the point of breaking down when they looked upon the limpid water of the "saqiya" and heard its tempting trickling. The example of their brethren, more resigned, soon made them pluck up fresh courage. The bonds of religious fraternity were tightened still more by this ordeal, and, having assisted each other to vanquish such terrible adversaries as hunger and thirst, Believers were ready to stand firm against the fiercest enemies among mortals.

During thirty days, without murmuring and with ever-increasing exaltation, the Ansars and the Moadjirun went through the first fast of Ramadhan. At last the crescent of the new month was about to appear: every terrace-roof and all the hills were crowded with the Faithful, all trying to get the first glimpse. The sun's golden disc was scarcely submerged in the blue waves of the desert's horizon when every eye scrutinised anxiously the depth of the sky of emerald-like limpidity. Suddenly, in the lower part of the shaded canopy of heaven, the thin silver bow appeared. A long-drawn sigh escaped from every breast, as if each had been pierced by invisible arrows, shot from this bow.

But the Faithful had heaved no sigh of deliverance. On the contrary, the sigh was caused by the regret at having so soon concluded the fasting ordeal, in easy payment of the debt of gratitude owing to the Benefactor. During this pious trial, each soul was fortified and each body strengthened. In order to pass through the frightful deserts that encircled before going forth to conquer the world, the Believers were training themselves to get accustomed, as if it were a more wholesome pastime, to endure the tortures

Group of Believers uncovering the Crescent of the Month or Ramadan.

of hunger and thirst that they were bound to undergo, later on, in the depths of these very wildernesses.

When, after such self-imposed deprivation, they were able to appreciate the real value of the benefit of food, the Prophet (Peace be on him) imposed upon them the "Sadaqat-ul-Fitr," the Alms of the Breaking of the Fast, forcing the faithful rich to give a share of their victuals to the Faithful poor.

PROPERTY BESTOWED IN ALMS, AND THE PROHIBITION OF FERMENTED LIQUOR

Mohammad judged that the obligation of feeding the poor once a year, the day after the fast, was insufficient. He completed his ruling by instituting the "Zakat-ul-Mal," the bestowal of property in alms, intended to safeguard the existance of pauper Mussulmans without overburdening rich folks.

This kind of almsgiving, being one of the five foundations of practical religion, is due upon all property and revenue whatsoever: gold, silver, flocks, grain; and varies from a third to a tenth of such resources. It should be bestowed with the greatest tact and humility:

"O ye who believe! make not your alms void by reproach and injury, like him who spendeth his substance to be seen of men. The likeness of such an one is that of a rock with a thin soil upon it, on which a heavy rain falleth, but leaveth it hard. And the likeness of those who expend their substance from a desire to please Allah, and through their own steadfastness, is as a garden on a hill, on which the heavy rain falleth, and yieldeth its fruits twofold; and even if a heavy rain fall not on it, yet there is a dew . . . if ye give your alms openly, it is well; and if ye conceal them and give them to the poor, this too will be of advantage to you . . . Those who know them not, think them rich because of their modesty. By this their token thou shall know them they ask not of men with importunity: and whatever good thing ye expend in alms are only to be given to the poor and the needy, and those who collect them, and to those whose hearts are won to Islam, and for ransoming, and for debtors, and for the cause of Allah, and the wayfarer. This is an ordinance from Allah." (the Qur'an, ii, 266, 267, 275. iii, 86. ix, 60.) By the foregoing verses was instituted the imposition of the "Zakat-ul-Mal", literally: "The Purification," because it serves, as it were, to "purify" wealth and excuse it.

The Prophet (Peace be on him) foresaw the universal ravages of alcoholism, as deadly in its effects as the worship of idols, and he forbade the use of fermented liquors. He had first received this Revelation: *"They will ask thee concerning vinous liquors . . . Say: In them is great sin, and advantage also, to men; but their sin is greater than their advantage."* (the Qur'an, ii, 216.)

Many among the Faithful gave up these beverages, whilst others could not bring it over their hearts to do so. A second Revelation brought this caution *"Come not to prayer when drunken, but wait till ye can understand what ye utter."* (the Qur'an, iv, 46.)

Ali caused this announcement. Having drunk to excess just at the hour of prayer, he recited: 'O ye Unbelievers . . . we worship what ye worship. Ye have no religion and I have no religion,' instead of saying: *"O ye Unbelievers, I worship not what ye worship! To you your religion; and to me my religion."* (the Qur'an, cix, 1, 2, 6.)

Formal prohibition was finally decreed in these imperative verses: *"O Believers! Wine and games of chance, and statues and the divining arrows, are only an abomination of Satan's work! Avoid them, that ye may prosper. Only would Satan sow hatred and strife among you, by wine and games of chance, and turn you aside from the rememberance of Allah, and from prayer: will ye not; therefore, desist from them? Obey Allah and obey the Apostle!"* (the Qur'an, v, 92, 93.)

AYISHAH IN THE HOUSE OF THE PROPHET

Ayishah, so kind, witty and learned, was only the Prophet's (Peace be on him) wife in his name. About this time, she became a member of his household.

CHAPTER THE FIFTH

Quoth Ayishah: "One day, surrounded by my companions, I was playing on a swing. Umm-i-Rumman, my mother, called me.

I ran to her without knowing what she wanted of me. She took my hand, and made me stop on the threshold until I had got my breath. She then washed my face and forehead and led me into the house. Many women of the Ansars were there and they said to me: 'Happiness do we wish thee, and blessings, and the best of luck!"

"My mother left me to the care of these women. They decked me out and had scarcely finished when Allah's Apostle suddenly came in . . . "

HOSTILITY OF THE JEWS AND THE MUNAFIQIN

In the beginning a certain number of Jews—and among them, the learned Mukhariq and Abdullah ibn Salam, were so moved by the advances and arguments of the Prophet (Peace be on him) that they came and were converted by him.

As for the others, their vanity was greatly flattered by the fact that the Temple of Solomon, their ancestor, had been chosen for the Qiblah, or direction in which Moslems were to pray. Their pride, therefore, led them to conclude that their Temple was immensely superior to that of Makkah, and consequently that the Jewish race dominated the Arabs.

When, following the orders of Allah, the Qiblah was changed from Jerusalem to the Ka'bah, they were deeply mortified. Besides, they soon found out how prejudical to their interests was the coming of Mohammad Al-Madinan. Thanks to his efforts, fraternity reigned among the Arab factions, whose feuds had hitherto been a source of profit. The Prophet, (Peace be on him) whose advent was foreshadowed in their books and on whom they founded great hopes, was born at last. They saw him in their midst, but he did not belong to their race which sprung from that of Ishmael. Mohammad brought with him the pure light of Islam which they sought to extinguish by every means in their power.

Not venturing to rely on their own strength, they sought to embroil Arab townsmen and met with valuable assistance granted by a few noblemen, whose prejudices were wounded by the principles of equality of the Qur'an. They felt belittled at merely becoming the brothers of those they scorned as being beneath them.

These fresh adversaries, who were called "Munafiqin," or Hypocrites, were particularly dangerous, for they mingled in the ranks of sincere Mussulmans and, to all appearances, professed the same doctrines. In this way, they wormed out secrets and sold them to Jews and Idolaters.

AL-JAHAD (THE HOLY WAR) AND HOW IT WAS INSTITUTED

The Prophet (Peace be on him) began to feel the urgency of taking up arms for the triumph of the faith, which could not be definitive until after the conquest of Makkah where stood the Holy Temple of the Arabs. He had received the Revelation of the warlike undertaking with orders to unsheath the sword in his struggle against idolaters: *"And fight for the cause of Allah against those who fight against you: but commit not the injustice of attacking them first: verily Allah loveth not the unjust: And kill them wherever ye shall find them, and eject them from whatever place they have ejected you . . . "* (the Qur'an, ii, 186, 187.)

Such were the ordinances of "Al-Jahad," "the Holy War" so violently criticised by Christians.

But did not Jesus—their Lord and ours—Himself declare: "Think not that I am come to send peace on earth: I come not to send peace, but a sword." (St. Matthew, x, 34.) "I am come to send fire on the earth; and what will I, if it be already kindled?" (St. Luke, xii, 49.)

If the institution of the "Jahad," destined for the triumph of truth over idolatry, stirred up strife among the families of Mohammad's fellow-countrymen for a few years, did not the words of Jesus, still more imperative in this connection, lead to much more terrible consequences; lasting too, for centuries among all Christian nations?

"For I am come to set a man at variance against his father, and the daughter against her mother, and the daughter-in-law against her mother-in-law." (St. Matthew, x, 33.) "If any man come to me, and hate not his father, and mother, and wife, and children, and brethren, and sisters yea, and his own life also, he cannot be my disciple." (St. Luke, xiv, 26.)

The "Jahad" was not instituted to attack the adversaries of religion only; it was also proclaimed against those enemies, no less perfidious, that lurk in every man's own heart. Quoth the Prophet: "The most meritorious Holy war is that which one declares against one's own passions."

Mohammad and the Believers had been patient quite long enough. Banished from the land of their birth after having endured pitiless persecution, did they not have the right, relying on the Revealed Verses, to resort to the force of arms? The site of Al-Madinah ensured victory, for that city overlooked all the caravan routes to Syria, of which the commerce formed the sole resource of Makkah, surrounded by barren wastes. By stopping these caravans, the Prophet (Peace be on him) could starve out the ungrateful town and force its citizens to beg for mercy. In this way, the Apostle would not be compelled to kill too many of his fellow-countrymen, whom he still loved despite their iniquity. He wanted to spare them, hoping to win them over and induce them to become steadfast supporters of religion.

Thus began the long series of campaigns called "Ghazwah" when the Prophet (Peace be on him) was personally in command; and "Saria," when one of his lieutenants led the van. We shall only mention the most characteristic of these innumerable expeditions; putting on one side the first minor skirmishes and come at once to the famous Ghazwah of Badr.

THE GHAZWAH OF BADR
(Year II of the Hegira, A.D. 624)

A caravan of exceptional importance, comprising a thousand camels, had been sent into Syria by the citizens of Makkah. It was to bring back the most valuable and highly-prized merchandise. This was the opportunity awaited by the Prophet (Peace be on him). If he succeeded in capturing the caravan, he would deal a ruinous blow at those who banished him and, as he hoped, without useless bloodshed, for the escort of the convoy numbered at most two score. These men could oppose no real resistance and would be obliged to surrender without fighting.

The Prophet (Peace be on him) arrived too late. The caravan had gone past. He made up his mind to fall upon it by surprise during its return journey. One of his partisans, posted by him to watch the roads, brought the news that the caravan had been seen, and would soon be near Al-Madinah, following the usual route, between the mountains and the sea.

Thereupon, the Prophet (Peace be on him) summoned all the Believers, of any origin whatsoever. The call was answered by more than three hundred men, all desirous of inflicting exemplary punishment on the idolaters. Seventy-three Mohadjirun joined the ranks and, for the first time, two hundred and forty Ansars stood shoulder with their brothers in Islam. Seventy camels were gathered together to carry water and food; and also to relieve men on foot who took it in turns to ride.

The expedition was poor in cavalry, possessing only four horses whose names were Beraja, Al-Bahrmi, Yasum and Sail. They were led riderless by the bridle, only to be used at some propitious moment during the battle. The "Liwa" or white banner, was confided to Musab-al-Abdri, and the flag of the Ansars was carried by Sad ibn Muaz.

Unfortunately, the organisation of such a numerous "qawm" could not be kept secret. The

"Hypocrites" and the Banu Israil, watching every step taken by Mohammad, found out what he was preparing and also his destination. They sent messengers to Abu Sufyan, the leader of the caravan, to inform him of the threatening danger. He sent an Arab of the Ghifar tribe, named Dhamdham, to beg for assistance and promised him a rich reward if, thanks to his diligence, the convoy could be saved.

All the inhabitants of Makkah had contributed, more or less, to the organisation of the great caravan and, counting upon its approaching return, they were already revelling in the fine profits that would accrue to them. All day long, in groups, they wended their way to the city gates, gazing, till their eyes ached, into the depths of the valley following the road to Syria, hoping to catch sight of a messenger.

At last there came a day when a man, swaying to an fro, by reason of the swift amble of his racing camel, appeared at the end of the ravine, advancing towards them. When he was near enough to enable his aspect and that of the animal to be made out, the stupefaction of the Makkans was inconceivable. To show his despair, the man, who was no other than Dhamdham, had rent his garments, turned his saddle around, slit the nostrils and cut the ears of his camel. As soon as he was near enough to make himself heard, weak from fatigue, gasping for breath, he cried out: 'Woe unto you, O men of the Quraish! Your caravan—your caravan' . . . '

In great anxiety, the Quraish gathered round him, besieging him with questions; and when he could breathe freely, he described the perilous plight of their caravan. Their fury broke loose. Just when they were on point of fulfilling their most dazzling hopes, this man Mohammad, of whom they thought they had rid themselves for ever, threatened them with ruin!

An urgent council, called together hastily, decided that there was not a moment to lose. To prevent such a catastrophe, every one, rich or poor, was ready to sacrifice riches and life. An army was immediately raised, composed of nine hundred and fifty men, having at their disposal one hundred horses and seven hundred camels. The idolatrous troops marched out of the town amidst frenzied cheers; groups of young singing-girls, each as dazzling as the sun; their faces radiant; their eyes sparkling; their garb of the brightest hues, glittering with gold and precious stones, headed the warriors. These girls shouted bitter mockery against the Mussulmans; or recited epic poems, accompanying their rhymes with the thumping of tabors, causing the hearts of their lovers to palpitate with burning ardour.

What spurred them on even better were the suggestions of Iblis (Satan) who, lurking in the recesses of their souls, filled the Unbelievers with dreams of victory and vengeance, although ready to desert his victims shamelessly in case Allah should exert His Might in favour of their adversaries.

"The Evil One had already bewitched them by exaggerated praise of their actions; and furthermore had said: 'No man shall conquer you this day; and verily I will be near to help you." (the Qur'an, viii, 50.)

The Prophet (Peace be on him) had no idea of his enemies' preparations. After having laid in a stock of water at Al-Rouha, he halted near the village of Safra; pitched his tents in the valley of Zufran, and sent out two scouts, Bisbas and Adi, to seek for information.

At early morn, the following day, he took to the road again, halting a few miles away from the wells of Badr. The two scouts, guessing that the caravan was heading towards this important spot for replenishing water supplies, reached there by having urged on their camels unmercifully. On arriving, they met two Bedouin women who were quarrelling loudly, while they filled their goat-skins. With insulting remarks, one claimed the repayment of a loan, and the woman in debt replied: 'Have patience until tomorrow or the day after, for by then the great caravan will have come back and thereby I shall have earned enough to settle with thee.'—'She is right,' broke in An Najd, chief of the Juhinna tribe, who happened to be at the well. 'They tell me that the caravan will certainly be here to-morrow or the next day.'

Having got to know all they wanted, Bisbas and Adi watered their animals and rode back in all haste to bring the news to the Prophet, (Peace be on him) well pleased to see that things had turned out exactly as he foresaw.

A few minutes later, however, he was rejoined by one of his partisans in his pay at Makkah. This friend brought bad news: the expedition of the idol-worshippers was coming by forced marches to the succour of Abu Sufyan. These tidings caused Mohammad the greatest anxiety: the ardour of the Mussulmans, who had set out to attack a caravan defended by a weak escort, might perhaps be damped upon finding themselves faced by superior forces? He did not intend to hide the gravity of the situation, but calling the head-men together, he laid the information before them, and asked where they thought it would be best to make their effort.

They were submerged by a great wave of vacillation. It must be confessed that the irresistible bait of booty added great charm to a wish to inflict punishment on the idolaters. Under the necessity of coming to a decision, some of them objected: 'Dost thou lead us to be slaughtered?' They were severely blamed for speaking thus. *"And remember when Allah promised you that one of the two troops should fall to you, and ye desired that they who had no arms should fall to you."* (the Qur'an, viii, 7.)

Then uprose Mikdad, protesting stoutly: 'O Prophet! go without hesitation whither thou art ordered. By Allah! we'll not tell thee as the Banu Israil told Moses. "Go fight by the side of the Lord and we'll await thy return here!" On the contrary, we say to thee: 'Go fight by the side of thy Lord and thou wilt find us with thee, always and everywhere.'

The Prophet (Peace be on him) called down divine blessings on the head of his courageous disciple; and then he added: 'Reflect, O my partisans!' He then turned towards the Ansars who might not have considered themselves bound by the oath of the Aqbah to do anything else than to protect him so long as he dwelt in their town.

But Sad ibn Muaz rose to his feet, pained to have to think that the devotion of the Ansars could be doubted, if only for a moment. 'Our confidence in thee is unlimited. We have given thee our word,' he exclaimed. 'Go where thou art ordered and I swear by Him who sendeth thee to bring about the triumph of truth, that shouldst thou ask us to jump in the sea, we would leap with thee!'

This declaration freed the Prophet (Peace be on him) from the anxiety that weighed him down, and which had prevented him from having recourse to the Ansars in preceding expeditions. His features were radiant with inspired, grateful emotion; and fixing his eyes on a vision that he alone was privileged to see: 'Rejoice, O men of my "qawm!" he cried. 'I look upon warriors fighting, and the enemy's troops are routed!' There was not a man but what understood that soon the battle would range and all made preparations with admirable confidence.

As for Abu Sufyan, ever since he had been warned that the Mussulmans were on the march, he was constantly on the look-out. He accelerated the speed of the caravan and, going on in front himself, arrived at Badr soon after the Prophet's (Peace be on him) scouts. He questioned An Najd who had not yet left the well. 'Hath no prowler been seen about here?'—'I only saw two camels, each ridden by a man; and they watered their animals.'

Abu Safyan hastened to the spot where the traces could still be seen, showing where the camels had knelt whilst their masters drew water from the well. He found fresh droppings, and, crumbling some in his fingers, picked out many date-kernels. 'By our gods! these camels hail from Al-Madinah, and the enemy is not far off!'—he thought, knowing that in all the country round, only the camels of Al-Madinah were fed on soaked kernels of dates.

Therefore, changing the direction of the caravan at once so as to leave the Badr well on one side, he turned off the direct road and took a westerly route along the sea-shore. He was thus able to escape from the soldiers of Islam; and when he was safe, sent another messenger to the Quraish, to inform them of what he had done, advising them to return to Makkah, as he no longer desired their aid.

'Nothing of the kind!' exclaimed their chief, Abu Jahal, carried away by hatred. 'Let us push on to the well of Badr. We'll camp there three days and three nights, passing the time in joyous revels, slaughtering cattle, enjoying the meat, and drinking our fill of wine. Every year a fair is held there, lasting a week, attracting Arabs from far and near. When they hear of our expedition to that spot, the echo of the news will have a great effect, inspiring all with salutary fear of our power!'

Puffed up with pride by reason of this speech, so flattering to their vanity, and allured by the festivals and liquors in store for them, the idolaters approved their chieftain's plan and continued on the march to Badr.

The Believers bent their steps towards the same goal, not knowing whether they would meet the caravan, the Quraish army, or both united. In order to find out, Mohammad sent Ali and Zubayr as scouts. They caught two young men seeking for a well from which to fill their empty goat-skins, strapped to their shoulders. They were made prisoners and taken to the camp to be interrogated, but as the Prophet (Peace be on him) was at his devotions, the scouts questioned the lads. 'We were looking for water for the Quraish army,' the two captives confessed.

The Quraish forces, therefore, were already in these parts? This seemed most unlikely, for the scouts did not know the strength of the enemy in camels and horses, and considered the prisoners' avowal to be a falsehood. So they fell brutally to beating the young idolaters. 'Think not that ye can hoodwink us with your lies,' said Ali and Zubayr. 'We know perfectly well that ye belong to the caravan of Abu Sufyan.'

Again they rained blows on the boys. To escape such unjust chastisement, and also to keep the Mussulmans in this state of error so profitable to Abu Jahal's plans, because it prevented Mohammad's men from suspecting how close their enemies were to them, the prisoners began to supplicate their tormentors. 'Mercy, my lords! Verily nothing escapeth your sharp sight! Yea, we confess it—we belong to Abu Sufyan's caravan.'

Proud of their perspicacity and content with having obtained this avowal, Ali and Zubayr set them free. Meanwhile the Prophet (Peace be on him) had finished praying, and as he knew how to read men's minds, he upbraided his disciples. 'What is all this? When your prisoners tell you the truth, ye beat them, and now they lie and ye set them free?' He continued the examination. 'Where are the Quraish?'—'On the other side of that high hill of sand.'—'How many are they?'—'We know not.'—'How many camels do they slaughter daily?'—'Nine or ten.'—'Oho! they number from nine hundred to a thousand,' said Mohammad to himself. 'Who is at their head?' the prisoners quoted the names of the most noted men of the city, and the Prophet (Peace be on him) shaking his head sadly, turned to his companions, saying: 'Of a truth, Makkah sends against us the best part of its liver!' (Meaning its best beloved children).

Nevertheless, the die was cast. The Mussulmans, who had set out to fall on a caravan protected by a puny escort, found themselves facing a force at least three times greater than theirs, assisted by formidable cavalry. At all costs, the well of Badr must be reached before the enemy. The Believers began their march again and attained the borders of the Wadi Superior which they found quite dry. Their supply of water was exhausted, and next day they suffered terribly from thirst: Satan tried to exploit these pangs by filling brains with most depressing thoughts. 'See where you are led by the man who pretendeth to be the messenger of the Almighty! Ye are surrounded by countless enemies, only waiting till your strength be broken by the agonies of thirst. They will then attack you and ye will be defenceless and an easy quarry.'

Every brain was bewildered. Luckily, their training during the fast of Ramadhan had accustomed the Believers to endure the torments of thirst and prevented them from breaking down. At the very moment when the heat, concentrated in the lofty heights of the Wadi, was on the point of making their position untenable, great clouds crowned the high peaks. The sombre veils darkening the sun were torn aside, and Allah let loose beneficial showers to drench His faithful servants. The Wadi, only just before filled with stones and sand, was transformed into a raging torrent.

The Believers were able to quench their thirst, and they dug holes all along the Wadi that was at once filled by the swelling of the waters. They washed their clothing, heavy with sweat, and performed their ablutions. Last, but not least, the shifting sands that rendered their advance so difficult, grew solid by the damp, and made the ground firm beneath their feet. *"He sent down upon you water from Heaven that He might thereby cleanse you, and cause the pollution of Satan to pass from you, and He might gird up your hearts, and stablish your feet by it."* (the Qur'an, viii, 11.)

For the idolaters, the storm was most disastrous. It overtook them in soil known as "Sabkha," signifying low-lying clay mixed with salt, churned by wet into greasy, sticky mud. Their camels slipped up and fell, their long legs comically gliding backwards, powerless to rise without the help of their drivers. Horses floundered, their hoofs sinking in the mire and, unable to find foothold, dropped back on their riders. The confusion and tumult cannot be described, and the effort of the Unbelievers to extricate themselves hampered their advance and exhausted them by fatigue.

The Believers, being cleansed, purified and refreshed, passed the night in invigorating sleep. They did not even take the trouble to post sentinels, relying blindly on the words of the Prophet (Peace be on him) who assured them that the angels would guard the camp. He alone remained wakeful, absorbed in prayer. *"Recollect when sleep, a sign of security from him, fell upon you,"* (the Qur'an, viii.)

The hour arrived when the fate of Islam was to be decided. It was on a Friday, the seventeenth day of the month of Ramadhan.

Hubbab-il-Ansari, renowned for his sage counsels, craved permission to be heard, 'O Prophet!' said he; 'hath the spot where we are now encamped been pointed out by a Revelation, and therefore we are forbidden to go forward or retreat? Or are we free to discuss the choice of ground befitting warlike strategy?'—'No Revelation hath imposed this place upon me, Speak freely and explain any stratagems that thou dost judge the most advantageous.'—'In that case, strike the tents,' Hubban rejoined, 'and with our troops, go down the channel of the Wadi and fill up every well we pass until arriving at the last. There thou must dig a reservoir that will fill itself with all the water running under the sand, whilst the wells higher up, which we shall have choked, will have run completely dry. I know the strength and direction of the stream. Thanks to this reservoir, our warriors, during battle, will be able to refresh their burning throats or relieve their sufferings if wounded, but our adversaries will not find anywhere in the surrounding country a single drop of water wherwith to slake their thirst.'

This piece seemed reasonable to the prophet, who carried out Hubbab's idea to the letter and so fixed the future battlefield, for the Unbelievers would be forced to come and try to wrest from him the only spot where water was to be found.

Then Sad ibn Muaz spoke: 'O Prophet! allow us to build for thee an "arish" (shelter from the sun's rays) on this hill, from which thou wilt be able to watch every move in the fighting. Near thee, thy she-camel shall be hobbled, and we will gallop into the enemy's midst. Should Allah grant us victory, thine eyes will be gladdened by the sight of our valour in defending the faith. Should fate be against us, thou wilt have naught else to do than to climb into the saddle and rejoin our rearguards, as devoted to thee as we are, and who will cover thy retreat.' The Prophet (Peace be on him) accepted, adding: 'Allah will reward you all by rendering assistance more efficacious than anything ye can imagine.'

The Believers cut down twigs of "araq" which they wattled, and so set up a shelter thatched with sheaves of "surfah." Mohammad retired therein in company with Abu Bakr, and when the advanced groups of enemy horsemen made their appearance, wheeling about defiantly before his eyes: 'O Allah!' he exclaimed, 'so there are the Quraish at last; urged on by monstrous pride to brave Thee and call Thy Messenger a liar!"

The enemy was assembled. After their efforts of the preceding day to extricate themselves from the briny mud of the "Sabkah," they had awakened with their throats afire; the storm, over too soon, not having filled any of the "ghadirs" and the wells of the Wadi having been choked up, the idolaters had not been able to find the least drop of water to allay the thirst that began to torture them. It was not to be wondered at therefore, that the sight of the sheet of water sparkling in the reservoir dug by the Believers and which reflected the sun's rays, blinding their eyes, should increase the fury of their revengeful feelings.

Some of the horsemen, reckoning on the speed of their steeds, dashed wrecklessly forward, hoping to reach the tempting liquid. The Prophet (Peace be on him) ordered his archers to let the mounted men get quite near, and when they were well within range, to riddle them with showers of arrows. All rolled on the ground, mortally wounded, with the exception of one rider, called Hakim.

Al Asad al Makhzumi, another idolater, instead of being discouraged by the result of this first attempt, felt his blood boiling in his veins and shouted loudly enough to be heard by both parties: 'By our gods! Lat and Uzza! I swear to slake my thirst in the cistern of Mohammad's "qawm". Then I'll demolish it and only death can stop me!'

He dashed forward, brimming over with arrogance. Hamzah went to meet him and, with a blow from his scimitar, sliced off one of his legs and sent it flying. Al Asad fell backwards, turned himself over, and hopping with surprising agility on both hands and his sound leg, tried to make his way to the reservoir and keep his oath. But Hamzah was there to meet him and finished him off just as he reached the goal.

Three champions came forward from among the ranks of the Unbelievers to challenge the Believers to single combat, and they were Utbah with his son, Al Walid, and his brother, Shaibah. Hamzah, Ali, and Obaidah were chosen by the Prophet (Peace be on him) to oppose them. Stalwart Hamzah and impetuous Ali soon rid themselves of their adversaries, stretching them bleeding and lifeless on the sand, but Obaidah and Utbah had no sooner crossed swords than they both wounded each other grievously.

Obaidah, one leg so deeply gashed that the marrow dripped from the bone, was on his back, at his enemy's mercy, when Ali and Hamzah came to the rescue and freed him by killing Utbah. They then lifted up their wounded comrade and carried him to the Prophet (Peace be on him) who supported his head lovingly on his knee, consoling him by the glad tidings of the reward awaiting him in Paradise. Obaidah soon breathed his last sigh and was thus the first martyr struck down in the Holy War.

After these single combats causing the hearts of all the lookers-on to palpitate with warlike ardour, the shock of the forces could no longer be postponed. The Prophet (Peace be on him) had drawn up his warriors in line, shoulder to shoulder, in serried ranks, like stone blocks cemented to form a wall, and it was all he could do to restrain the impatience of many who, outstripping their brothers-in-arms, would have run to face certain and useless slaughter.

Such an one, Sad ibn Quzai, was far in advance of the post assigned to him. So as to make him take his proper place, Mohammad struck him on the breast with the shaft of an arrow he held in his hand. 'Thou didst hurt me, O prophet!' cried Sad. 'As a messenger from Allah, sent to bring about the triumph of Right and Justice, thou dost owe me reparation on thine own body.'—'Satisfy thyself!'—'Thou art clothed, whereas my flesh was naked.' The Prophet (Peace be on him) laid bare his breast, saying: 'Give me as good as I gave, O Sad!'

Profiting by the permission, Sad threw himself on Mohammad, took him in his arms and pressed his lips to his body. 'Why do thou this thing?' asked the Prophet.—'O Messenger of Allah! Death faceth me and I desired that for my last farewell, my flesh should touch thy flesh!'

Moved by such fierce devotion, Mohammad called down the blessing of the Most High on Sad. Then, having ordered his men to wait without flinching for the enemy's attack, he went back with Abu Bakr to the *arish* of which the entrance was guarded by Sad ibn Muaz, sword in hand. The Prophet (Peace be on him) prayed: 'O Allah, remember Thy promise! If this day, Thou dost let the army of the soldiers of the faith be exterminated, no-one will be left on earth to adore Thee!'

Uneasy at the great disparity of numbers, Mohammad renewed his supplicating prostrations. His mantle slipped from his shoulders. Abu Bakr picked it up and threw it over him again, saying: 'Rest easy, O Prophet! Allah will surely do what He promised!'

Overwrought by excess of fatigue and anxiety, the Prophet (Peace be on him)lost his sense, and his eyes closed for a second, only to re-open almost immediately. A smile lit up his features. 'Good news, O Bakr!' he cried. 'The angel Jibra'il flieth to our assistance, I see the sand rising in a whirlwind under his horse's hooves!'

Leaving the "arish" abruptly, he called out to his army: 'Our enemies are routed! Already I see their backs turned in wild flight! I swear by Him who holdeth Mohammad's soul in the hollow of His hand, that any Believer killing a foe hath the right to his spoils; and any Believer killed face to the enemy will be immediately welcomed by Allah in the gardens of Paradise.'

Amir ibn Hammam, listening to these promises, held a handful of dates, and was about to lift them to his mouth, when he threw them on the ground with a sudden gesture of disdain, and shouted in tones of joyous exaltation: 'Bakr! Bakr! Consider that between me and my entry into Paradise there is only the slight barrier of death at the hands of the men over there.' Without finishing the sentence, he drew his sword and fell on the idolaters, digging a blood road through their ranks, until he succumbed outnumbered.

Another among the Faithful, having heard the Prophet (Peace be on him) declare that Allah would consider the martyr fighting with no armour other than that of his faith to be more deserving than any, threw off his breastplate and followed Amir's footsteps until he, too, fell cut to pieces, but not until he had sent many Unbelievers to the infernal regions.

From that moment, it was impossible to restrain the Believers. The Apostle scraped up a handful of dust, throwing it in the direction of the Quraish. 'May their faces be covered with confusion!' he cried. 'Forward! O Believers! Forward!

The Faithful, like a human hurricane, threw themselves on the Unbelievers and frightful noises rent the air. The clashing of weapons, cries of despair and triumph, reverberating again and again by reason of the echoes of the valley, were accompanied by a strange uproar, sounding jerkily, like the beating of a drum.

Quoth an Arab idolater of the Banu Ghifar: "I went with one of my cousins to the top of a hill overlooking the battlefield, so as to find out which side was victorious, meaning to join the conquerors and plunder the vanquished.

CHAPTER THE FIFTH

All of a sudden, at the very moment when the warriors of Islam attacked, I saw rising up behind them, from the depths of the valley, a great pillar of sand approaching with marvellous velocity. In its tawny spirals that threatened the clouds, fantastic and terrifying visions appeared and faded. It was like a gigantic combat of the Earth rebelling against the Heavens!

Sounds quite as strange escaped from the whirlwind, freezing my blood with horror. There was the neighing and trampling of galloping steeds; the beating of great wings; the roll of loud drums and, dominating the tumult, an imperious voice shouting: 'Forward, Haizum!'

In less than the twinkling of an eye, the whirlwind overtook the Believers, falling with them on to the ranks of the idol-worshippers. It soon reached us as well, smothering us in its yellow darkness. I lost sight of my companion, and was nigh fainting with fear. Powerful gusts of wind drove me hither and thither, and I had to cling to projecting rocks so as not to be swept away like a wisp of straw. My ears were deafened by atrocious clamours. The curses and the groans of the wounded; the blasphemy of the vanquished, mingled now with the rumbling of thunder. In the yellow, foggy obscurity, flashes of lightning gleamed; swords and spears glittered.

"At last, when the whirlwind passed away, I saw my comrade prone on the ground, his breast torn open, showing the membrane of his heart and, like trees uprooted by a hurricane, countless dead bodies strewed the bed of the Wadi; and in the distance, lit up by a ray of sunlight, the soldiers of Islam pursued the enemy in flight."

This whirlwind was the track of Jibra'il riding his horse, Haizum, that Mohammad had seen at the head of three thousand angels flying to his aid. The whirlwind of sand, uplifted by the tempestuous wind, allied itself to the human whirlwind swept along by the stormy breeze of faith and both, at one bound, rushed upon Allah's foes. The shock was irresistible. The furious billows of the raging sands struck the idolaters straight in the face, blistering the flesh, filling the nostrils, blinding eyes, so that they knew not where to strike, nor where to defend themselves.

The Believers, on the contrary, felt their impetuosity increased by the pushing of the hurricane, and their eyes, freely open, enabled them to avoid their adversaries' attack, and cut them down to a certainty. Better still: unknown, supernatural strength increased the strength of their arms tenfold, to such an extent that they fancied they struck at empty air because they felt no resistance to the impact of their weapons. "Scarcely did I threaten a head with the edge of my blade," one of the conquerors narrated later, "than I saw it fly off my adversary's shoulders and roll on the ground, even before my weapon touched it".

"So it was not ye who slew them, but Allah slew them." (the Qur'an, viii, 17.) Seventy idolaters bit the dust; and, among them, all the conspirators who tried to assasinate the Prophet (Peace be on him) at Makkah. Twenty-four of the dead belonged to the highest aristocracy: Utbah, Al Walid, Shaib Umaiyah ibn Khalaf, Abu Bulhtari, Hanzalal, Abu Sufyan's son, and, most important of all, the chief of the expedition, the famous Abu Jahal.

Knowing that the latter was the life and soul of the plots weaved against the Prophet, (Peace be on him) the Faithful sought for the arch-conspirator everywhere in the fight. One of them, Muaz ibn Amr, having succeeded in falling across him, pierced his thigh with a furious lunge. Ikrinah, Abu Jalal's son, rushed to his fathers assistance and, with a scimitar, avenged him by hacking the left arm of Muaz. It hung from his shoulder by a strip of flesh. His movements hampered by the useless, swinging limb, Muaz stooped, and placing his foot on it, tore it off by roughly standing erect again. He threw it far from him and went on fighting.

Two young Ansars, sons of Afrah, coming to the rescue, dragged Abu Jahal out of the saddle and left

The Muezzin calling the Faithful to Prayer.

him for dead, riddled with wounds.

The Prophet's mind was more engrossed with the fate of Abu Jahal than with that of any other of his foes. Ibn-i-Masud went out to search, and found him at last, in the midst of a pile of corpses. The chief of the idolaters was still breathing. Ibn-i-Masud placed his foot on the dying man's neck, even as one stamps on a Viper, but just as he lent over, Abu Jahal, to brave him, seized him by the beard, and gazing at his death rattle sounding in his throat: 'Hast ever seen as noble a fellow as I, murdered by such vile ploughmen?'

To put an end to the infidels' insults, Ibn-i-Masud cut off his head and brought it to the Prophet. (Peace be on him) At the sight of the bloodstained face of his enemy, Mohammad exclaimed: 'Verily, this man was the detestable Pharaoh of his nation!'

Corpses soon became decomposed, exposed to the sun's torrid rays; the tumefied faces of the dead took on the colour of pitch. This phenomenon proved to the Believers that the infidels had been struck down by celestial warriors, for were they not already carbonized by the flames of hell? Mohammad scoured the whole of the battlefield, ordering all the dead bodies he came across to be buried at once, no matter of which creed. Huzaifah, one of the early Islamic adepts, accompanying Mohammad, suddenly came upon the remains of Utbah ibn Rabiyah, his father. The son's features became distorted and blanched with mortal pallor. 'Hast thy fathers death shattered thy soul?' asked the Prophet. 'No, by Allah! but I knew my father was endowed with intelligence, goodness and generosity. I had hopes that he would have trodden the path of salvation. His death depriveth me of that hope. Hence my grief!'

The Prophet, (Peace be on him) impressed by the reply of this stoical Mussulman, called down the blessings of the Lord on his head. Mohammad then had his she-camel led to him and, mounting, rode to a dried-up well in which he ordered twenty-four of his best-known enemies to be buried. He stopped his she-camel in front of the mouth of this well and called on the dead by name: 'O such an one, son of such an one! And thou, such an one, son of such a none! Would ye not have preferred this day to have obeyed Allah and His Messenger? Of a surety, we have found that which Our Lord promised us; but you-have ye found that which your divinities promised you?'—'O Apostle!' said Ura, 'why dost thou speak to soulless bodies?'—'By Him who holdeth in His hands the soul of Mohammad!' he replied, 'I swear that thou dost not hear my words as distinctly as they!' By this he meant to inform Ura that these infidels, now dwelling in Hell, were compelled to acknowledge the truth of words that he had ofttimes repeated to them when they were in the land of the living. Thus does a "hadis" of Ayishah explain this scene, for it is said in the Qur'an:

"Verily then, thou canst make the dead to hear." (xxx, 51). The Believers only lost fourteen men, six Mohadjirun and eight Ansars, winning eternal glory as the first fallen in the Holy War.

The prophet (Peace be on him) remained three days on the field of battle to bury the dead and gather together the booty which he left to be guarded by the family of the Najjar. He then got ready to go back to Al-Madinah.

Two couriers, Zayd, his adopted son, and Ibn-i-Ruhah, sent on to carry the glad tidings, reached there before him. They arrived at the moment when the situation of the Believers in the city was becoming critical. Gravediggers had not finished cleansing their hands from the earth with which they had just covered the last resting-place of Roghaid, Mohammad's daughter, married to Usran. She had been carried off by painful illness. "Hypocrites" and Jews put the most alarming rumours in circulation concerning the Prophet's (Peace be on him) fate and they were getting ready to attack his supporters.

The good news spread all over the town with lightning rapidity; causing confusion in the haunts of "Hypocrites" and Jews, reassuring the Faithful and causing great enthusiasm in their ranks. All of them-a vast crowd of men, women and children-went forth to acclaim the conqueror, the procession marching to the cadence of drums. They sang in chorus the chant with which he had been welcomed when he first arrived: "The full moon hath risen above our head-Emerging from the Sanniyat-ul-Wida;-Numerous are the thanksgivings we must offer up to Allah-With the purest fervour of our supplications.-O thou His Messenger among us-The orders thou dost bring us shall be piously executed!"

Ever since this battle, for ever memorable, which by its results eventually changed the whole face of the world, although only fought out by a small number of men, the Wadi of Badr is visited yearly by thousands.

It is written by the traveller Abul Hosain ibn Zubair: "A small market-town, surrounded by ramparts, stands now upon its site . . . What was once the well where the Unbelievers were buried, is now a clump of palm-trees, and a little farther off are tombs of the martyrs.

To the left of the road leading from Safra, is the Mountain of Mercy- A Rhmah- by which the Angels descended from Heaven.

The "arish", the shelter where Mohammad stood, is said to have been erected on the slope of a sandhill, called Jabl-ul-Tabl, the Mountain of the Drum, because the roll of supernatural drums is frequently heard there by pilgrims; mysterious martial music, "celebrating the remembrance of the first victory of Islam."

There were as many prisoners as dead: three score and ten, mostly belonging to the best families among the idolaters.

Two of them, Aqbah and An Nazir, whose insults to the Prophet (Peace be on him) were beyond all measure, suffered the death penalty after condemnation.

Abbas, Mohammad's uncle, compelled by his pecuniary interests to remain behind in Makkah, had not yet made up his mind to embrace the Islamic faith. He had gone to the aid of the caravan in danger, and was taken prisoner. His commanding stature and bodily vigour stood him not in good stead, for he was captured by the weakest warrior among the Ansars and remained petrified with surprise. The ropes that bound him cut cruelly into his flesh. He sighed heavily in pain. One of the Faithful, recollecting the captive's handsome behaviour and that he was a relative of the Prophet (Peace be on him), loosened his bonds most charitably. Hearing of this and not admitting that a member of his family should be favoured, Mohammad ordered the bonds of all the other prisoners to be loosened in the same way.

It now remained to decide the fate of the captives. Abu Bakr, pretexting the ties of blood uniting victors and vanquished, was of opinion that a ransom should be accepted. Fierce Umar, recalling the fact that all the prisoners had made themselves conspicuous by their persecution of the Mussulmans and were responsible for the Prophet's (Peace be on him) banishment, proposed that they should be pitilessly exterminated. Both opinions rallied an equal number of partisans.

The Prophet (Peace be on him) sided with Abu Bakr. He gave orders to respect luckless valour and to treat the captives with the greatest humanity. He caused them to be freed from their bonds and had them guarded by all the Mussulmans in turn who, faithfully obeying his commands, deprived themselves of bread in favour of their prisoners, being content with dried dates.

The ransom was fixed according to each prisoner's wealth. Abbas, Mohammad's uncle, had to give the largest amount; the others were liberated without paying anything. Nevertheless, Mohammad required that, before being set free, each captive knowing how to read and write should give lessons to two children of the Ansars.

Among the prisoners was Abul's As ibn Rabiyah, a rich man in high repute. He had married Zainab, the daughter of the Prophet (Peace be on him) before the Revelation, and was still an idolater. For the ransom of her husband, Zainab sent from Makkah a sum of money and a necklace, a wedding-gift from her mother Khadijah. The Prophet (Peace be on him) recognising this piece of jewellery which he had ofttimes seen round the neck of his beloved and regretted Khadijah, was unable to repress his emotion and put this question to his disciples: 'If ye do not oppose me, I will send her husband back to Zainab, and renounce all claims to ransom.' No object being raised, Mohammad told his prisoner that he was free. 'But only on one condition. Restore my daughter to my arms, for a woman of the Mussulmans cannot remain in the power of an idolater.' The captive accepted most reluctantly, and as soon as he was again in Makkah, he kept his word.

The Quraish, however, hearing of Zainab's departure, started off in pursuit of her, and one of them, Hibar, struck her so brutally with the shaft of his spear that he threw her out of her "hawdaj," (a kind of litter), and she dropped from the back of her camel to the ground. Shortly after her arrival at Al-Madinah, the poor woman, not having recovered from her fall, and being pregnant, died from the effects of the ill-treatment she had thus undergone.

Under the influence of grief and despair, the Prophet (Peace be on him) gave orders that anyone putting his hand on the villain Hibar was to burn him alive. But it was not long before Mohammad cancelled this cruel command, declaring: 'The Master of the Worlds alone hath the right to inflict the torture of Fire!' This was an allusion to the flames of Hell.

As for Abul'As, retaken by the Mussulmans while conducting a caravan back from Syria, he was again liberated by the Prophet (Peace be on him) and became a convert to Islam.

Mohammad thus let no opportunity escape to prove his generosity to the prisoners, his own fellow countrymen. The Prophet's (Peace be on him) clemency resulted immediately in the conversion of no small number of Makkans, marvelling at the tales told by the captives who, upon regaining the bosom of their families, bore witness to the kindness with which they had been treated.

Perhaps the fact of such compassion towards the enemies of Islam constituted peril in the future? So said a Revelation to the Prophet (Peace be on him) blaming him at the same time. Mohammad was overwhelmed with profound sadness, at the thought that his generosity would cause the death of many Believers, as he dared not hope that goodness would sweep away all feeling of enmity.

As soon as the victory was won, the division of the booty was near to causing serious quarrels among the Faithful. Each man desired to keep to himself all he had plundered. Those who had fought without thinking of stripping the dead put in a claim, saying to their comrades who wanted to keep that which they had taken: 'Had it not been for us, ye would have been unable to seize any booty at all.' Finally, the men of the rear-guard also complained: 'If we had not considered the Prophet's (Peace be on him) safety above all things, we should have fought with you and pillaged as ye did.' The debate seemed to be turning out badly when a Revelation put an end to the dispute: *"They will question thee about the spoils. Say: The spoils are Allah's and the Apostle's."* (the Qur'an, viii, i.)

Back again in Al-Madinah, Mohammad divided the booty with the most scrupulous fairness, and gave out that not only the rearguard should receive their share, but also a few of the Faithful who had remained in the city to uphold the cause of Islam during the absence of their chief.

Thus did Mohammad succeed in contenting everybody. So far as he was concerned, he only took the same share as a common soldier; but it was settled that in future the fifth part of the booty *"should belong to Allah and to the Apostle and to the near of kin and to orphans, and to the poor and to the wayfarer."* (the Qur'an, viii, 42.)

The Makkans were joyfully celebrating the return of the great caravan that had caused them such immense anxiety, when the remains of the routed army began to straggle back.

At first, the citizens refused to believe such dire disaster, so great had been their confidence in the superiority of the numbers and equipment of their soldiers. The fugitives were considered to be cowards deserting before the battle had begun.

But when doubt was no longer possible, profound consternation overtook Allah's enemies. The fury of Abu Lahab, the real organiser of the expedition, was inconceivable. In his presence, one of the fugitives told of the miracles he had witnessed and which, in his opinion, were an excuse for the defeat. 'The Mussulmans, assuredly, were granted supernatural succour, for I saw, with my own eyes, in the whirling tempest, many warriors gifted with superhuman strength, wearing white tunics, mounted on dapple-grey horses, and fighting side by side with our enemies.'—'By Allah! verily, they were angels!' exclaimed one of those present, Abu Rafiah, a servant of Abbas, Mohammad's uncle.

Abu Lahab, enraged at the impression of terror produced by this story and the remarks that had followed, hurled himself on Abu-Rafiah, threw him down and beat him unmercifully in the most savage fashion—'Art thou not ashamed thus to profit by the master's absence to strike his serving-man?' the wife of Abbas, revolted at the sight, shouted to Abu Lahab. Catching up a spear, she struck him in the face with it, and drew blood. The punishment was so well deserved that no one protested. Abu Lahab, humiliated in the eyes of all, hastened to hide his shame and rage in the most secluded part of his dwelling. Not being in the best of health just then, he could not master the exasperation he felt. His blood was turned; the whole of his body broke out in reddish pustules, known as "adsah", and he was carried off in less than a week.

As for Abu Sufyan and his wife, Hind, in despair at the death of their son, Hanzalah, and debased by the defeat, they showed themselves conspicuously as being athirst for vengeance. Abu Sufyan exercised his authority by prohibiting all show of grief. 'Weep not for your dead,' he proclaimed. 'Do not give way to the usual funereal lamentations. Let poets be careful not to compose elegies. O Makkans! avoid causing the joy of our foes by the sight of your sadness. Let only one thought absorb your mind—that of vengeance!'

He took a solemn oath to abstain from going near his wife or making use of his perfumes until the day when striking revenge should bring balm to his heart.

The effect of the Prophet's (Peace be on him) victory spread far and wide among all the tribes of Arabia. The tidings crossed the seas; the Prophet (Peace be on him) despatched an emissary to the Najashi of Abyssinia, to announce the result of the battle and to inform all the Believers, who had taken refuge at this monarch's court, that they would be in safety behind the walls of al-Madinah, at Mohammad's side.

يا أيها الذين آمنوا إذا لقيتم فئة فاثبتوا
واذكروا الله كثيرا لعلكم تفلحون

CHAPTER SIX — Decorative plate.

وَلَا تَهِنُوا وَلَا تَحْزَنُوا وَأَنْتُمُ الْأَعْلَوْنَ إِنْ كُنْتُمْ مُؤْمِنِينَ

CHAPTER THE SIXTH

ALI'S MARRIAGE

By reason of admirable devotion, indomitable courage and the absolute purity of his way of living, Ali had become one of the most popular heroes of Islam, but his extreme poverty forced him to hire himself out to Ansar, a garden landlord. When Ali was not engaged in prayer, he passed the hours in watering date-trees. He deserved that this lowly situation, bearing no comparison with his exploits, should have been changed so as to give him new e in the eyes of the people.

Abu Bakr and Usman, finding him one day busily engaged in drawing water from a well, bade him halt in his work, and reminded him of a former desire of his, when he had thought of marrying Fatimah, the Prophet's (Peace be on him) daughter. Ali got out of temper. 'Ye know how poor I am,' he told them. 'It's cruel of you to bring up a dream that can never come true!'

But they were so persistent, affirming that he could rely upon their good offices that Ali repressed his timidity, and carrying his sword, armour and sandals, that constituted his sole wealth, went and knocked at the Prophet's (Peace be on him) door. Mohammad welcomed him with these words: 'Here stands a man more dear to me than any other.' Ali remained silent, with bowed head. 'Speak!' commanded Mohammad.—'O Prophet!' Ali made up his mind to reply at last, 'thou didst bring me up, an orphan boy, with a father's love. This day I arrived at an age when a man should have a home of his own. Once more I seek thine aid. I come to ask thee to give me thy daughter Fatimah in marriage'—'What dower bringest thou?'—'Thou knowest my poverty. I bring thee all I possess: my sword, armour and sandals.'—'Thy sword belongeth to thy religion, I cannot accept it. But thy good right arm is strong enough to defend thy breast better than any cuirass. Go sell thine armour and bring me the price thereof to sell as my daughter's dower.'

Ali, all his wishes gratified, sought out a buyer. Usman offered him a good price and then gave him back his armour, begging him to accept it as a wedding-present.

The marriage was soon arranged; ratified by Mohammad saying to Ali: 'Verily, Allah gave thee my daughter in Heaven before I gave her to thee in this world.'!

A great number of the faithful, summoned by Bilal, were present to listen to the "khutbah" (sermon) of their chief, who wished to apprise them of the betrothal of his daughter to Ali. Bilal was charged to procure the few simple things indispensable in a household. Half the dowry served to buy a mattress and a pillow of palm-fibre, a goat skin for water and a few earthenware platters. With the other half were purchased butter, dates and flour, forming the frugal betrothal repast.

When according to custom, a group of women came to fetch the bride and lead her into her husband's room, the Prophet, (Peace be on him) in memory of her whom this duty would have devolved, namely Kadijah, Fatimah's mother, was overtaken by a profound fit of sadness. Showers of tears coursed down his cheeks. When he had mastered his emotion, he placed Ali at his right hand, with Fatimah at his left, saying to them: 'May Allah cause to be born to you noble descendents, who shall be an honour to our race!'

For three days and three nights, the newly-married couple remained absorbed in prayer. It was only on the fourth night that chaste Ali, to whom Mohammad declared that he hoped a long line of male children would spring from this marriage, dared to approach his wife in whose veins coursed the blood of the Prophet (Peace be on him).

Nine months later, Fatimah brought into the world a son who was named Hasan. A year after the birth of Hasan his brother Husain was born. The offspring of Hasan and Husain, called *Sharifs*, are the sole descendants of the Prophet (Peace be on him).

Hafsah, daughter of Umar and widow of Khunes, wished to marry again, but she was of such a haughty disposition that no one came forward to offer to be her husband. Abu Bakr, and Usman after him, to whom her hand had been proposed, both declined. Umar, greatly annoyed at his daughter's humiliation, opened his heart to the Prophet (Peace be on him) who replied: 'Usman will marry a better woman than Hafsah will marry a better man than Usman.' Mohammad gave his daughter Umm-i-Kulsm in marriage to Usman, whilst to honour Umar, the Prophet (Peace be on him) took haughty Hafsah to wife.

Shortly afterwards Mohammad also espoused the widow of Ubaidah, the martyr of Badr. She was a woman whose charity was inexhaustible and earned the surname of "Ummu'l-Masakin," (the Mother of the Poor).

The inhabitants of Makkah could not console themselves for the defeat at Badr. The future seemed to them black indeed. Their caravans dared not to venture on the Syrian road, blocked by the Prophet's (Peace be on him) bold stroke. Ruin and famine were inevitable at an early date. To guard against such impending disaster, they decided to devote the large profits made by their great caravan to arming an expedition which would avenge their dead and grant them commercial security. Allured by offers of money, numerous Bedouins of the vicinity came forward to proffer assistance. Already worked up by the inflammatory satires of the poets Kab ibn Ashraf and Abu Uzd, these tribesmen, called "Habash," or Confederates, were enrolled in the ranks of the army raised by Abu Sufyan.

At the head of these troops, three thousand strong, were Safunah and Ikrimah, sons of Ibn-i-Khalaf and Jahal, two of the mighty dead of Badr, and Khalid ibn Walid, the unconquerable soldier. The women's thirst for revenge was equally ardent; and Hind, the wife of Abu Sufyan, bore along behind her a horde of her companions resolved to stop any warrior who might be tempted to run away.

In the fertile plains, north of Al-Madinah, the fellahs were peacefully engaged in their work of agriculture, or watching over their grazing flocks, when all of a sudden, the soldiers of Abu Sufyan, who had taken the greatest precautions to hide their rapid advance, debouched from the ravines of the western mountains. All resistance being impossible, the ill-fated peasants fled in great haste to escape being massacred, and to warn their fellow-citizens of the invasion of Allah's enemies.

From the top of their ramparts, the dwellers in Al-Madinah looked down on a sight that made their agriculturists' hearts bleed. Like a swarm of gigantic locusts, the camels of the idolatrous army ravaged the verdant meadows, whilst horsemen slaughtered cattle and, madly rushing, the riders trampled down and scattered the golden harvest, with all the disdain of traders for the work of husbandmen.

CHAPTER THE SIXTH

In the face of this havoc wrought before their eyes, the Faithful found themselves in a state of most irritating powerlessness. The plain afforded commodious space for the manoeuvres of their enemies' countless cavalry, and the Believers had no mounted men to put in the field. Their sole resource was the wisdom of Allah's Apostle; so, ready for any sacrifice, they gathered round him.

Now Mohammad had dreamed that he saw his sword-blade notched; his foes slaughtering his flocks, whilst a breastplate was close to his hand. The Prophet (Peace be on him) told his followers of his dream and explained what it signified. 'The notched blade means that I shall be wounded. The slaughtered flocks show that a great number of my disciples will die; and the breastplate near me symbolizes the ramparts of Al-Madinah which alone can save us from disaster. Let us shut ourselves up in the city and we shall have nothing to fear from our adversaries. Should they attack, they can easily be repulsed and made to suffer cruel losses; and if they fall back without attacking, they will be crushed in their retreat by the shame of not having dared to fight us.'

Such had always been the tactics of the people of Al-Madinah from time immemorial; but the quality of their Mussulmans and their victory at the battle of Badr had changed all their ideas. Thinking that they were now and forever invincible, they no longer had the patience to remain impassive while their gardens were laid to waste. Furthermore, those who had not fought at Badr were burning with desire to show that they too were full of courage. The worst that could befall them was martyrdom to which they sincerely aspired.

Abdullah ibn Abi Salul, chief of the "Hypocrites," was alone opposed to an advance. For once in a way, the Prophet (Peace be on him) agreed with him. Nevertheless, in the face of unanimity and the enthusiasm of the true Believers, Mohammad considered that he ought to give way, and resolved to order the march out that he disapproved of in his foresight. After having recited the afternoon prayer, *Asr*, he went back into his house to buckle on his armour.

The warriors, too, were ready. A compact crowd surrounded the dwelling of the Prophet (Peace be on him) who soon appeared, girt with his coat of mail, helmet on head, sword by his side, shield on his shoulders, and spear in hand.

Whilst waiting, the faithful had had time to reflect. They began to regret their hasty decision, and their chiefs, ashamed at having upheld different ideas to those of Allah's Chosen One, said to him: 'We ought to have bowed down to thy judgment. We feel inclined to remain where we are. Thou canst put aside thine armour.'—'When a Prophet hath buckled on his breastplate,' replied Mohammad, 'he forfeits the right to take it off until the fight is finished.'

The army of the Believers numbered a thousand foot-soldiers, but possessed only two horses. The standard of the Mohadjirun was confided to Musab ibn Amir; that of the Aus to Uqaid; the banner of the Khazraj being born by Habbab. Just before sunset, the column went forward, taking a northerly direction.

Scarcely had they passed the ramparts, when they were rejoined by a troop of six hundred men, all well-armed. They were Jews; allies of Abdullah, the "Hypocrite," and it was thanks to his counsel that they offered their assistance to the Prophet. (Peace be on him) 'Allah's aid sufficeth,' he answered, as he sent them away, for knowing their secret sympathies, he feared they might betray him.

Abdullah, belittled by the rejection of his allies, lost no time in trying to spread anxiety in the soldiers' ranks by perfidious remarks such as these: 'Mohammad listens to the chatter of good-for-nothing folks, and spurns the good advice I give him. Why go to face certain death?' In this way, he succeeded in decoying a third of the little army, thus reduced to about seven hundred men and, at the head of the deserters, he turned back on the road to Al-Madinah, followed by the hooting of the true Believers.

The next morning, on a Saturday, the eleventh day of the month of Shawwal, before daybreak, the Prophet (Peace be on him) ordered the tents to be folded. He asked for a guide clever enough to lead his troops, unseen by the enemy, to the Jabl-ul-Uhud, a mountain rising isolated in the plain. Abu Haythama came forward and led them through the orchards and palm-tree plantations of the Banu Harith.

The owner of these gardens, a "Hypocrite," named Mirba, his eyes eaten away by ophthalmia, rose up as he heard Mohammad's footsteps at the head of his troops, and shouted to him: 'If even it were true that thou art the Prophet of Allah, I would not authorise thee to go through my garden! if I did not fear to strike someone else, I would hurl this earth in thy face.' The Believers wished to punish the insolence of the "Hypocrite" by taking his life, but Mohammad (Peace be on him) restrained them, saying: 'Kill him not, for he is blind. His heart is as blind as his eyes.'

Along this by-path, and concealed behind the thick foliage of the orchards, the Mussulmans reached the mountain of Uhad before sunrise, without having been caught sight of by their foes.

The Prophet (Peace be on him) arranged his forces for the fight. They had the mountain behind them; their left wing being covered by the pass of Ainin, so that there was no fear of being turned. To be more sure, he posted Ibn Jubayr above this defile, with fifty of his most skilful archers, to whom Mohammad gave the following strict order: 'If the idolaters' cavalry attempt to outflank us, slipping through the ravine, repulse them with a shower of arrows. But whether the enemy should be above or below us, remain steadfast at your post, and whatever befalls, take care not to go forward!'

At this juncture, a loud outcry was heard resounding in the direction of the plain. The Makkans had just perceived the Believers who, with the oblique rays of the sun playing on their spears, stood out in glowing relief on the rocky slopes of the Jabal-ul-Uhad. Exactly as the Prophet (Peace be on him) had foreseen, the enemy's army, its right wing directed by Kalid ibn Walid, the terrible, and it's left wing commanded by Ikrimah, son of Abu Jahal, spread itself out in a semi-circle, so as to surround and turn the Mussulmans.

Abu Sufyan, chieftan of the Infidels, trying to wound the vanity of the Banu Abdi'd-Dar, guarding the flag, called to them thus: 'O ye who carried our standard at Badr, remember the disaster for which the blame must be laid on you. A soldier should follow the flag, but ye fled with it. If this day ye fear to be unable to defend it, let me confide it to other hands.' Stung to the quick by such an insult, the Banu Abdi'd-Dar threw up their heads boldly. 'We shall know how to guard our flag,' said they; 'and if we are alive tomorrow thou shalt do justice to our valour.'

Hind now came forward, leading her companions to take their stand behind the guardians of the flag. And the women sang:

"Courage! O sons of the Abdi'd-Dar!—Courage! O defenders of the women at your heels!—Strike with every blade!—We are daughters of the star of Tariq—Our feet glide on soft carpets—Pearls glisten in our necklaces—And musk perfumeth our tresses—If ye show a bold front to the enemy, we will embrace you!—Should you flee from the foe, we shall repulse you—And you will die dishonoured eternally by our scorn!"

On the side of the Believers, the Prophet (Peace be on him) was not sparing of encouragement. 'Who among you,' he exclaimed, offering a glistening sword, 'is capable of giving this weapon its due?'—'And what is its due, prithee? asked Abu Dujana, coming forward.—'Its due is to strike with its blade till it be twisted!'—'Well then, I swear to give it its due!'

Abu Dujana was a redoubtable warrior. He received the sabre from Mohammad's hands and rolling around his head a red turban that he never wore, except on great occasions when death was nigh, he strode superbly up and down in front of the ranks. 'Such a defiant bearing would give rise to Allah's wrath,' the Prophet (Peace be on him) declared, 'on any other occasion but this.'

Among the enemy was an inhabitant of Madinah, Abu Amir, converted to Christianity and nicknamed "Ar Rahib," which means "the Monk." Having got it into his head that he could lead a few of his fellow-countrymen in the Aus tribe astray from the cause of Islam, he went and stood before them, saying: 'O "quam" of the Aus!' tis I, Abu Amir, a son of your soul. Will ye not hear me out?'—'May Allah refuse thee all favour, O scoundrel!' they replied. Choking with shame and rancour, "the Monk" went away, after picking up a pebble which he threw in fury at them.

When "the Monk" had retired, an idolater of terrible appearance, bestriding a gigantic camel, advanced; challenging the Believers thrice. At the third provocation, Zubayr stepped out of the ranks. With the leap of a panther, he sprang on to the camel's rump, threw his arms round his adversary, and rolling with him on the ground, never let go his hold until he had torn his throat open.

Seeing the combat beginning, Abu Dujana could restrain himself no longer. He drew his sword. 'There is no good fortune in the ranks of cowards!' he exclaimed. 'I strike with the sword of Allah and his Prophet!' The scarlet turban was seen digging into the very centre of the enemy's massed troops like a glowing brand.

By dint of prodigies of audacity, he struck down all those he met on his way, when suddenly he found himself facing a strange being who, vomiting forth the vilest blasphemy, was followed by a crowd of girls playing on tabors. Abu Dujana brandished his blade over his adversary's head, but on hearing the piercing shrieks uttered by Hind, he recognised her. The sword of the Prophet (Peace be on him) was rendered generous by him, for he knew it ought not to strike a woman.

Following Abu Dujana's onslaught, the battle raged furiously and all the combatants were at grips. Arshah, the Quraish standard-bearer, was struck down by Hamzah, and showed all his teeth in the snarling grin of death. Siba-al Ghassani picked up the flag, and challenged his companion's conqueror. 'Come a little nearer, O son of the procuress!' replied Hamzah; and at a single stroke, he made him share the fate of Arshah.

Wishing to avenge his uncle Tahaimah, slain at Badr by Hamzah, Zubayr ibn Mutam promised to free his Abyssinian slave, Al-Uhayha, if he succeeded in killing Hamzah.

Thus spoke Al-Uhayha: "During the battle, I had no eyes but for Hamzah. When I caught sight of him, he was like a rutting grey camel, throwing down all he met with such terrible blows that none of them rose again. Not daring to face him, I dogged his footsteps, skulking behind bushes or rocks. At last, he neared the spot where I was hidden. I am skilled at throwing the Abyssinian javelin and rarely miss my mark. Just as Hamzah cut Siba down with a blow on the head, I balanced my spear and sent it hissing at him. It struck in his groins coming out between his thighs. Terrible in his wrath, Hamzah turned to attack me, but his strength failing him, he fell down in a huddled heap and died on the spot. I then came out of my place of concealment, tore my spear from his dead body and left the battlefield. I only struck at Hamzah to gain my freedom."

The standard-bearer of the Mohadjirun, Mussab ibn Amir, was slain at the Prophet's (Peace be on him) side. His murderer, Qaumiah-al-Lissi, thinking that he had killed Mohammad himself, returned to his comrades. 'I've slain Mohammad!' he bawled, puffed up with pride.

Ali seized the standard that had slipped from Mussab's grasp, and accepted the challenge of Abu Sad ibn Abi Talhah, the idolaters' standard-bearer, who uttered these jeering words: 'O companions of Mohammad! ye maintain that our swords send you to Paradise whilst yours despatch us to hell! By Lat and Uzza! ye lie in your teeth, for ye take good care not to rush on our blades!'

Ali did not allow him to say anything else. No sooner did the two men meet, than the mocking idol-worshipper was sent rolling in agony to earth. Ali's arm was lifted to finish him off when suddenly the young man averted his head and turned away: Abu Sad, in falling, had exposed his nakedness to his conqueror.

A furious fight took place round the flag of the Quraish, and many other Infidels passed from life to death. Two defenders of this banner, Mishfah and his brother, Al Zulas, both pierced through and through by arrows, dragged themselves along to their mother, Sulafa, one of Hind's Companions. The two lads, vomiting streams of blood, rested their heads in the lap of the woman who had brought them into the world. 'O my poor boys!' she cried, her voice choked with sobs, 'who dealt you these terrible blows?'—'When we fell,' her sons replied, 'we heard a voice saying: 'Take these darts from me. I am Asim, son of Allah!' And Sulafa swore that Asim's skull should be fashioned by her into a cup from which she would drink vinous liquors.

The balance of victory was clearly in favour of the Believers. The Quraish flag was laid out on the ground, close to a heap of dead bodies, and no idolator dared to lift the banner. The rout of Allah's foes had begun. The fury of Hind, her serving-girls, and her female friends was changed to terror. They lifted their draperies, showing their legs, in order to flee more easily in wild haste. The archers, posted near the ravine on the slopes of the Uhud, could see all this better than anyone else, and they stamped with hot impatience, fearing that they would not be able to take a hand in plundering the vanquished.

In vain their chieftain, Ibn Jubayr, tried to restrain them by bidding them to remember the Prophet's (Peace be on him) strict orders, and their duty which was to cover the army's flank by guarding the mountain pass. 'The fight is finished,' they answered in ill-humour. 'Victory is ours! We mean to have our share of the booty, or deserve the crown of martyrdom.' Like a living torrent, they rushed down the declivity of the ravine, disobeying Allah and his Messenger.

"Already had Allah made good for you His promise, when by His permission ye destroyed your foes, until your courage failed you, and ye disputed together about the order, and disobeyed, after that the Prophet had brought you within view of that for which ye longed." (the Qur'an, iii, 145.)

Khalid, the valiant, farseeing warrior commanding the Quraish left wing and who, till then, recognised that it was impossible to turn the position, perceived the fault of the archers. At the head of his cavalry, he charged Ibn Jubary, surrounded by a handful of men remaining faithful to him, and after they were crushed beneath the hoofs of the horses, Khalid took the Mussulmans in the rear while they were engrossed with the thoughts of plunder.

At the same time, a woman of the idolators, Amir bint Alqamah, lifted the standard abandoned by the Makkans who, ashamed at their own cowardice when they saw what this courageous woman had done, went back and fought again. In triumphant tones, dominating all clamour and clash of arms, the voice of Qumiah, slayer of Musab, rang out: 'Verily, Mohammad hath just been killed!'

The current of the combat deviated. The day, that had begun so favourably, became a day of calamity. Attacked in the rear, maddened by the fatal news, the Mussulmans gave way, and a number fled to Al-Madinah. Even Usman, in despair, allowed himself to be led away.

A great many of the most noble combatants fell martyrs in the fight, and Allah's enemies rained showers of arrows and stones on a small group of the Faithful surrounding the Prophet (Peace be on him). One stone, thrown by the son of Abu Waqas, struck Mohammad, splitting his lip, breaking a front tooth, on the right. Another projectile smashed the rings of his helmet, driving them into his cheek.

Abu Ubaidah, by biting the rings forced into flesh, managed to drag them out. Little he recked when he broke a tooth on each; and he sucked in ecstasy the blood flowing from the wounds of Allah's

Chosen One. Moved by such fierce devotion, Mohammad said to him: 'He who hath sucked my blood hath naught to fear from the flames of Hell; but how can those men prosper who have shed the blood of their Prophet?'

Meanwhile, the situation became more and more critical. During the thick of the fight, Mohammad was knocked down, and thrown into a deep hole that he had not noticed behind him. Ali and Talha helped him out at once.

Then Ali, together with Abu Bakr and Umar, both wounded, hurled themselves on the assailants whose forces increased unceasingly threatening to encircle the Believers. There were moments when the Prophet (Peace be on him) had no one with him except Abu Dujana, shielding him with his body riddled by arrows, and Abu Talha who protected Mohammad by means of a leather buckler.

Abu Talha was an archer so strong that he broke three bows by bending them. He said to Mohammad who rose up to see the result of the fighting and give directions: 'O thou for whom I would give father and mother in ransom, lie down, I beg of thee. Thou might be struck by an arrow. Let my breast protect thy breast.' At that moment, a foeman's dart, that he dashed aside, mutilated his hand. No longer able to use his bow, he unsheathed his sabre, but was so greatly exhausted by fatigue that, overcome by sleep, he closed his eyes and his weapon fell from his grasp.

Ummi-Amr, a heroine of the Ansars, a goat-skin on her back, flew along the ranks of the Believers, pouring water in their mouths to refresh them. She seized a sword and fought with manly vigour near Mohammad, until, she fell, badly wounded.

Ali Abu Bakr and Umar had been separated from the Prophet (Peace be on him) in the ebb and flow of the fight; and the shouts of the Infidels announcing his death deprived them of all courage. The three Believers were like soulless bodies and they did not even think of defending themselves. Seeing them in this state, Anas ibn Nazir shamed them: 'What aileth you that you are so downcast?'—'The Prophet is dead.'—'Well then! what have ye to do with life, now that he is gone? Die as he died.' Setting the example, he dashed forward, and fell covered with so many wounds that only his sister was able to recognise his dead body, and that by a peculiarity of his fingers.

This was a rallying signal. Abashed by their own despondency, Ali, Abu Bakr and Amur, followed by a few of the Faithful, copying Umar, rushed to a part of the battlefield where the enemy masses were furiously attacking a few men still standing.

Suddenly, among these heroes resisting with superhuman energy, Kab ibn Malik recognised the Prophet (Peace be on him) in person, whose eyes sparkled under his helmet. 'O Mussulmans! O brothers!' shouted Kab, in stentorian accents. 'Good news! Look at the Prophet of Allah! He is safe and sound!'

This cry awakened fresh courage in the heart of every man. On all sides, the Mussulmans rushed recklessly to the spot whence the glad cry proceeded. After having disengaged the Prophet, (Peace be on him) they were afire with irresistible ardour and cut a bloody path through the overthrown enemy's ranks as far as the ravine of Ainin, which they never ought to have abandoned. The effort of the idolators to storm this impregnable position was unavailing. Ubi ibn Khalaf cried out in his fury: 'O Mohammad! where art thou? Shouldst thou be still alive, I swear thou shalt not escape me!'

The Prophet (Peace be on him) would not allow his partisans to tear Ubi limb from limb as they wished to do, but dragging a spear from the grasp of Al Haris, Mohammad drove its steel into Ubi's throat. He dropped forward on his horse's neck and, after vainly trying to save himself by clutching at the mane, fell heavily to the ground. The idolators, exhausted, gave up the idea of avenging his death. The fight was finished.

Finding a little water in the hollow of a rock, Ali filled his shield and offered it to the Prophet (Peace be on him). But he turned against the smell of this water and refused to drink it. So Ali then used it to wash the wounds of Allah's Chosen One, but in vain, his blood continuing to flow freely as to give rise to great uneasiness. Fatimah, who in a state of great anxiety, had arrived at the scene of battle with a few of her companions, caused some fragments of a rushmat to be set on fire and covered her father's wounds with the ashes. This dressing put a stop to the haemorrhage.

The Prophet (Peace be on him) recited the midday prayer, but remained seated, in consequence of extreme fatigue and the suffering brought on by his wounds. Behind him, also seated for the same reason, all the combatants prayed with him, and gave thanks to the Almighty for having saved them despite their disobedience.

The death-roll numbered three score and ten, equalling the count of the idolatrous prisoners of Badr. Many of the Believers considered that this coincidence formed a punishment for having accepted a ransom in their greed for worldly profit.

The bodies of the martyrs of Uhud were in a parlous state. A thirst for vengeance, the women of the Quraish had thrown away their tabors in order to hurl themselves on the corpses and mutilate them odiously. Hind, their mistress, was the most ferocious of them all. Taking out her earrings, pulling off necklaces, bracelets and ankle-rings, she handed them all to Al-Uhayha, the slayer of Hamzah and, in place of her gewgaws, adorned herself with necklaces and bangles fashioned with noses and ears sliced from the heads of her foes. Like a filthy hyena, she squatted on Hamzah's remains. With ensanguined fingernails, she tore his body open and dragged out the liver with fury, making her teeth meet in it. She then climbed on the top of a lofty rock and turning towards the soldiers of Islam, howled with all the strength of her lungs:

"We have paid you back for the day of Badr!—I was tortured by the remembrance of my father—my son, and of my uncle, murdered by you!—My soul is now at rest and my vengeance is glutted.—My "uhayha" (grief) hath been softened by thee—O Uhayha! O conqueror of Hamzah! I'll sing thy praises—Until my bones crumble into dust in my grave!"

Abu Sufyan, searching every nook and corner of the field of battle in the hope of finding Mohammad's lifeless body, stopped short in front of Hamzah's corpse at the same time as Jalis, chief of the Arab Confederates. Abu Sufyan amused himself by striking the corners of the dead man's mouth with the point of a spear. 'Take a good taste of the bitterness of rebellion,' he said.

Seeing this, Jalis, although an idolator, was greatly shocked. 'O Banu Kinana!' cried he to his partisans, admire the behaviour of the Lord of the Quraish towards his cousin now that he is lifeless!' Abu Sufyan, alive to the fact that his conduct was vile, drew Jalis on one side and supplicated him. 'Keep all this secret, O Jalis, for I am ashamed of what I did just now in thy presence.'

He then drew near to a spot within hail of the Faithful, entrenched on the slopes of the Uhud, and called out to them: 'Is Mohammed with you?' There being no answer, he joyfully concluded that the Prophet was dead. Before going away, he bawled as loudly as he could: 'Assuredly, war is a game of chance. This day avengeth the day of Badr; Hubal, our god is victorious. He is the All-Highest!'

At this blasphemy, the Prophet ordered Umar to reply. He cried out: 'Allah is the Most High; the Most Majestic!' Recognising Umar's voice, Abu Sufyan asked him: 'O Umar! I conjure thee, inform me if we have killed Mohammad.'—'No, by my faith! He is even now listening to thee.' Abu Sufyan, disappointed, rejoined: 'Evidently, I am bound to believe thee in preference to Ibn Qamiah who boasts of having killed him. But I swear to meet you next year at Badr.'—'That is understood!' replied Umar. 'We pledge our word to meet thee there.'

The Prophet despatched Ali to track the Infidels. 'Take heed how they carry themselves,' Mohammad impressed upon his scout. 'See if they ride their camels and lead their horses by the bridle. That will certainly denote that they gave up all hope of battle and are going to Makkah. If, on the contrary, they mount their steeds and drive their camels before them, it is a sure sign that they are bound for Al-Madinah with the intention of cutting us off. In that case, there is but one thing to be done: to hurl ourselves upon them without loss of time, so as to attack them and hack our way through.'

A few minutes later, Ali returned. He had seen the Quraish alight from their horses, bestride their camels and set out in the direction of Makkah.

Reassured as to the enemy's intentions the Believers busied themselves with the burial of the martyrs. First of all, the Prophet sought to find the body of his uncle Hamzah. Mohammad discovered it in a hollow of the Wadi, the belly ripped open; and with ears and nose cut off. 'Were it not that I feared to grieve Safiyah (Hamzah's sister), and to set an example which would perhaps become law, I would leave these remains unburied, until they should disappear in the entrails of jackals and vultures; thus keeping alive the hope of revenge. If the Almighty should ever deliver into our hands the wretches who have thus treated thee, I swear to exercise most terrible reprisals.'

The Prophet then received this Revelation: *"If ye make reprisals, then make them to the same extent that ye were injured: but if ye can endure patiently, best will it surely be for the patiently enduring."* (the Qu'ran, XXVI, 127.) Thus warned, Mohammad relinquished his ideas of retaliation, and earnestly urged the Faithful to abstain from mutilating their enemies.

The news of the disaster having reach Al-Madinah, all the women, and Safiyah among them, came in crowds to attend to the wounded and mourn for the dead. The Prophet charged Safiyah's son, Zubayr ibn Awam, to send his mother away, to prevent her seeing her brother's corpse, so atrociously disfigured. 'I have been told that my brother was mutilated for the cause of Islam,' she replied, 'and I shall be resigned no matter how horrible the sight, please Allah!' She went straightway to where Hamzah was lying and after having prayed over him with fervent firmness, she departed.

Funerals then began. After having led that of his uncle Hazmah, the Prophet, so not as to fatigue the Believers who were already exhausted, had the dead bodies buried two by two, or three by three, in the same grave, and without being washed according to custom. 'For I bear witness for these martyrs,' he declared. 'Those who have been struck down on Allah's Road will be resuscitated on the Day of Resurrection when their wounds will appear fresh and bloody; smelling sweetly of musk.' When it came to his ears that several families had carried their dead to Al-Madinah to buy them there, he upbraided them there, and ordained: 'Henceforward, ye shall bury your dead where they fall.'

The battle of Uhud did not result fatally for Islam as might reasonably have been feared. There were grievous losses; but several advantages accrued from the fight. The defeat was due to having disregarded the Prophet's first idea, and to disobeying his orders on the field. In future, the Believers submitted entirely to him; they were resolved to carry out his commands to the letter even in case he should be killed, according to the verse alluding to the momentary despondency of Ali, Abu Bakr, Umar: *"Mohammad is no more than an Apostle; other Apostles have already passed away before him; if he die, or be slain, will ye turn upon your heels?"* (the Qu'an, III, 138.)

Moreover, defeats, when faith is fervent, serve only to sharpen energy: *"And how many a Prophet hath combated an enemy on whose side were many myriads? Yet were they not daunted at what befell them on the path of Allah, nor were they weakened, nor did they basely submit! And Allah loveth those who endure with steadfastness."* (the Qur'an, III, 140.)

Clemency henceforward was not to be shown to the idolators: the savage mutilation of the seventy

"Es Soujoud", or the Prostration.

martyrs proved that compassion was inadmissible.

A distinction was also clearly established between the true Believers and the "Hypocrites" such as Abdullah ibn Salul and his partisans. The Prophet (Peace be on him) knew what they were, but the majority of his disciples were ignorant of these double-faced men's perfidy, as demonstrated by their cowardly desertion in the hour of danger. Concerning the Uhud, quoth Mohammad: "That mountain loveth us and we return its affection! O Allah! Abraham declared the territory of Makkah to be sacred. I declare the territory of Al-Madinah, situated between the harrah, to be sacred also."

THE MARRIAGE OF MOHAMMAD AND ZAINAB

Zayd, the enfranchised slave and adopted son of the Prophet, had taken Zainab bint Jahsh to wife, but the marriage had not been concluded easily. Zainab was of noble birth. Ali, sent to make the matrimonial demand, found it rejected by her and her brothers. The union was only brought about when the Prophet came forward in person, and Zainab continued to behave most haughtily towards the freed man now her husband.

Having gone one day to Zayd's dwelling to speak to him, Mohammad was received by Zainab who, hidden behind a curtain, said 'Zayd hath gone out; but come in and wait awhile.' The Prophet refused and was about to depart, when a gust of air having lifted the hanging, he involuntarily caught sight of Zainab. She made a great impression on him; so much so that as he turned to go, he could not help exclaiming: "Glory to Him who inclineth all hearts!"

This cry filled Zainab with boundless pride. When poor Zayd returned, he was received with more scornful haughtiness than ever, and she hastened to let him know the effect produced upon Allah's Apostle by her radiant beauty. Zayd began to feel that life with his spouse, already hard to please, would soon be unbearable. He made up his mind to see Mohammad; and then he told him: 'Maybe Zainab pleaseth thee? If so, I'll get rid of her.'—'Go back to thy wife and keep her to thyself,' replied the Prophet.

But Zayd had had enough of her. Ever since the sight of Zainab had forced a cry of admiration from the prophet, her husband did not dare to approach her and considered that he would have no peace until after he had divorced her. So he went back to Mohammad. 'O prophet!' said he, 'the way Zainab talketh to me is worse than ever. I wish to repudiate her.'—'Fear Allah,' replied Mohammad, 'and keep thy wife to thyself.'—'But I'm no longer master in my own house!'—'If that is so, put her away from thee.'

As soon as she was repudiated, Zainab had but a single thought: to become the wife of the Prophet; (Peace be on him) and she never ceased intriguing to gain her ends. At last a Revelation came down to Mohammad: *"And when Zayd had settled the necessary matter of her divorce, We married her to thee."* (the Qur'an, XXXIII, 37.) So he resolved to be wedded to Zainab.

The Jews and the "Hypocrites" declared this was scandalous. 'Mohammad marries his son's wife!' was their cry, and they worked with a will to make capital out of the incident and bring him into disrepute. The following verses, however, stopped every true Believer from listening to the discreditable group: *"Name your adopted sons after their fathers: this will be more right before Allah, But if ye know not who their fathers are, still let them be your brethren in the faith, and your comrades Mohammad is not the father of any man among you."* (the Qur'an, XXXIII, 5, 40.)

The adoption of Zayd, dating from before the birth Islam, and which might have proved a serious stumbling block in the political career of its chief, was thus annulled, and the freed man, called Zayd ibn Mohammad, now went by his real name: Zayd ibn al-Haris. But the affection that Mohammad had for Zayd, and his son Usamah, was strengthened by this solution which put an end to all feelings of restraint.

Such is the adventure of Zainab, which all the historians who are enemies of Islam have passionately exploited in order to sully the Prophet's (Peace be on him) memory. We shall not discuss the subject, because, in our opinion, the details of the life of a man like Mohammad cannot be isolated from the whole of his work and judged separately. In common with all Prophets (Peace be on him), without exception, Mohammad doubtless had what some call "moments of weakness," but they have nothing to do with his inspiration. Moreover, the historians of Mohammad enjoy the unusual honour of having felt such great respect for his memory, that they refused to discuss his conduct.

When the historians of other Prophets cut out of their lives all that they consider may belittle them in the eyes of posterity, the writers set themselves up, in reality, as critics of their heroes' acts. In the foregoing narrative, which has served as a pretext for so many pamphlets, we find the most incontestable proof of the sincerity of the Arab Prophet's (Peace be on him) biographers. Following their example, and as a token of our impartiality, we thought it our duty to relate this episode, although of secondary interest, and greatly inferior to other events for which we have not found space in this work.

THE GHAZWAH: OR EXPEDITION OF ZAT-IR-RIQUA *(Year IV of the Hegira, A.D. 626)*

Having heard that the Banu Muharib and the Banu Saliba of the Najd were preparing an expedition against him, the Prophet (Peace be on him) decided to be beforehand with them, and set out to meet his foes. In his haste, he had only been able to get together a small number of camels; one for six men who took it in turns to ride. The Believers were compelled to bind up their cruelly wounded feet, from which the nails were torn by the sharp stones of the Hammadas, with "ruqqah": fragments of their apparel. Hence the name of Zat-ir-Riga bestowed on this expedition. After having camped at Nakhl, Mohammad's soldiers came in sight of the assembled enemy. The two armies remained motionless, face to face, neither making up its mind to begin the hostilities; the Mussulmans, because of their numerical inferiority out of all proportion; and the infidels, in consequence of their terror arising from the influence of the recent victories of Islam. It was in these circumstances that the Prophet (Peace be on him) instituted the "Salatu'l-Khauf", the Prayer of Peril. He divided the Believers into two groups; one saying the prayer, and the other keeping a vigilant eye on the enemy.

Greatly impressed by the resolute bearing of the Mussulmans, whom their foes hoped to surprise, but who had come out and showed fight, the allies began to retreat, one after the other, so that, passing from extreme vigilance, as shown at first, the Believers became a prey to exaggerated confidence.

During the torrid heat of the middle of the day, they were scattered here and there enjoying their "siesta" in the shade of the numerous "talhah" (gum-trees), growing in the valley, and had posted no sentinels to keep watch and ward. A Bedouin of the Banu Mustaliq perceived this lack of precaution. By crawling along on hands and knees, he succeeded in approaching the Prophet (Peace be on him) and lifting the silver-hilted sabre hanging to the branches under which the Apostle was resting, the tribesman said: 'O Mohammad! dost thou not fear me?'—'No, Why should I fear thee?'—'Art thou not afraid of the weapon I hold?'—'No, for Alla protecteth me,' replied the Prophet, (Peace be on him) with the greatest calm, gazing boldly at his aggressor.

Petrified at such indifference in the face of danger, the Bedouin was overwhelmed with supernatural emotion which paralysed his heart's action. Cold sweat bathed his brow; his fingers, gripping the sword hilt, opened out involuntarily, and the sabre fell at Mohammad's feet. He picked it up quietly. 'And now, what will save thee from my blows?' he asked.—'Thy generosity!' replied the downcast brigand.

He was right. The Prophet (Peace be on him) let him depart without compelling him to embrace the Mohammedan faith, for he wished to accustom idolaters to the generosity of Islam, so that they should come to it of their own accord. The Bedouin, who before leaving his own bivouac, had boasted that he would bring in Mohammad's head, declared to his people: 'I have just met the best of men.' And he went back to the Prophet (Peace be on him) and became a convert to Islam.

THE GHAZWAH: OR EXPEDITION OF THE BANU MUSTALIQ *(Year V of the Hegira, A.D. 627)*

Now it was the turn of the Banu Mustaliq to get restless and conspire against Islam. The Prophet (Peace be on him) resolved to punish them, and, at the head of his troops, he came upon them on their own territory at Qudid, near the wells of Al Misisiyah. The two armies crashed together in their shock, and many were slain on both sides. Allah routed the Banu Mustaliq; and an enormous amount of booty—camels, sheep and captives, fell into the hands of his warriors.

Among the prisoners was the daughter of the Lord of the Mustaliqs, beautiful Juwairiyah. As a result of drawing by lot, she fell to Sabit ibn Qais, but promised her master a heavy ransom in exchange for her liberty. She then sought out the Prophet (Peace be on him) and told him: 'I am Juwairiyah, daughter of Haris, Lord of the Mustaliqs. Thou knowest my unlucky fate. I know thy magnanimity and I come to implore thy help to pay my ransom.'—'I will settle thy ransom,' he replied; 'and I'll marry thee, if so be thou art willing.' She accepted, and despite Ayishah's jealousy, aroused by the charm and grace of Juwairiyah, the marriage was decided.

In the meantime, Haris had arrived, bringing his daughter's ransom. Mohammad gave him back Juwairiyah, but only to ask him immediately for her hand, offering as dower the sum of four hundred drachmas. As soon as the news of this union was noised abroad, the Believers said: The Prophet (Peace be on him) hath allied himself to Banu Mustaliq. We must therefore look upon them as our allies.' The Faithful gave back all the booty; together with all the captives who had just been shared among them. Few women ever brought such a blessing to her tribe as this Juwairiyah.

After the severe fighting, whilst the soldiers were watering their panting camels at the well Al Mirisiyah, a violent quarrel was nigh bringing Ansars and Mohadjirun to blows.

Jajjah, leading Umar's horse by the bridle, hustled Simana ibn Ubair, an ally of the Banu Auf ibn Khazraj, in order to deprive him of his turn at the well. Simana turned upon him, and the two adversaries, locked in murderous embrace, rolled on the ground, Simana shouting: 'Help! O comrades of the Mohadjirum!'

They were hauled apart and for the moment the quarrel come to nothing. But on both sides, great effervescence reigned in the minds of the tribesmen. The "Hypocrite," Abdullah ibn Abi Salul, an eyewitness of the scuffle, worked up the men's exasperation to the highest pitch by these words: 'O citizens of Al Madinah! have ye seen the impudence of all these Quraish? They pick a quarrel with us in our own country, abusing our hospitality and relying on their numbers. Such is the result of your candour, when ye opened your doors to them and shared your property with them. How true is the saying of our ancestors: Feed thy dog and he will devour thee! Once back in Al Madinah, will not the strong make up their minds to drive out the weak?'

Zayd, son of Arquam, reported these wicked remarks to Mohammad. By his side stood Umar who flew into a violent passion. 'O Prophet!' he cried, 'Wilt thou not order Abbad ibn Bashir to put this impostor to death?'—'How cometh it, Umar, that thou canst give such a piece of advice?' rejoined the Prophet (Peace be on him). 'If people are able to say: Mohammad cutteth his companions throats, what a fine stir there would be in Al Madinah. No, no,' he went on, turning to Abad, 'but give out orders to depart at once.'

The sun was at its zenith; the heat overpowering. It was not a favourable moment for folding the tents. Nevertheless, the Prophet (Peace be on him) lashing his she-camel on the tender skin of her belly, to increase her speed, led his soldiers in a forced march lasting all day, all night, and all through the morning of the next day till noon.

It was then, seeing his brave warriors beginning to stagger, that he called a halt. All his men, worn out by fatigue, dropped on the ground, overcome by deep sleep where they fell, without having been able to give vent to the feeling of fury seething in their hearts and which might have caused most sanguinary conflicts among them.

The "Hypocrite" Abdullah had a son who also called Abdullah. He was a sincere Believer and he went to the Prophet. (Peace be on him) 'They tell me,' quoth the young man, 'that thou didst intend to kill Abdullah, my father. In that case, charge me to bring thee his head for by Allah, thou shalt know that among the Khazraj, there is no son more devoted to his father than I. If thou shouldst charge any other to execute him, I should not be able to bear the sight of his murderer going unpunished and I should kill him. Therefore I should be slaying a true Mussulman in order to avenge a Mussulman "Hypocrite", and render myself deserving of Hell-fire.'

The Prophet (Peace be on him) tranquillised the stoical Believer by these words: 'Give no credit to what thou didst hear. On the contrary, we look upon thy father as our friend and comrade so long as he remaineth with us.'

THE TAYAMMUM: OR THE CEREMONY OF ABLUTION PERFORMED WITH SAND

It was during this expedition that the following Revelation came down: *"But if ye are sick, or on a journey, or if one of you come from the place of retirement, or if ye have touched women and find no water, then take clean sand and rub your faces and your hands with it."* (Qur'an, V, 9.)

Thus was established the Tayammum, or purification by sand, destined to prevent Believers from ever forgetting their salutary duty; for this did away with the pretext, so frequent in their deserts, that lack of water hindered the performance of ablutions.

THE BATTLE OF THE DITCH *(Year V of the Hegira, A.D. 627)*

A deputation of Jews from the tribe of the Banu Nazir, and a few malcontents of the Wayls journeyed to Makkah to offer the Quraish an alliance. The Ghatafans, a tribe hailing from the north of the Hijaz, and the "Habash," or Arab Confederated, joined them. Thus was organised a vast conspiracy, threatening Al-Madinah on all sides.

This time, when the Prophet (Peace be on him) got to hear of this expedition, he had no difficulty in persuading the Believers that the only way to save themselves was by entrenchment in the town and there awaiting the advent of the enemy.

Al-Madinah was protected in almost every direction, either by ramparts, fortlets, or gardens. At the north only would it have been possible for the enemy to arrange a formidable assault. A learned Persian, Salman-i-Farisi, recently converted, explained to the Prophet a system of efficacious protection. It was by means of a ditch, and Salman had seen it practised in his own country. Mohammad was so struck by the Persian's arguments that this ditch was ordered to be dug immediately. All the Believers, confiding in their chief's farsightedness, set ardently to work.

Nevertheless, they were in a state of extreme distress. An icy north wind, such as blows frequently in winter on these table-lands of the desert where there is intense radiation, benumbed their shivering bodies. Roads where the work of revictualling was carried on were blocked by the enemy; provisions were lacking. The pangs of hunger would have paralysed their strength if it had not been kept up and rekindled by faith, for all they had to eat were a few grains of barley cooked in rancid, nauseous mutton-fat.

Meanwhile, the shovelfuls of earth accumulated, thrown up with great spirit by the workers, and the ditch had reached a good depth, when suddenly the pickaxes struck against a rock which they were powerless to uproot. Mohammad filled his mouth with water and spat it out on the stone, at the same time as he implored the help of the Almighty. The diggers again applied themselves to their task and the vigour of their arms, increased tenfold by the certainty of success which the Prophet's (Peace be on him) action had instilled into their hearts, met with no further obstacles. It seemed to them that the hard stone had become as friable as the sand, the rock splitting into countless fragments under the attack of their tools.

Scarcely was the ditch ready, when the entire plain was covered by the tents of the enemy's army, ten thousand strong: the Quraish, Banu Kamanah, Ghatafans, Arabs of the Tuhamah and of the Najd etc. Despite their great superiority of numbers, the Infidels were not sanguine as to the result of their conflict with the Prince of Apostles, and they cast about for new allies. Huwai ibn Akhtab, an enemy of Allah, approached Kab ibn Asad, Prince of the Jewish tribe of the Banu Quraizah who, although deeply hostile to the Prophet (Peace be on him) had signed a treaty with him. Ill at ease, Kab repulsed his visitor in these terms: 'O Huwai! the step thou dost take is fraught with great danger for my tribe. I have signed a treaty with strict fidelity.'—'Open thy door to me, O Kab, for I only wish to partake of thy Shisha,' (a kind of soup). Kab let him in, and Huwai immediately broached the subject that brought him there. He vaunted the power of the ten thousand Confederates encamped near the Uhud, and demonstrated how he was certain of ridding the world of Mohammad. 'Thou bringest me ugly business, O Hawai!' replied Kab, still hesitating. 'Tis an empty raincloud in which only thunder and lightning remain. I see no advantage for me. What have I to do with all this?'

His interlocutor never left off until he had coaxed Kab into cancelling his contract with Mohammad and forming an alliance with the Infidels.

The rumour of this defection coming to the Prophet's (Peace be on him) ears, he sent Sad ibn Muaz, Sad ibn Ubaidah and Chuat ibn Zubary to see if it was true. When these envoys reminded the Banu Quraizah of their pledge, the following reply was made: 'Who is this Prophet of Allah of whom ye speak? There exists no treaty between him and us.'

This was downright treachery, for the Banu Quraizah was marvellously well informed as to the Believer's secrets and weak points of the town. To guard against the anxiety that such treason might create among his disciples, Mohammad, when his envoys returned, exclaimed: 'Allah is Great! Here we have good news! Hearken, O Moslem comrades!' In this way he predicted that the spoils accruing from the overthrow of the Banu Quraizah would soon enrich the Believers, thus brazenly betrayed.

The sight of the ten thousand sparkling spears that made the plain look like a field of darts, produced, nevertheless, a great impression on the Believers lining the ramparts. The "Hypocrites", as was their wont, instead of exhorting the citizens to pluck up courage, tried to sow the seeds of panic. 'Admire Mohammad' they would say. 'He promised us the treasures of Chosroes and of Cæsar; and yet, this very day, he himself is not certain of having a roof over his head!'

To put an end to these gloomy forebodings, the Prophet (Peace be on him) made his troops sally forth and posted them behind the ditch. They were covered in the rear by the Sala hill. At that juncture, some of the soldiers whose courage was on the wane asked the permission of the Prophet (Peace be on him) to return saying: 'Of a truth, our houses are left defenceless'. But they were not left defenceless: *"verily their sole wish was to flee away. If the enemy had effected an entry at all points, and they had been asked to promote rebellion among the Believers, they would certainly have done so; but only a short time would they have remained in."* (Qur'an, XXXIII, 13, 14.)

Frankly, great anxiety reigned; but the faith of the sincere Mussulmans and the unchanging serenity of the Apostle got the best of it. On the other hand, the Confederates despite all their advantages, were still smitten with terror at the thought of the mysterious forces that they always found facing them each time they fought against Allah's warriors; and dared not risk an attack before making sure that it would not turn out to be another miserable, humiliating failure. So they were contented with drawing near to the walls.

For twenty days and twenty nights, hostilities were limited to encircling the city and a few flights of arrows, without any result. Ashamed at last, of their inaction, several horsemen of the Quraizah and Kinanas, got ready for the fray. In close rank, they broke away from the enemy front. Their breasts pressed to the necks of their steeds, they dashed forward in a frenzied charge, swallowed up in the orange tinted whirlwind of dust . . . Then suddenly, the living hurricane stopped dead, and when the clouds of sand enfolding the idolatrous riders lifted, they were seen petrified with affright in front of the deep ditch in which they had nearly been engulfed; whilst the horses, with twitching nostrils, their mouths twisted and bleeding by reason of the sudden jerk of the bit, stopping them in their forward bound, remained with stiffened, trembling legs on the edge of the trench.

'By our gods!' swore the Infidels, 'this is a trick that Arabs never play!' They sought for a spot where the moat was the most narrow, and savagely spurring on their steeds, they lifted them in fantastic jumping efforts and so reached the other side. Ali, followed by a few soldiers, when out to meet them. Getting between them and the ditch, he cut off their retreat. One of the men on horseback, Amr ibn AdbiAud, of frightful aspect and gigantic stature, howled the vilest curses and challenged the Believers to single combat. With the permission of the Prophet (Peace be on him) who buckled on his own breastplate, rolled his turban round his head and placed his sword in his hand, Ali stood face to face with the giant. At the sight of his assailant, only a boy, Amr the terrible, made a gesture of scorn and pity. 'I am loth to shed thy blood,' he said, 'for thy father was my friend.'—'As for me,' retorted Ali, 'I shall have no compunction in shedding thine.'

At these words, Amr foamed with rage, and Ali bade him remark that if he despised his young adversary, he did not disdain to profit by remaining on horseback to defend himself against an enemy on foot. Amr jumped off his horse and hamstrung it; thereby showing that he did not wish to use it for fight or flight. Mad with rage at the mocking challenge of so youthful a foe, he beat his own face with his clenched fists. Then he rushed at Ali, aiming a fierce blow which glanced lightly off the lad's forehead, after having smashed his shield to pieces.

As quick as lightning, Ali sprung on one side and, by an unexpected bound, got behind his adversary. Carried forward by the violence of his advance, the monster was bewildered and staggered when he tried to turn round. Ali seized the opportunity at once and made a skilful thrust. The blade pierced Amr's throat, cutting the carotid artery. An enormous gush of blood spurted from the gaping wound; like a drunken man, the colossus, with hoarse hiccups proceeding from his severed throat, made a few faltering steps and fell in a heap at the feet of Islam's champion.

At this sight, the Mussulmans sang the "Takbir", and the other Infidels, overwhelmed by consternations, fled at a wild gallop. One of them, Nuhfil ibn Abdullah, having miscalculated his jump rolled with his mount down into the ditch where he was slowly being killed by showers of stones, when

Zubayr put an end to the torture by a cut from his scimitar, which after having cleft his body in twain, was stopped by the saddle.

Safiyah, the Prophet's (Peace be on him) aunt on his mother's side, kept an eye on the foe from the top of a fortlet belonging to Hasan ibn Sabit, who remained by her side. She caught sight of a Jew wandering round the ramparts and said to Hasan: 'Seest thou that Jew prowler? Without a doubt, he seeketh to find a weak point in our walls, and whilst the Prophet and his soldiers are busy on the front facing the enemy, other Jews will be fetched to follow the spy and capture our fortlet. Go down and kill him!'—'May Allah pardon thee! O daughter of Abdul Muttalib, I am not a warrior accustomed to the use of arms. I am a poet.'

Shrugging her shoulders, masculine minded Safiyah seized a mace and went down. Gliding behind the Jew, she felled him by dint of dealing repeated blows on his head; and then went back to Hasan. 'Now thou canst go down and strip the Jew of all he possesseth, for it is not seemly for a woman to undress a man.'

Several skirmishes of slight importance took place at long intervals; but if an attack was not to be feared, thanks to the precautionary moat which had upset the Confederates' calculations, the garrison might have been mastered by famine. Great uneasiness prevailed in their ranks.

Meanwhile, Naim, Prince of the Ghatafans, sought out Mohammad, saying: 'O Prophet! I have become a Mussulman and my people know it not. I am entirely at thy disposal.'—'Of what use is all thy courage? Thou art alone! But couldst thou not help us by provoking relinquishment among the Confederates? In all wars, there are tricks which are licit.'

Naim understood at once the part he had to play. He went to the Banu Quraizah, having often broken bread among them when he was an idolater.

'O Banu Quraizah!' said he. 'Ye know how I feel towards you all?'—'Verily, and we have entire confidence in thee.'—'Being so, listen to me. The Quraish and the Ghatafans, your allies, are not in the same position as you. This part of the country is yours: here is your property; here dwell your families. Ye cannot abandon your land for another. They, on the contrrary are only here to fight Mohammad and his companions; their belongings and families are beyond their enemies reach. If the fortune of war turneth against them, they will return in tranquillity to their own country and leave you in yours, to do the best you can with this man. Will ye be able to resist him, once ye face him alone? Fight therefore no more with these "qawms" without claiming hostages chosen from their noblemen, so as to make sure that you will never be left in the lurch before ye have brought Mohammad to his knees.'—'Of a truth, the advice is good!' they declared unaminously. Naim then went to the Quraish idol worshippers and talked to them. 'Ye know how I feel towards you all.'—'Aye'—'I have been able to ascertain something that I consider is only right that you should be told at once. But swear to keep it secret.'—'We swear!'—'This is it,' he went on. 'Know that the Jews regret having annulled their compact with Mohammad and consequently have sent him this message: "Most certainly do we regret that we did, but if thou dost consent to pardon us, we will give up to thee several hostages chosen amongst the most noble of the Quraish or the Ghatafans we have seized; and we will remain thy faithful allies until thine enemies are exterminated." Mohammad having accepted, the Jews therefore will come and claim hostages, pretexting that they are certain of never being thrown over whilst holding these sureties. Take care never to give them a single hostage!'

He said the same thing to the Ghatafans, his fellow-countrymen, and was just as successful with them. The Quraish and the Ghatafans swore they would be on their guard. One night, on the eve of a Saturday in the month of Shawwal, Abu Sufyan and the chieftains of the Ghatafans sent Ikrimah to the

Banu Quraizah, charging him to say to them: 'We can no longer sojourn in these parts, so unsuitable to our horses and camels. Be ready to fight Mohammad tomorrow. We must get done with him!' They made answer: 'Tomorrow is a Saturday, the Sabbath day, which means obligatory repose in our religion. But, at any rate, we cnnot fight by your side unless ye grant us hostages chosen from the most noble among you, as a guarantee that ye will not abandon us before having crushed our common enemy.' When Ikrimah repeated these words, the Quraish and the Ghatafans cried out: 'By all our gods, what Naim told us concerning the Banu Quraizah was perfect truth!' The Confederates immediately sent another message, declaring plainly: 'By our gods, we'll not give you a single hostage!'

It was now the turn of the Banu Quraizah to find out how correct was the information vouchsafed by Naim and they came to rupture with the Confederates. This piece of news, reported by Naim, made the Prophet (Peace be on him) rejoice exceedingly; but being desirous of knowing the effect produced by this rupture in the ranks of the Quraish and the Ghatafans, he said to Huzaifah: 'Make thy way, this very night, into the enemy's camp and find out what they may be planning. Come back and tell me without letting anyone know.'

Thanks to the pitchy darkness of that wintry night, Huzaifah glided among the enemies tents. A high, icy wind had put out all the fires and blown down the cooking pots. The whistling gusts deafened all ears; and the shivering idolaters huddled together, wrapped in the folds of their mantles. 'Keep an eye on your companions!' was the watchword shouted by Abu Sufyan, meaning: 'Beware of spies!' Huzaifah, with great presence of mind, seized the hand of an Infidel standing close to him and demanded in threatening accents: 'Who art thou?'—'Such an one, son of such an one.' Huzaifah let him go, and the Infidel, forced to exonerate himself, never thought of putting questions as well.

The relinquishment of the Banu Quraizah; the difficulties with regard to feeding camels and horses; and, above all, the disorder arising from that calamitous night, caused Abu Sufyan to be discouraged. After a short discussion between him and the other Quraish chieftains, in the hearing of invisible Huzaifah, the return of the besiegers to their dwellings was decided.

Having got to know all he wanted, Huzaifah went back to his camp. He found the Prophet (Peace be on him) praying and beckoned to his disciple to approach. When Huzaifah was close to him, to warm his messenger, he covered him with part of the mantle spread out on the ground in lieu of a praying carpet. When Mohammad had finished his devotions, he listened to the intrepid scout and congratulated him on the success of his mission.

Next day, the plain was clear of the enemy; and the Prophet, (Peace be on him) leaving the ditch, led his troops back to Al-Madinah. 'The Quraish came here to attack us for the last time,' he declared. 'Henceforward it will be for us to go and beard them in their dens.'

The Prophet (Peace be on him) dreamt that he entered Makkah in the midst of his companions and then marched to Mina, in the Valley of Sacrifices. This vision embodied the greatest desire of his heart; and all the Believers felt the same, as they suffered from not being able to visit the Holy Places since the Hegira. So Mohammad determined to satisfy their craving.

In the month of Zu'l-Qadah, he went out of Al-Madinah, and took the road to Makkah at the head of fourteen hundred pilgrims, driving seventy camels for sacrificial purposes. To show that his intentions were peaceful, he caused garlands to be hung round the victim's necks. Furthermore, at Zu'l Halifah, he solemnly put himself in the state of "Ihram", which consists in assuming the pilgrim's garb of double cloths without seams, and abstaining from all that is forbidden during the visit to the holy places:

approaching women; the use of perfumes; cutting the beard, hair or nails; fighting or quarrelling; and the slaying of animals other than those sacrificed. His disciples followed his example and he gave out the "Talbiyah": *I stand up for Thy service, "O Allah!"* which they all repeated in chorus.

At Osfan, he met with Bishr ibn Al-Kaab on his return from Makkah whither he had been sent to glean information, and who told him: 'O Prophet! the Quraish know that thou art on the way. They have called upon the Saquifs and the Habash who are coming to face thee, bringing with them their wives and children, to stop themselves from even thinking of flight. They also lead their she-camels and the young camels, so as to be certain not to suffer from lack of meat or milk; and the warriors have covered their bodies with skins of panthers as a token that they will never give in, but fight to the last gasp. At this moment, they are encamped at Zu Sua. Khalid ibn Walid, at the head of their cavalry, is in ambush at Kurrat-ul-Ghamin.'

'Who can guide us along some other road than that by which they expect us?' asked the Prophet. (Peace be on him) A guide of the Aslams proffered his services and led the army of the Believers through an unknown path, but it was frightful to look upon. It meandered through an inextricable chaos of wild ravines, jagged rocky heights, abrupt ascents and descents, strewn with pointed pebbles that cut the feet of men and animals.

After having mastered exhaustion and fatigue, the Believers debouched in the sandy bed of a broad wadi which seemed to their bruised and bleeding feet like a carpet of the richest pile. They offered up thanksgivings to the Compassionate, and obeying the commands of their inspired leader, they cried out: *"We implore the forgiveness of Allah and we repent in His Presence!"*

Then they went through the pass of Al Morar, and arrived at the foot of the hill of Al-Hudaibiyah, situated partly on holy ground and partly in ordinary territory, a day's jouney from Makkah. At this spot, Qaswa, the Prophet's (Peace be on him) she-camel, suddenly knelt and refused to get up. 'Is she restive?' asked his companions.—'No, she is not restive,' replied Mohammad; 'but she is stopped by Him who formerly stopped the elephant of the Negus Abrah, and prevented him entering Makkah.' And the Apostle gave orders to pitch the tents.

The enemy, surprised at not having met Mohammad, and knowing he was not far off, soon found out that he had taken a new road. They turned back in the greatest haste, sending their horsemen on in front to bar the way to their city. They despatched Budail and several Arabs of the Khuzzah tribe, to sound the Prophet (Peace be on him) as to his intentions.

Budail, having heard from the Prophet's own lips that all he wanted was to make a pilgrimage to the Holy Places and not to wage war against his fellow-countrymen, returned to inform the Quraish. But they had no faith in the Khuzza men whose secret sympathy for Mohammad was known, so they sent him another messenger, Al Halis ibn Alqamah.

'Let the victims be paraded in front of him,' ordered the Prophet (Peace be on him) when he saw him arrive. When Al Halis had seen the long rows of victims going by with garlands round their necks which were shorn at the parts where their throats would be cut, he thought it would be useless to continue and went back to the Quraish to give them an account of his observations.

'Sit down,' they told him. 'Thou art naught else but a simpleton of the Bedouin tribes and thou dost not understand the cunning of Mohammad who haileth from our part of the country.' Al-Halis got out of temper. 'O Assembly of the Quraish! Ye do not respect the terms of our compact. No one hath a right to drive away from the Temple of Allah the man who cometh to glorify the Most High! By Him who holdeth in His hands the soul of Al-Halis, ye will let Mohammad finish his pious visit in peace; or else we Confederates will break off with you—and at once!' They shrugged their shoulders. 'Pshaw! let us be until we have achieved what we have planned.' And they charged Ora ibn Masud, a chieftain of the Saquifs, with the mission which, in their judgment, had been badly carried out by the previous messengers. 'O Assembly of the Quraish!' he objected; 'I have hearkened to the bitter words with which ye welcomed the return of your men sent to the enemy. Ye know me by my mother; I am on your side, for I belong to the folks dwelling in the Makkah valley. If ye suspect me in the least, lay your hearts bare ere I depart.'—'Thou art in the right. We know thee. We are not at all distrustful of thee.'

Ora came into the presence of the Prophet (Peace be on him) and bowed down to him. 'O Mohammad,' he said, 'thou hast gathered together a horde of people of all countries and thou dost come back to thy egg (birthplace) to smash it with their assistance! Now the Quraish have sworn a most solemn oath, to the effect that never, so long as their eyelashes quiver on their eyelids, shalt thou set foot again in Makkah, unless by force of arms. And, by our gods! the scum surrounding thee must flee from thy side, before the sun setteth on another day!'

At these words, a flame of indignation lit up the eyes of the companions, standing, the lower half of their faces veiled, behind the Prophet. (Peace be on him) From out of the group, strode Abu Bakr. He went up to the Infidel and shouted to him: 'Be gone and bite the belly of Lat, thine idol! Dost thou think for a moment that we could abandon Allah's Messenger?'—'Who is this man, O Mohammad?' queried Ora.—'The son of Abu Kuhafah.'—'By our gods!' Ora went on, turning to Abu Bakr, 'if I were not bound to thee by a debt of gratitude, I would have rewarded thee according to thy deserts. But, by thine insult, we are quits for the future.'

The messenger now went up to Mohammad, and while speaking to him, plucked familiarly at his beard, as was the custom in those days between people engaged in discussion. 'Take thy hand away from the Prophet's face before I come to rid thee of thine arm!' cried another of the companions. 'Who is this boor?' asked Ora.—'Dost thou not know him?' replied the Prophet (Peace be on him) with a smile. 'He is thy brother's son, Al Mughairah Shuba.'—'O traitor!' exclaimed Ora to his nephew, 'hast thou so soon forgotten thy crimes that were pardoned thanks to my intervention?' He then continued his conversation with Mohammad who treated him with the respect due to his rank. The Prophet (Peace be on him) reiterated his statement that his intentions were purely pacific. During his sojourn in the camp of the Believers, Ora was able to see how boundless was their veneration for their chieftain. When the Prophet (Peace be on him) performed his ablutions, his companions rushed to share the water he had used. If he had his head shaved, not a hair fell to the ground without being picked up and treasured. So Ora, on his return, said to those who had sent him forth: 'I have seen Chosroes in the midst of his sumptuous Persian court; Caesar, in the proud Senate of Roman patricians; the Negus, at the head of his formidable bodyguard of Abyssinian warriors. Well then, I swear that I have never met with a monarch who, surrounded by the noblemen of his court, held the same position as Mohammad among his companions. And what is more remarkable, contrary to what taketh place around the mighty, Mohammad's followers expect nothing from him; neither favours, riches, nor honours! That is what I have ascertained. Now act as it pleaseth you.'

Although the Quraish were deeply affected by his declaration, they persisted in their delusion and sent forty or fifty of their partisans to prowl round the Believer's army, with the idea of surprising and capturing a few soldiers of Islam. The Believers were on their guard and it was they who took a certain number of Infidels prisoner. They were led before the Prophet, but resolved not to belie his own words of peace, he pardoned and freed them, although by having been caught attacking perfidiously, they deserved death.

Just then, Mohammad wanted to send Umar with a message to the noblemen of Makkah, but he

E. DINET

The Prayer of El Fithero, or breaking the Ramadan fast.

made the following reply. 'O Prophet! the Quraish know my feeling towards them as manifested by many inimical acts of mine. I have everything to fear from them, because there is no longer any member of my family in Makkah. But I can show you a man whose influence is much more efficacious than mine. I mean Usman ibn Affan.'

Mohammad, recognising this to be sound advice, despatched Usman to Abu Sufyan and the noblemen of the city, to assure them that he was actuated by pacific sentiments, and to inform them of his wish to do honour to the "House of Allah" by a pilgrimage. When the Prophet's (Peace be on him) envoy had finished explaining the object of his mission to the men of Makkah, they replied: 'O Usman! if thou dost desire to perform ritual circuits of the "Tawaf" we authorise thee to do so.'—'I will not accomplish them unless following in the footsteps of Allah's Messenger.' This answer exasperated the citizens of Makkah who threw Usman into prison, despite his quality of ambassador. Finding that Usman did not return, the Believers concluded that he had been murdered and they were overwhelmed with the most profound indignation. Mohammad hesitated no longer and proclaimed: 'We will not go away until we have punished the "qawm" of the Infidels for the abominable crime they have just committed!' Umar, acting under the Prophet's orders, cried out with all the strength of his lungs; 'O Believers! come and take the Oath—the Oath! Come while ye invoke the name of Allah!'

The Prophet, (Peace be on him) seated in the shade of a gumtree, awaited the coming of the Faithful who went in haste to him. They quivered with enthusiasm, and resolved to follow him blindly even if they had to make war in holy territory. They struck their palms against his to swear fidelity till death. Just then, the news of Usman's murder being denied on the best authority, the Prophet (Peace be on him) clapped his hands together so as to take the oath in place of Usman and acknowledge it.

Meanwhile, the intense agitation manifested on this occasion, in the ranks of the Believers, was notified by spies to the Quraish. They grew uneasy and sent Sohail ibn Amr with a flag of truce, giving him the following instructions: 'Offer peace, to Mohammad, but claim as condition that he turneth back this year, for never could we put up with the sarcasms of the Arabs who will maintain that he came into our city in spite of all we said. Next year at the same spoch, he may accomplish his pilgrimage to the Holy Places, an it pleaseth him.'

Sohail went back with these proposals and the Prophet (Peace be on him) accepted, despite Umar's vehement protestations. 'I am the servant of Allah,' Mohammad told him. 'He leadeth me not astray, and I cannot disobey the orders He sendeth me. How now, O Umar? I decide; and thou must perforce oppose my decision?' Umar, hearing these words, was overtaken by such confusion that he trembled in every limb, and icy sweat poured off him. Quoth Umar: 'From that day forth, I have never ceased praying, fasting, giving alms and freeing slaves, so as to be granted pardon for my error.'

'O Ali!' said the Prophet, at this juncture, 'write: in the name of Allah, the Merciful, the Compassionate!'—'I cannot accept that wording,' protested Sohail. 'Write simply: in Thy name, O Allah!'—'So be it! Write: in Thy name, O Allah! it hath been agreed between the undersigned, Mohammad, Prophet of Allah, and—,—'If I acknowledge that thou art the Prophet of Allah,' interrupted Sohail, 'I should not be at war with thee!'—'Well then, write: 'between Mohammad ibn Abdullah and Sohail ibn Amr: hostilities shall be suspended for a period of ten years. Anyone escaping from Makkah and taking refuge with Mohammad shall be given up to the Quraish. Mohammad and his followers will turn back, and not attempt to enter Makkah this year, against the will of the Quraish. Next year, the Quraish will cease opposition to the visit of the Mussulmans to the Holy Places where they may sojourn for three days, but only carrying the arms permitted to pilgrims: sheathed sabres.' Hearing these clauses, seemingly so disadvantageous for them, the Mussulmans were roused and shouted: 'O Prophet!

is it thou who signeth such a compact?'—'Assuredly!' replied Mohammad with a smile. 'Those among us who take refuge with the idolaters being insincere, we need not regret them; and Allah will have rid us of them. As for the Makkan Mussulmans who take refuge with us; if we give them up, Allah will not abandon them, for He will know how to succour them.'

The treaty had scarcely been signed by the leading Believers and principals among the idolaters when Abu Jindal, Son of Sohail, who had become converted and kept a prisoner, suddenly made his appearance, still dragging round his ankles the links of his broken chains. He rushed into the midst of his Moslem brethren who welcomed him with the transports of joy.

Sohail flew into a passion at this sight. He lashed his son's face with a thorny twig; and, seizing him by his garments, drove him into the Prophet's (Peace be on him) presence, saying: 'O Mohammad! here is the first fugitive. I call upon thee to give him up to me; the treaty having been concluded before he arrived.'—'Thou has right on thy side.'—'O my Mussulman brethren!' cried Abu Jindal, 'am I thus given back to the idolaters who persecute me on account of my religion? See to what state they have reduced me!' The whole of the stoical Believer's body was indeed covered with traces of the ill-usage from which he had suffered. 'Be resigned, O Abu Jindal,' said the Prophet, 'and put thy trust in Allah. He will not abandon thee; nor you; nor the "Mustazifin" (those who are oppressed like thee); and He will deliver thee when the time cometh . . . But we have concluded a treaty on these terms, with the "qawm" of the Quraish and on no account can we break our word.'

Nevertheless, the Prophet (Peace be on him) made overtures to Sohail, asking him to give up Abu Jindal in exchange for a ransom; but Sohail refused unmercifully. Umar, in his turn, approached the ill-fated Mussulman, saying: 'Patience, O Abu Jindal! Thou art in the power of infidels whose blood hath no more value than that of dogs,' and he showed him his sword, hoping thereby to incite him to murder his father. Despite everything, the son loved his father tenderly and thus did he reply: 'Why dost thou not slay him thyself?'—'The Prophet (Peace be on him) hath forbidden us to do so.'—'Well then, must not I also observe the condition imposed by Mohammad?'

When Muqirris ibn Hafz, one of the Makkans who had accompanied Sohail, witnessed this distressing scene, he was overcome with pity, and swore to protect Abu Jindal against his father and all his persecutors.

But whilst their companion was dragged away in the direction of Makkah, the Believers were heartbroken. Their sanguine enthusiasm, arising from the fact of their expedition, gave place to gloomy discouragement; and when the Prophet, to show them that all was finished, sent forth his order: 'Sacrifice the victims and shave your heads!' it seemed as if they had suddenly lost their hearing.

Loudly invoking the name of Allah, Mohammad slew the first victim with his own hand. He then sat down and was shaved by Khurash ibn Umaiyah. Recovering from their state of prostration by this example, the Believers repented, and ashamed at having shown such little eagerness in obeying their leader, they imitated him at once by sacrificing the victims and cutting off their own hair. Allah (Glory be to Him) sent a high wind that whirled away the shorn locks and carried them within the precincts of the Holy Temple.

The sojourn of Mohammad at Al-Hudaibiyah extended over nineteen or twenty days. He gave the signal to return; and his soldiers who, until the last moment secretly hoped to march on the enemy, obeyed him without murmuring, despite their deep disappointment. On arriving at Al-Madinah, fresh scenes of the kind they had just witnessed, produced a heart-breaking effect. Notwithstanding, they were much gratified to find that the Prophet (Peace be on him) refused to give up to the idolaters several Moslem women who had fled from Makkah, such as: Ummi-i-Kulsum bint Ogbah, Sabiyah bint

AlHaris etc., a Revelation having taught him that women were not to be included in the treaty: "*O Believers! when believing women, fleeing from idolatry, come over to you as refuges, then make trial of them . . . and if ye have ascertained them to be Believers, let them not go back to the unbelievers; they are not lawful for them, nor are the believers lawful for these women. But give the husbands back what they spent for their dowers.*" (the Qur'an, LX, 10). By way of compensation, the clauses of the treaty concerning men were scrupulously respected.

Like Abu Jindal, there was a Believer named Abu Basir who had escaped from his persecutors and he was given back to a tribesman of the Banu Amar, accompanied by a slave; these two having been sent to Al-Madinah to claim the refugee. They took him away in full view of the Believers who would have preferred to sink into the earth sooner than be forced to remain powerless and witness such a sight. Alone, among them all, the Prophet who saw what they could not see, remained unmoved and promised freedom by the aid of the Almighty to his ill-fated disciples.

At Zu'l Holifah, the three men sat down in the shade of a wall to rest awhile. The tribesman of the Banu Amar, priding himself on the success of his mission, thought he would act the part of an invincible hero and, unsheathing his sabre, flourished it, bawling: 'With this good sword, I could cut down Ansars from daybreak to nightfall and never feel tired!'—'Is thy blade really so sharp as all that?' asked Abu Basir. 'Let me see if it is, O my brother!'

Blinded by pride, the man of the Banu Amar cast all distrust from his mind. He allowed the edge of the steel to be examined by Abu Basir who suddenly pulled it out of the conceited wretch's hands, brandished it over the Infidel's head, and with a single blow, stretched him dead at his feet. Seeing this, the slave, overcome by terror, fled to Al-Madinah where he implored Mohammad's protection. At the same moment, Abu Basir arrived, bestriding his victim's she-camel which he had captured. He made the animal kneel before the Mosque and, with the sabre in his grasp, he went and addressed the Prophet, (Peace be on him) saying: 'Thou canst not be blamed for what hath occurred, for thou didst remain true to thy word in giving me into the hands of my enemies. But Allah hath delivered me from their persecution! Here are the spoils. A fifth part is due to thee. Take it!'—'I can touch no plunder coming from that foe without being false to my oath. Away with thy booty; and now, go whither it pleaseth thee.' When Abu Basir was gone, after taking leave of him, the Prophet added: 'Woe to his people! That man is a brand of war! Would that he were accompanied by a few comrades as determined as he!'

Abu Basir went to Al-Aish, near the seashore on the road to Syria trodden by the Quraish caravans. Once there, he was met by Abu Jindal and seventy other Mussulmans who, having heard that the Prophet (Peace be on him) could not be held responsible for those who freed themselves without his assistance, had made good their escape from the idolaters. These refugees were quite as determined as Abu Basir. They elected to remain in the part of the country because it was very woody and well suited to the irregular warfare of partisans in ambush. They captured all the convoys venturing in those regions and their success and the enticement of booty caused them to be joined by many Arabs of the Ghifar, Aslams, and Buhaunah tribes etc., who became converts to Islam and formed a "jihsh" of more than three hundred highwaymen.

It was then that the Believers began to fathom the reason for the Prophet's placidness when he accepted the paragraph, seemingly so unfavourable, concerning the restitution of fugitives. Hungered by the stoppage of all revictualling caravans, the Quraish finished by sending written entreaties, begging him to suppress the very clause which at first pleased them so much. They informed Mohammad that all Mussulmans who should get out of Makkah to join him, could remain under his protection; and he was begged to recall Abu Basir and his fellow raiders. So it turned out that when Mohammad gave the

Theology students in the courtyard of the University of El Azhar in Cairo.

Quraish satisfaction, he had the advantage of doing a generous act at the same time as he increased his fighting strength to a most appreciable extent.

THE TREATY OF AL-HUDAIBIYAAH
(Year VI of the Hegira, A.D. 628)

The results, therefore, of the expedition of Al-Hudaibiyah, to all appearances so poor, were of great importance. In the Qur'an it is set down as being almost equal to the battle of Badr. In fact, at the moment when the Mussulmans thought they ought to attack the Holy City, all of them, whether Makkah Mohadjirun, or Ansars of Al-Madinah, took the oath of fealty without hesitation. After the Prophet's death, the tree under which he accepted the pledge was so celebrated that numerous were the Faithful who came to pray in its shade; and Umar was obliged to have it felled, because he feared lest it became the object of a cult tainted with fetishism.

To crown all and complete these results, the following verses came down: *"Well pleased now hath Allah been with the Believers when they plighted fealty to thee under the tree; and He knew what was in their hearts: therefore did He send down upon them a spirit of secure repose, and rewarded them with a speedy victory. And with the rich booty which they took."* (Qur'an, XLVIII, 18.)

CHAPTER SEVEN — Decorative plate.

إنا فتحنا لك فتحا مبينا

CHAPTER THE SEVENTH

Mohammad was never able to get the Jews to ally themselves with him, despite all his advances, and the encouragement he had lavished on them. As we have seen already, they could not admit of the expected Prophet (Peace be on him) belonging to any other race but theirs; nor pardon him for having, by means of religious fraternity, put an end to the secular quarrels of the citizens of Al-Madinah, which, in olden days, had been a source of abundant profit. To sum up, the victories of the Islamic Arabs led the Jews to fear that they would never be able to free themselves from the Arabic yoke. Therefore each fresh success of the Mussulman armies increased the jealousy of the Jews and their perfidy soon degenerated into open hostility, necessitating a long series of expeditions against them.

For the sake of clarity, we gather into one chapter the whole of these expeditions, although they took place at long intervals.

EXPEDITION AGAINST THE QAYNUQA JEWS
(Year II of the Hegira, A.D. 524)

An Arab woman, seated close to the shop belonging to a jeweller of the Qaynuqa Jews, was the victim of a most insulting practical joke. Without her knowing it, someone had hooked the lowest edge of her robe to the part of her apparel covering her shoulders, so that when she rose to her feet, her nakedness was displayed to the gaze of the Jews in the shop, who were all overtaken by a fit of the indecent hilarity.

An Arab, very indignant, struck down the insulter with a blow from a club. He was felled in his turn, by the jeweller's relatives. Other Arabs rushed to avenge him, and a pitched battle took place in the open, blood flowing on both sides.

Jews being the aggressors, the Prophet (Peace be on him) knowing their deep-rooted inimical feelings, profited by the opportunity to demand in due form that they should become converts to Islam. At first he tried persuasion: 'By doing so, you will be making a loan to Allah which will bring you in marvellous interest,' he told them.—'Allah must be very poor,' they replied, 'since He is reduced to borrow of us who are rich'.

At this blasphemy, the Prophet (Peace be on him) threatened them with exemplary punishment, unless they embraced Islam immediately. They shrugged their shoulders. 'Thou art proud indeed by reason of thy victory over soldiers of no account,' said the Jews. 'Try now to attack us and thou wilt see that we are in no wise like thy fellow-countrymen of Makkah'.

Mohammad called upon the Mussulmans to come to his aid, and the Banu Qaynuqa, losing their arrogance as soon as Allah's warriors showed themselves, ran away and took refuge in neighbouring strongholds belonging to their co-religionists. After holding out for a fortnight, they had to surrender and beg for mercy. The Prophet (Peace be on him) ordered their throats to be cut as an example to the other Jews that would deliver them from the temptation of copying their slaughtered brethren. Abdullah, the "Hypocrite", with whom they were allied, interceded with Mohammad in their favour. Twice he answered: 'Let me be.'

Abdullah placed his hand on the heart of Allah's Apostle and supplicated him, saying: 'I cannot stand by and see them massacred! It would be black ingratitude on my part!'—'They are at thy disposal,' the Prophet (Peace be on him) told him at last. 'But their belongings are ours.'

The Qaynuqa, saved by the intervention of the "Hypocrite", had to go into exile in Syria, and their property was divided among the victors.

EXPEDITION AGAINST THE JEWS OF THE BANU NADIR *(Year III of the Hegira, A.D. 625)*

The Jews of the Banu Nadir having claimed money compensation for the death of two of their brethren killed by the soldiers of Amr, the Prophet (Peace be on him) went among the tribesmen to enquire into the matter.

He had just given them satisfaction; and, whilst conversing with a few companions, the Prophet was seated in the shade of a house, when a Jew, son of Jahsh ibn Ka'b, climbed stealthily on to the flat roof with the intention of crushing Mohammad with great stones already brought there. By celestial inspiration, Mohammad looked up just as the son of Jahsh was about to commit the crime. The Apostle of Allah moved quickly away from the wall, dragging his companions with him.

As soon as he returned to Al-Madinah, he called his warriors together, and set out with them to punish the authors of this treacherous act. The Banu Nadir, having failed in their attempt, shut themselves up in their strongholds, but after holding out for six days, they had to follow the example of the Qaynuqa and surrender unconditionally, throwing themselves on the mercy of their conqueror.

Their lives were spared, but of all their immense wealth, each man was only allowed the load of one camel.

EXPEDITION AGAINST THE JEWS OF THE BANU QURAIZAH *(Year V of the Hegira, A.D. 627)*

The Confederates, being dispersed following their defeat at the Battle of the Ditch, the Mussulmans laid down their arms. One day, when taking their siesta, recuperating after passing sleepless nights and undergoing great fatigue during the siege, they were suddenly awakened by the voice of the Mue'zzin. Acting under the Prophet's (Peace be on him) orders, he shouted: 'Let all who hear and obey refrain this day from saying the prayer of "Asr" (afternoon) unless in the midst of the Banu Quraizah.'

Mohammad judged that the treachery of these tribesmen, renouncing their alliance and joining his enemies, deserved immediate punishment. The same day, he camped with his soldiers at the well of Enna, in front of his enemies' citadels; and after a blockade of twenty-five days forced them to capitulate.

The Aus, to whom the Banu Quraizah had long been allied, begged the Prophet (Peace be on him) to spare their lives, as in the case of the Qaynuqa. The Prophet, (Peace be on him) however, considered that the treachery of the Banu Quraizah was a much more serious matter and he was not at all inclined to let himself be mollified. At last, desirous of meeting them half-way, he said: 'O Assembly of the Aus! will ye not consent to let one among you become arbitrator and decide what shall be done with your allies?'—'Then let one of your chieftains, Sa'b ibn Mu'adh, seal their fate.'

Now, Sa'b ibn Mu'adh had been badly wounded during the Battle of the Ditch by an arrow which had severed an artery in the arm and he prayed Allah let him live long enough to punish the Banu Quraizah for their felony. Sa'b, corpulent and too weak to walk, had himself placed on the back of an ass; where propped up by cushions and supported by two Believers, he was led to the assembly of the Mahadjirun and the Ansars, who stood up to do him honour, saying: 'The Prophet hath commissioned thee to decide the fate of their allies.'—'Will ye swear by Allah that my decision be carried into effect!'—'We swear it!'—'Well then, I decide that the men shall be slain, their property divided, and their wives and children sent into bondage.'—'Thy decision hath been inspired by the will of Allah!' concluded Mohammad.

Seven hundred Jews paid for their unjustifiable treachery with their lives. The wish for which Sa'b had lived was fulfilled. His old wound burst open, causing the last drops of his blood to flow away, and he earned the crown of martyrdom.

EXPEDITION AGAINST THE JEWS OF THE KHAIBAR
(Year VI of the Hegira, A.D. 628)

Notwithstanding these grave defeats, the power of the Jews in Arabia was not definitively crushed.

The land of Khaibar, about ninety-six miles north of Al-Madinah, still belonged to them and it was richer and more important than the territory they had lost. Many Jews, driven from the neighbourhood of Al-Madinah, had taken refuge there; and by their thirst for revenge they rekindled the hatred which the inhabitants already felt towards Islam.

The Jews of Khaibar, fancying themselves safe from any attack of the Mussulmans, never let an opportunity escape to do them harm; and copying the manner in which Mohammad had proceeded against the Jews found out a good way to satisfy their rancour. The region between Khaibar and the sea was inhabited by the tribe of Ghatafans, their allies, and they had come to an agreement to block the road and stop all Mussulman caravans leaving Al-Madina to travel to Syria. The damage inflicted from these tactics had often made the Prophet (Peace be on him) think about sending an expedition against the Jews of Khaibar, but he was too busy round about Makkah, to carry out this plan.

On returning from Al-Hudaibiyah, the ten year's truce, signed with the Quraish, freed him from all anxiety as regarded them, and the Revelation he received at that moment. *"He rewarded them with a speedy victory. And with a rich booty,"* (the Qur'an, XLVIII, 18–19), seeming to him to apply to Khaibar, and nothing else, he hesitated no longer, and decided to march against this fortress, the last stronghold of the Jews in Arabia.

The Ghatafans, secretly forwarned by Abdullah, the "Hypocrite" rushed to the aid of the Jews, their allies, but on arriving at the Wadi'r Raji, they found that the Mussulman forces had outstripped them and thus they were cut off from the road to Khaibar. Whilst brought to a dead stop, disagreeably surprised, they heard noises behind them, near their tents, and imagining that part of the Mussulman "qawm" had been diverted to take them in the rear, they turned back in great haste.

The palm-gardens of Khaibar, spreading between the sombre heights of the Harra like an emerald lake whence emerged rocky, citadel-crowned islets, came suddenly into view, after passing through a ravine. To be able to take possession of them, the Prophet (Peace be on him) invoked the aid of the Almighty. But, night coming on, Mohammad postponed the attack till the following day. When the first rays of the sun gilded the tops of the date-trees, the Khaiber husbandmen left their strongholds to go in their gardens; their spades, pickaxes and baskets hanging from their shoulders. Suddenly, they found themselves confronted by the Believers' army debouching from the Harra; spearheads and swords reflecting the light of the rising sun in ensanguined radiance.

'Mohammad and his Jihsh!' they cried, and throwing away implements and baskets, fled as fast as their legs would carry them. 'Allah is great!' proclaimed the Prophet. (Peace be on him) 'Khaibar shall be destroyed. When we swoop down on the territory of a nation, its awakening is terrible! Lo and behold the sinister omen! On our behalf, its inhabitants abandon their tools that will serve to undermine their ramparts and dig their graves.'

The first of many Khaibar citadels to fall into the Mussulmans' hands was that of Na'im. It was there they had to mourn the loss of Mahmud ibn Maslama, who, tired of having fought all day in the sun, wearing heavy armour, had imprudently gone close to the rampoart to rest in the shade. A mill-stone hurled from an embrasure, smashed the valiant soldier's helmet, split his skull, and caused the skin of his forehead to fall down over his eyes. In that parlous state, the wounded man was brought into the presence of the Prophet (Peace be on him) who put the strip of flesh back in its place, fastening a turban round it; but the best of attention was unavailing in face of such a serious injury, and it was not long before Mahmud gave up the ghost.

The citadels of Natha, the next to be attacked, resisted, more obstinately. In order to force the besieged to capitulate, the Prophet (Peace be on him) gave orders to cut down under their eyes four hundred palmtrees of their oasis, but all in vain. He therefore put an end to such devestation, contrary to his principles, for as he said: 'Among all trees, there is one which is blessed like a Mussulman: 'tis the palm'.

The siege continuing, famine began to make itself felt, discouraging the besiegers, when Umar, having taken a jew prisoner, the captive, to save his life, offered to give the Prophet (Peace be on him) valuable information. In the cellars of Sa'b ibn Mu'adh, one of the Natha citadels, called after the man, instruments of warfare of all kinds were stored: battering-rams, catapults for siege purposes; and armour, shields, pikes, lances and swords for the equipment of combatants. Just then, this fort happened to be weakly garrisoned, and the Jewish captive undertook to take the Musssulman inside by means of a secret itinerary, known to him alone.

Mohammad, having accepted the offer, seized upon Sa'b easily and thanks to the machines he found therein, which he used to destroy the ramparts, he captured the remaining fortresses of Natha, one after the other. They all contained provisions in abundance. While taking one of these forts, the poet Amr'ibn u'l-Uhayha, pursuing one of the enemy, dealt him a furious sabre-cut, aiming at his legs to stop him in his flight. But the blade, too short, striking the empty air, rebounded from the force of the blow and pierced Amar's knee, setting up such a strong haemorrhage that he expired soon afterwards, being sacrificed by his own hand, whilst fighting for Allah.

The most important of all the Khaibar citadels was still standing: that of Al-Qamus, in which Kinana, Prince of the Banu-Nadir, had taken refuge. It was defended by Marhab al-Yahudi, an illustrious warrior. Built on top of a vertical black rock, with smooth sides, and surrounded by cleverly designed fortifications, this fort was said to be impregnable. After ten days of desperate efforts against the ramparts, the Believers however, succeeded in effecting a breach, into which leapt the Prophet (Peace be on him) setting the example to his companions; but after having been in the greatest danger, he was compelled to retrace his steps.

The shooting pains of neuralgia forcing him to take forty-eight hours rest, he entrusted the standard to Abu Bakr, who led an attack through the breach, with the most ardent courage, but he also had to beat a retreat at last. Umar took his place, accomplishing prodigies of valour, likewise without success.

Hearing of their failure Mohammad declared: 'By Allah! to-morrow I'll confide the flag to an intrepid fellow, to whom flight is unknown. He loveth Allah and His Messenger, and by them he is beloved. 'Tis he who will capture Al-Qamus by sheer strength.'

Next day, all the companions clustering close to the Prophet (Peace be on him) were anxious to learn who was the man among them to be so greatly honoured. But without glancing at the group, he sent for Ali who had to remain in the rear because he was suffering from painful ophthalmia. Led by a friend, he came into the Prophet's (Peace be on him) presence. Ali's eyes were covered by a bandage.

'Come hither, close to me,' said Mohammad. 'Take this flag and keep a hold on it until the Almightly shall open a way for thee through these ramparts.'—'I suffer cruelly from my eyes, O Prophet!' replied ali. 'I cannot even see to walk.'

Mohammad made Ali rest his head in his lap; separated the young man's swollen eyelids, and rubbed the bloodshot eyes with a little saliva. All inflammation vanished immediately and every vestige of pain disappeared. The Prophet (Peace be on him) then buckled his own breastplate on Ali and armed him with his own sword, celebrated under the title of "Dhul'l-Fiqar".

Ali went towards the fortress, planting in the ground, close to the ramparts, the white flag on which stood out in bold relief, embroidered in black letters, the Islamic profession of faith. He then got ready to storm the breach. Al-Harith, at the head of the Jews, tried to bar the way and drive back the Mussulman hero, but the leader of the children of Israel succumbed, struck down by Ali; and the soldiers who had followed all ran away.

The brother Al-Harith Marhab, famous and feared, came now to the front, eager for revenge. He produced an effect of terror by his gigantic stature, double armour, a pair of swords, a three-headed spear, a double turban; and his helmet on which sparkled a jewel as big an an egg. His eyes, too, glistened like two carbuncles. Puffed up with pride, he strode to the breach. 'The whole of the land of Khaibar, from end to end, knoweth my valour! When war rageth, sometimes I pierce with my lance; and sometimes I slice with my sword! Doth there exist in all the world a champion who dare stand up against me?'

Without being moved by this bragging bombast, Ali showed himself to take up the challenge: 'I'll be that man! Verily I, called by mother Haydra, the lion cub, in memory of my father, known as the Lion. With my sabre I'll give thee good measure!'

Hearing this reply Marhab became purple with rage. Brandishing his scimitar, he rushed at Ali. The formidable blade hissed through the air and it seemed as if the champion of Islam had just been annihilated. But the sword of the terrible Jew was stopped by Ali's shield in which it penetrated deeply and stuck therein. Without giving his adversary time to drag it away Ali loosened his hold of the buckler, now useless and in his way, and replied to the attack by a wonderful cut that split the helmet, turban and skull of his enemy, scattering the brains in every direction. The steel was only stopped by the Jew's teeth, forming a barrier. The giant fell in a huddled heap, like a tower ruined by an earthquake, in a cloud of dust, with noise as of thunder.

Seized with affright, the Jewish soldiers fled, pursued by Ali's men. He tore from its hinges the heavy door of the ramparts and it served him as a shield in place of the one broken in the fight. Resistance was cut short and Al-Qamas, the impregnable, was captured by the warriors of Islam.

When the fall of the famous fort became known, the Jew of Fadak and of Wadi'l-Qura, two places a few day's march towards the north, sent in their submission. In concordance with their co-religionists of Khaibar, they supplicated the Prophet (Peace be on him) to let them live as farmers on their estates which they alone knew how to cultivate properly: and to allow them to take half the crops as remuneration for their labour. Mohammad consented, on condition that the Believers would have the right to alter this decision, should they deem it necessary.

Khaibar was the most fertile land of all the Hijaz; the spoils were therefore considerable. One half was set apart to defray the expenses of the pilgrimage to take place during the current year; the rest was distributed among the warriors. The land, with the exception of the portion due to the Prophet (Peace be on him) and to orphans was divided in such a way that each man received one share, and each charger two shares: making three shares for each horseman. This was done with the aim of encouraging the breed of horses. A supplementary gift fell to the lot of any soldier being the owner of a pure-blooded courser.

IMPORTANCE OF HORSE-BREEDING ACCORDING TO THE PROPHET

These measures show the importance attributed by the Prophet to the equine race in the lift of the Arabs.

Up till then, horses were very rare in Arabia, being looked upon as articles of luxury as it were. Led by the bridle by the side of the camels ridden by the warriors, the steeds were only called upon when charging or pursuing the enemy. The Prophet completed these arrangements by founding race-meetings destined to develop emulation among breeders and horsemen. In the Qur' an, so as to inspire Believers with the fear of the Day of Retribution, horses galloping are breathless called to witness: *"By the panting chargers! And those that dash off sparks of fire. And those that scour to attack at morn! And stir therein the dust aloft! And cleave therein their midway through a host! Truly, Man is to his Lord ungrateful! And of this he verily is himself a witness And truly he is vehement in the love of this world's good. Knoweth he not, then, that when that which is in the graves shall be turn forth, And that which is in men's breasts shall be brought out, Verily their Lord shall on that day be well informed concerning them?'* (the Qur'an, C, 1-11.)

Unfortunately, tame translation is powerless to give an idea of the dizzy, whirling rythm and the panting, galloping, neighing—if one may venture so to write— assonance of the first verses of this surah. One of the most celebrated horsemen of that epoch, Abdullah ibn Abi Sarh, afterwards governor of Egypt and who inflicted cruel defeats on the Romans, by land and sea, was such an enthusiastic admirer of this surah that it was always on his lips, and he recited it even on his deathbed.

Thanks to the vigorous impulsion given by the Prophet (Peace be on him) to horse-breeding, the race of pure-blooded barbs, unrivalled in the world, was soon formed, to be kept up ever afterwards.

THE POISONED LAMB

After sunset, when the Prophet (Peace be on him) had said the prayer of "Magrib," he went back to the camp. Near his tent, he saw seated the Jewess Zainabl, daughter of Al-Harith, and wife of Sallam ibn Mishkam. She awaited Mohammad's coming to give him the present she had brought: a lamb spitted on a spear, and which had been roasted at a fire fed with aromatic wood from the desert. He thanked the woman, and when she had taken her leave, he invited his companions to sit down and partake of the roast. Its crisp, golden outer skin looked very tempting.

The Prophet (Peace be on him) was the first to fall, twisting off a shoulder into which he bit and began to chew a morsel. Following his example, Bishr ibn U'l-Bara took a mouthful of meat, masticating and swallowing it. The other guests had already reached out their hands in like fashion, when the Prophet spat out the piece he was chewing and stopped them abruptly shouting: 'Hold your hands! This shoulder hath just told me that it is poisoned!'—'By him who is Generosity incarnate!' exclaimed Bishr, 'I thought that my mouthful had a peculiar flavour and guessed what it meant; but seeing thee chew thine, I could not spit it out, saving your reverence. If this poison should destroy thy life, what liking can remain to me for mine?'

Scarcely had Bishr uttered these words than his face, overspread by a blackish hue, became distorted, and he writhed on the ground, a prey to unbearable suffering.

The Prophet (Peace be on him) sent at once for the Jewess and said to her: 'Thou hast poisoned this lamb?'—'Who told thee so?'—'This!' and he showed her the fragment of shoulder he held.—'It is true,' she confessed.—'Why didst thoud do this thing??'—'My father, my uncle, my husband and many of my people have suffered the sad fate thou knowest of, by thy fault. And I did think: if Mohammad is naught but a monarch, I end his days and glut their vengeance and mine. If, on the contrary, he is truly a Prophet (Peace be on him) he is in no danger, because his Allah will warn him of my purpose.'

This clever answer calmed the Prophet (Peace be on him) and he was perchance on the point of pardoning the guilty woman for her abominable crime, when Bishr expired at that moment. Mohammad delivered the Jewess into the hands of the dead man's relatives who came clamouring to be avenged. Zainab was crucified and the remains of the fatal lamb were burnt.

Although the Prophet (Peace be on him) spat out the perfidious piece of meat almost as soon as it passed his lips, the poison filtered through his body as far as his entrails, and he never fully recovered from its pernicious effects. Three years later, when fatally ill, Bishr's sister coming into his house to task after his health, he told her: 'The vein of my heart was torn by the food I ate with thy brother, at Khaibar'.

AMRATU'L QADA OR THE PIOUS VISITATION

(Year VII of the Hegra, A.D. 629)

At the same time as the expeditionary forces, laden with spoils came back from Khaibar, the last emigrants arrived from Abyssinia. Among them was Jafar, son of Abu Talib and brother to Ali. Their return made Mohammad very joyful. With sincere effusion, he kissed Jafar between the eyes and declared: 'I know not which causeth me the greatest joy: the taking of Khaibar, or the return of Jafar.'

Among those returning was also Umm Habiba, daughter of Abu Sufyan, the Prophet's (Peace be on him) mortal enemy. She had emigrated with her husband, Ubaydu'llah ibn Jahsh, but he was a convert to Christianity and had died in Abyssinia, while she remained steadfast to Islam. As a reward for such fidelity, as well as hoping to disarm the alliance of one of his most fierce adversaries, the Prophet (Peace be on him) had sent Amr ibn Umayya to the Negus, asking to be married by proxy to Umm Habiba and to have her sent back afterwards with the other emigrants. This being done, Umm Habiba, on arriving at Al-Madinah, was received in the dwelling of her illustrious husband.

As for the emigrants, Mohammad proposed that they should be allowed a share of the Khaibar booty. This arrangement being ratified by unanimous consent, they were thus compensated for having sacrificed their property and left their country in order to remain true to their faith.

The date on which the treaty of al-Hudaibiyah gave the Prophet (Peace be on him) the right to come to Makkah with his disciples to visit the Holy Places having arrived, he was now on the point of being able to fulfil one of his most ardent aspirations and also see his native land.

Followed by the same number of pilgrims, and driving before him the same number of camels, destined to be sacrificed, as in the expedition of Al-Hudaibiyah, he made his partisans disarm and leave in the valley of Batn Ya'jiju a great quantity of weapons, brought as a precautionary measure, in the care of a guard, two hundred strong, commanded by Aws ibn Khawli. 'We only penetrate into the Holy Land,' declared the Prophet, (Peace be on him) 'carrying the arms of the traveller: our swords in their scabbards, according to the terms of our oath, but if we detect in the glances of the idolatrous Quraish the slightest sign of treachery, our other weapons will be found handy.'

An Arab horseman from the Desert.

He then pushed on. Self-communing, he climbed the Kuda hill, in order to descend into the valley near the cemetery of Al-Hajun where rested his beloved Khadijah (May Allah welcome her in His Grace!). When he cast eyes on the first houses of Makkah, unspeakable emotion overpowered him by reason of the remembrances and hopes they evoked. Fearing lest treachery, on the part of the Infidels, should force him to order reprisals, causing the blood of his fellow-countrymen to sully the streets of the city where he was born, he cried out: 'O Allah, spare us all misfortune in the Holy City!' He never ceased repeating this request until he left the precincts of Makkah.

On the approach of the Believers, the leading citizens, exasperated at the triumphant return of the men they had banished, went out of town and hid their impotent rage in tents pitched in the neighbouring ravines. As for the mass of the inhabitants, like all mobs, they were dominated by a feeling of curiosity and clustered either on the heights of the Jabal Qu'ayqu'an, or on the terrace-roof of the "Darun-Nadwa", House of Council, from which they were able to look down into the interior of the Temple. From the gossip of the crowd could be gathered the general hope that the Prophet (Peace be on him) and his partisans would arrive in a state of complete exhaustion, their blood and bodies impoverished by the torrid summer heat and pernicious fevers of Al-Madinah.

Forewarned by divine inspiration, Mohammad cautioned his companions 'Allah will be merciful to those,' said he, 'who this day display their bodily vigour.'

With the exception of the common people mustering on the roof of the "Dar-un-Nadwa," the city was quite empty. The Prophet (Peace be on him) could have captured it without striking a blow; but his soul, incapable of such treachery, was entirely engrossed by pious thoughts. Riding his she-camel, Qaswa, its bridle held by Abdullah ibn Rawaha, and surrounded and followed by his disciples, he passed through the outlying districts, under the eyes of enemies, without even honouring them a single glance. He alighted on the Temple threshold, wrapping himself up in the folds of his mantle, by throwing one end over his left shoulder, leaving his right arms and shoulder at liberty. Followed and imitated by all the Faithful, he kissed the Black Stone and performed the "Tawaf", the seven ritual circuits round the Ka'bah. The three first were made with swift, measured strides (called "Ramal" or "Harwala"), with a view to proving the fine state of health of the Believers to the Infidels looking on. They shook their heads gloomily, saying to each other: 'So these are the men described to us as enfeebled by the heat and fevers of Al-Madinah!'. At the bottom of their hearts, the Unbelievers were forced to confess that such men as these, their mental well-being surpassing even their bodily health, were unconquerable. The four remaining circuits were made with slow dignity, as Mohammad had no desire to demand useless efforts from his partisans; and ever since that day, this manner of performing the "Tawaf" is religiously copied by the pilgrims.

The Prophet then ordered Bilal to call the faithful to prayer. When the idolaters heard the resounding accents of the black freed slave reverberating in the echoes of the valley, they were so deeply annoyed that they envied the fate of their illustrious dead, Abu Jahal and Abu Lahab, prevented from hearing this call by the weight of the earth piled on their graves. After the prayer, Mohammad again bestrode his she-camel, to perform the "Sa'y", which is the run between the two hills of Safa and Marwa. His example swept away the believers' scruples; for, until then, they had hesitated about going through this ceremony, being embarrassed by the presence of the idols Isaf and Na'ila, set up at the spot.

By the performance of these rites, instituted by Abraham and perpetuated by the Arabs, the Prophet had in view a nationalist and political goal, which he wished to combine with his religious aims. If he kissed the Black Stone, it was not by reason of a feeling of superstitious worship which would have contradicted all the principles of the Qur'an much too flagrantly, but solely through a feeling of reverence for this relic of his glorious ancestor.

Quoth Ibn Abi Shayba, following Isa ibn Talha: "Addressing the Black Stone, the Prophet (Peace be on him) declared: 'Verily, I know that thou art nothing more than a stone, powerless to do harm, or be of any use." Then he kissed it. In this conjuncture, Abu Bakr, followed by Umar, one after the other, came and kissed it, declaring: "By Allah! I know that thou art nothing more than a stone, powerless to do harm or be of any use, and if I had not seen the Prophet kiss thee, I should not have kissed thee!"

In like fashion, by the "Sa'y" and the ablutions at the well of Zamzam, Mohammad kept alive the touching remembrance of the Arab's ancestor Ishmael and of his mother Hajar (Hagar). Being too weak to carry any farther her wretched child succumbing athirst in a horrible desert, Hajar placed her offspring on the ground in the shade of a shrub and ascended a hill, hoping to see from afar a well or spring; but all in vain. Then, fearing that the soul of Ishmael might have escaped from his body, she came back, panting to his side and climbed another hill for the same purpose, but with no more success than before. So she went down again, tortured by the same anguish.

"Seven times did she run in despair between two hills until, maddened, she thought she would only find a corpse, when she caught sight of her beloved son quenching his thirst at a spring which, by order of the Compassionate, had gushed forth under the heel of the poor child. And to this miraculous well was given the name of Zamzam."

In imitation of Hajar, pilgrims pass seven times along the path of agony which she trod between the two hills known as Safa and Marwa, and it is their duty to drink and perform their ablutions at the Zamzam spring.

On the following day, in commemoration of the sacrifice of Abraham, the victims were immolated in the valley of Mina. Their flesh was shared among the pilgrims who, having shaved their heads, were once again in the state of "halal", ordinary life, which they had relinquished since Zu'l-Holifah.

While still in the state of "ihram," Mohammad, thanks to the special privilege derived from his position as Allah's Messenger, married a woman of Makkah, named Maimunah. She was fifty years of age and extremely poor; but this matrimonial alliance was bound to bring notable recruits to Islam. In the first place, her brother-in-law, Al-Abbas, was Mohammad's uncle. He was her "wakil," or guardian, and decreed the union with the Prophet (Peace be on him). But the marriage was only consummated at the first halt on the return journey to Al-Madinah.

Despite the rage of the idolatrous Quraish, who could not bear to look upon the sight of their enemy's pilgrimage, the Prophet (Peace be on him) had gained his end: to inform the Arabs of the whole of the Peninsula that he had no intention of abolishing their secular traditions; but on the contrary, would devote all his efforts to consolidate them, by restoring their primitive purity.

The "Amratu'l-Qada" was thus the cause of great reaction; bringing about immediate conversions; among others, those of three great pesonages: Uthman ibn Talha, Amr ibnu'l-As and Khalid ibn Walid, besides preparing the minds of the majority of the Arabs to follow their example.

THE PROPHET SENDS AMBASSADORS TO THE PRINCIPAL MONARCHS OF THE WORLD

The definitive defeat of the Jews rallied a great part of Arabia to the Prophet; and the rest of the Peninsula was fatally bound, in course of time, to come under the sway of Islam.

It was then that Mohammad turned towards neighbouring empires. Allah's presence filled the universe and Islam, which counted already in its ranks disciples of many different origins, was not destined to be merely confined to the land of the Arabs. It spread over the whole world. As it is written in the Qur'an: *"We have not sent thee otherwise than to mankind at large."* (XXXIV, 27.)

To the most powerful monarchs of Europe, therefore, Mohammad despatched envoys carrying letters inviting these potentates to embrace the religion of Allah, the Only one; and the missives bore a seal on which the Prophet (Peace be on him) had caused to be engraved these words, set out in three lines: "From Allah — the Prophet — Mohammad."

On receipt of the message, Al-Mundhir, King of Bahrayn, and Badhan, Persian Satrap of Yaman, became converts to Islam. Al-Muqawqas, Viceroy of Egypt sent rich presents, among which, as well as Duldul, a white mule, and Ya'fur, an ass, was a young slave, Mary the Copt. She at once became Mohammad's concubine. Hirqal, (Heraclius), the Roman Emperor, and the Najashi, (Negus) of Abyssinia, both replied by most courteous letters.

Kesra (Chosroes), King of Persia, swore he would punish the Prophet (Peace be on him) for his audacity and the Almighty immediately chastised the monarch, for he was murdered by his son Shiru'e, (Siroes), who took his father's place on the throne. Al-Harith, son of Abu Shamar, was fated to see his kingdom torn asunder, even as he had torn the letters delivered to him by the Prophet's (Peace be on him) envoy.

Only one of these ambassadors, Al-Harith ibn Amr, was received with contumely and afterwards treacherously murdered near Karak in the Balqua region, following orders given by Shurabil al-Ghassani who governed this region under Roman rule.

THE EXPEDITION OF MUTAH
(Year VII of the Hegira, A.D. 629)

When the news of the outrage on his ambassador came to the Prophet's (Peace be on him) ears, he determined to be instantly avenged, although he did not conceal from himself the dangers of the undertaking.

This time the Believers had to face, not only the Syrian Arabs, outnumbering those of the Hijaz, but also the Roman troops who occupied the Balqua-Land. The Prophet placed Zayd ibn al-Haris at the head of three thousand men; but foreseeing that in this unequal struggle, his army might be deprived of its leader, he nominated in advance, as successor, Jafar, son of Abu Talib; and if misfortune befell Jafar, Abdullah ibn Rawaha; and lastly, in the cast of anything unluckily happening to the latter, it was left to the soldiers to choose a commander themselves.

A Jew was present at the council of war and made the following remarks: 'O Abul Qasim! (a surname of Mohammad), 'if thou art really a Prophet, all the men thou hast appointed are irretrevably lost. When our prophets of Israel, after having placed a general at the head of their armies, used to add: "and if he is killed, name such an one in his place," that infallibly meant that he was bound to lose his life.' Then, turning to Zayd, he went on: 'I swear to thee that if Mohammad is a true Prophet, thou wilt never return from this expedition.' Zayd replied simply: 'I swear to thee that Mohammad is the Prophet of Allah.' Then the Apostle tied the white "Liwa" (flak) to a spearhead and gave it into the hands of Zayd.

Filled with funereal sentiments, Mohammad accompanied his troops to Sadiyat-ul-Wida, (the Pass of Farewells). It was there that he halted and gave them his final instructions: 'Remain ever in fear of Allah. Fight in his name and kill His foes who are yours. But leave in peace such men as dwell in the seclusion of monasteries. Spare women, children and the blind. Destroy no monuments; cut down no trees; and when ye shall have avenged the death of Al-Harith ibn Amr, summon the Arab tribes of Syria to Islam.'

Shurahbil, anxious as to the results of his cowardly outrage, called upon all the Arabs of the surrounding country; the Banu Bahra, the Banu Lakhm, the Baliyy, etc., and he notified his fears to Theodurus, lieutenant of Heraclius, who sent him all the Roman troops then occupying the land.

Shurahbil had therefore mustered an army of nearly a hundred thousand men before the Mussulman forces arrived at Mu'an. When they found themselves confronting such formidable cohorts, the Believers remained two days and two nights in consultation and many among them proposed that a messenger should be despatched to the Prophet who would then decide whether they were to turn back or fight. Perhaps he might send them reinforcements. But the utterances of Abdullah ibn Rawaha revived the courage of the Believers. 'O comrades! how is it that ye seem to fear the very thing ye come to seek: martyrdom in the Holy War? We reckon not on numbers to gain the victory, but on the faith with which Allah hath inspired us!'—'Thou dost speak truly!' they cried and hesitating no longer, advanced towards the enemy, coming in contact with him at Mutah, a little village situated south of the Karab fort.

Like lions, they dashed into the centre of their massed foes, whose chief, Malik ibn Rafila, was killed by a spear-thrust. Recovering from their first surprise and profiting by their great numerical superiority, the Infidels were not long in getting the best of the struggle and they encircled the Mussulmans completely. Outnumbered, Zayed ibn Al-Haris died the death of a hero; and Jafar, obeying the Prophet's instructions, bounded forward to uphold the standard that Zayd's contracted fingeres still gripped, and to take command in his place.

Jafar rode a magnificent chestnut charger, but seeing the immediate danger, he alighted and hamstrung his steed, so that if the master succumbed, his horse should not be captured by the enemy to be used against Islam. By his example he was able to rally the Believers and lead them in an enthusiastic charge, whilst waving the Islamic standard which proudly spread its wings above their heads. But soon, like an eagle wounded in its flight, the flag fell down; the hand that held it being hacked off by a blow from a scimitar.

Jafar picked up the standard, grasping it in his left hand, when another sword-cut sliced his unwounded wrist. Jafar stooped, and seizing the flag between the bleeding stumps of his arms, he kept it aloft by pressing the staff against his breast, and with sublime heroism, continued to charge the enemy until he fell, riddled with ninety wounds.

Abdullah ibn Rawaha succeeded him and met with the same fate shortly afterwards. The Mussulmans, attacked on all sides, seeing their leaders struck down, gave way and began to flee in disorder. Arqam ibn Amir stopped them. 'O comrades!' he cried out, 'tis better to be struck in the breast than in the back!' Picking up the standard, he passed it on to Khalid ibn Walid who refused it as first, saying: 'Thou hast a better right to this honour than I, for thou wert a Badr.'

But Arqam insisting Khalid took charge of the flag. His impetuous energy instilled fresh courage and confidence into the hearts of the Believers, ashamed of their momentary weakness, and being skilful strategist as well as a valiant soldier, he succeeded with the help of Allah, in freeing the Mussulman troops and reorganising the fighting front in such masterly fashion that the Infidels were unable to claim the victory.

At sunrise, the next day, he was first to attack, so as not to give the enemy time to recover from his partial defeat. To deceive him with regard to the numerical weakness of the Islamic forces, he restored to the following stratagem: by rapid evolutions of various sections of his army, he made the rearguards pass to the van guards, and *vice versa*, in such a way that the enemy, continually seeing fresh adversaries confronting him, imagined that the Mussulmans had been greatly reinforced during the night. The Infidel's certainty of triumph, mainly founded on their numbers, vanished; and seized with indescribable terror, they gave way, pursued by the Believers who slaughtered them ruthlessly. During that memorable day, Khalid had nine sabres broken in his hand.

By divine inspiration, the Prophet (Peace be on him) was informed of the ordeals of his army. After general prayer, he went up in the pulpit, his eyes full of tears, and cried out three times: 'The Gate of Good! Know ye all that Zayd hath fallen a martyr; implore the mercy of Allah in his favour. Then Jafar and Abdullah died martyrs; implore the mercy of Allah for them. Then the standard was upheld by Khalid ibn Walid, who is the sword among all the swords of Allah. And the Almightly granted him victory.'

Mohammad afterwards went to see Asama bint Omis, the wife of Jafar, and bent down over his children to "smell" them, tears welling up in his eyes and trickling pearl-like down his beard. 'O Prophet! asked Asama, 'what maketh thee weep? Hast thou had news of Jafar and his comrades?'—'Aye and now they are no more!'

The wretched woman dropped down, groaning in despair and lacerating her cheeks with her nails. Attracted by her shrieks, the other wives imitated her and the whole house resounded with lugubrious lamentation. The Prophet (Peace be on him) ordered one of his companions to impose silence on the women. 'It is not fitting,' said Mohammad, 'to mourn thus for Jafar. Hath he not obtained the great reward? I pray Allah that He may permit the father's place on this earth to be taken in posterity by the most accomplished among his children!'

Suddenly he lifted his eyes to heaven and murmured: 'The Salvation and Mercy of Allah be upon you!'—'To whom dost thou speak, O Prophet?' asked one of his followers.—'I have just seen Jafar go by in the midst of a procession of angels. He was mounting to Paradise with ruby-stubbed wings in lieu of his amputated hands. He greeted me and I returned his greeting.'

Sohail, who recorded this tradition, is careful to add: 'Such are merely images: the wings are symbols of the supernatural strength of Jafar's soul; and the rubies are the precious drops of his blood.'

In the midst of the universal mourning at Al-Madinah, the Prophet ordered the funeral repast known as "Al-Oudhim," to be prepared. It was destined for the families of the martyrs; for it is hard for those whose souls are saddened to have to think about preparing nourishment for the body.

When the return of the army was announced, the whole of the population of the city, rich or poor, went out to meet it. The Prophet (Peace be on him) ordained that the mounted men should lift up the children and give them a ride on the pummels of the saddles. He took the son of Jafar in his arms and seated the child in front of him. The soldiers, on arriving, confirmed the tidings of their leaders' death and the people of Al-Madinah, thinking that these heroes had not been fully avenged, threw handfuls of dust in the soldiers' faces and inveighed against them: 'O cowards! ye fled, even when ye trod the Path of Allah!'

The Prophet bade the crowd be silent and made this declaration: 'On the contrary, these warriors deserve your greatest praise, for they returned and charged courageously!'

THE TAKING OF MAKKAH
(The 21st day of Ramadhan Year VIII of the Hegira, January 11th A.D. 630)

It was not long before the idolaters of Makkah violated the ten years truce, signed at Al-Hudaibiyah.

By surprise, one night, they massacred a score of Mussulmans belonging to the tribe of the Khuza'a, encamped at the well of Al-Wati. In face of such terrible treachery, the Prophet (Peace be on him) threw all scruples to the winds. Determined to attack, he proposed to organise an expedition.

The Makkans, well aware that their crime would not go unpunished, delegated Abu Sufyan to go to Al-Madinah, to offer compensation and ask for the truce to be maintained. On arriving, Abu Sufyan went to the dwelling of Umm Habiba, his daughter, who, as we know, was one of Mohammad's wives. But, when he made as if to sit down on a carpet, Umm Habiba, guessing his purpose, quickly folded up the rug and placed it on one side. 'O my daughter,' said Abu Sufyan in offended tones, 'dost find thy father unworthy of that carpet, or is that carpet unworthy of thy father?'—'That carpet belongeth to the Prophet,' she replied. 'Now thou art a worshipper of idols; therefore in a state of impurity, and thou wouldst sully it with thy impiety.'—'Of a surety, O my daughter, some misfortune hath happened, bringing disorder to thy mind, since the day thou left us!'

Understanding, by this kind of welcome, that there was no hope for him in that quarter, he sought out the Prophet (Peace be on him) from whom no reply was obtained. Then he made desperate attempts to circumvent Abu Bakr; and tried his best with Umar and Ali, supplicating them to intercede in favour of his fellow-citizens, but with no greater success. Full of apprehension, he mounted his camel and went back on the road to Makkah.

The steps taken by Abu Sufyan no longer allowed the Prophet (Peace be on him) to conceal his designs. His sole care was to hurry on with his preparation, so as to surprise the men of Makkah before they had time to place the city in a state of defence. On the tenth day of the month of Ramadhan, after having left Abu Ruhm Kulthum al-Shifari as his lieutenant at Al-Madinah, the Prophet (Peace be on him) set out, followed by an army of no inconsiderable strength, increased on the way by numerous tribes joining, and the total forces soon numbered ten thousand men.

The fast of Ramadhan was strictly kept by all the Faithful but when they reached the well of Al-Kadid in the middle of the day exactly, the Prophet (Peace be on him) judged that their constancy had been sufficiently tested. Fearing the deprivation of drink, joined to extreme fatigue, might have a dangerous effect on their health, he asked for a jar filled with water to be brought to him. Overlooking the crowd on his tall she-camel, he swallowed a mouthful in front of all, so as teach by his example that they might break their fast when on a journey as soon as they felt their strength exhausted. Thus prescribes the Qur'an: *"But he among you who shall be sick, or on a journey, shall fast that same number of other days."* (the Qur'an ii, 180.)

After that halt, the Prophet (Peace be on him) hastened the march of his army so actively that he camped at Marru'dh-Dhahran, close to the town gates, before the Quraish were able to find out anything about the important strength of the Mussulman troops, or the road they had taken.

Abbas, Mohammad's uncle, kept in Makkah till then by his business functions as superintendent of the water supply, joined the Believers at Al-Juhfa, with the whole of his family. The sincerity of his conversion had not caused him to forget the love he felt for his fellow-citizens. He was most uneasy about their fate, in case they should behave in such a way that Mohammad would be forced to take the town by murderous onslaught.

Quoth Abbas: "When the tents were pitched, I rode the Prophet's (Peace be on him) white mule and went to Al-Ark, on the road to the Arafa, hoping to meet a carrier of wood, brickmaker, or pilgrim whom I might charge to take a warning to the Quraish and exhort them to go and implore the mercy of Allah.'

"Whilst advancing with due precaution in the dark, two men passed quite close to me. They were hidden from my sight by big boulders and they talked in whispers. One of them, his mind engrossed by the myriads of golden stars that the camp-fires of the Faithful caused to scintillate on the hills beneath the real silvery stars of the firmament, said: 'Never have I seen so many lights as this night on those mountains.'—'They are probably the camp-fires of the Khuza'a, determined to wage war to avenge their dead.'—'The Khuza'a are not so numerous. No, truly, these cannot be their fires!' replied the first speaker whose voice I recognised. It was that of Abu Sufyan. 'O father of Handala!' I called to him.—'O father of Al-Fadl! if'tis thee what dost thou want of me?" he returned, having also recognised my voice.—'O Abu Sufyan! the Prophet is here at the head of such a great army that all resistance is impossible. To-morrow the Quraish will be cut to pieces!"—'What is to be done! Canst thou advise me?'—'If thou art taken prisoner during the fight, thy head will be cut off. Doubt it not. But get up behind me on my mule. I will take thee to Mohammad and implore him for thee.'

Abu Sufyan, understanding that this was his last hope of safety, could only submit. He got up behind me and we went on in front of his companion Budayl, who made up his mind to follow us.

Every time the flicker of one of the many camp-fires lit up our little group, on the dark background, sentinels stopped us, asking: 'Who is that man?' But when I told them that I was Abbas, the Prophet's uncle, and as they recognised the mule, they allowed us to pass.

All went well until we came to the light of Umar's tents. He came forward to meet us and also demanded: 'Who is that man?' Just then, the flame of the brazier lit up the face of my companion who held me tightly. Umar knew him again, and cried out in sudden joy: 'Ah!' tis thee, Abu Sufyan, with no treaty or safe-conduct, O enemy of Allah! The Almighty be praised for delivering thee into our hands!'

He ran to the Prophet's (Peace be on him) tent. I made the mule gallop along, outstripped him and jumped off, going into Mohammad's tent; but Umar arrived, almost at the same instant. 'O Prophet!' he shouted. 'Here is Abu Safyan, Allah's enemy, without treaty or safe-conduct, given up to us by the Almighty! Charge me to cut his head off!'

I interfered: 'O Prophet! He is under my protection. No one but me shall go near him this night.' As Umar kept on manifesting still greater hatred, I said to him: 'Softly, O Umar! If Abu Sufyan was one of the Banu Adi ibn Kad, thy relatives, thou wouldst not behave in this way; but he is one of the Banu Abd Manaf, related to the Prophet (Peace be on him) which thou must not forget!'

Umar made answer: 'Softly, O Abbas! Know that thy conversion gave me more pleasure than that of my father, Al Khattab, would have caused me, for he lived and died in idolatry; for the sole reason that, as I know well, the Prophet (Peace be on him) attached more importance to thy conversion than to that of my father.' Allah's Messenger cut our dispute short by saying: 'Take away Abu Sufyan, O Abbas, and tomorrow at dawn, come back here with him.'

I obeyed. Abu Sufyan passed the night in perfect safety in my tent, but seeing all the Mussulmans rise up at one bound at the first glimmer of daybreak, he was overcome by anxiety. 'O father of Al-Fadl!' he asked, 'What are they about? Do they want to kill me?'—'Be not alarmed,' I told him in reply. 'They only want to pray.'

At the sight of these ten thousand men, the mysterious light reflected by the rosy dawn playing on them; all piously repeating every gesture of the Prophet (Peace be on him) bowing down when he bowed down and prostrating themselves when he prostrated himself, he could not refrain from exclaiming: 'By Allah! I have never seen kings obeyed as this man is obeyed; not even Chosroes, nor Cæsar, nor any of the most powerful monarchs of the universe!'

'Come,' I told him, when prayers had been said. 'I will intercede for thee; and thou wilt intercede for thy qawm.'—'How now?' ask the Prophet (Peace be on him) when the idolater came before him. 'Dost thou not acknowledge, O Abu Sufyan! that there is no God but Allah?'—'By my father and my mother! How patient, generous and conciliatory thou art! Yea, I acknowledge it. If with Allah there were other gods, they would have given me some little help.'—'Dost thou acknowledge that I am the Prophet of Allah?'—'But my father and my mother! As for that, there is still some doubt in my mind. I will see later.'—'Woe unto thee! O Abu Sufyan!' I exclaimed, indignant at his reply. 'Hasten to bear witness to the whole truth, or I deprive thee of my protection and thine head will fall from thy shoulder!'

Abu Sufyan still hazarded a few objections: 'What wilt thou do with the state of Al-Uzza that is in my dwelling?'—'Thou shalt throw it in the privy!' shouted an angry voice. It was that of Umar, listening behind the canvas of the tent, hoping to be ordered to execute the man who had been an enemy of Allah. 'Woe unto thee, O Umar! thou art an indecent fellow, Let me come to terms with my uncle's son.'

Having made up his mind by this time, he recited the profession of Islamic faith integrally, at the same time as his companion Budayl, who had just rejoined us.

I remarked to the Prophet (Peace be on him) 'Thou knowest how proud is Abu Sufyan. Invest him with some authority no matter what, and he will be bound to us definitively.'

My idea met with Mohammad's approbation and he gave out the following proclamation: 'He who taketh refuge in the dwelling of Abu Sufyan will be in safety, he who taketh refuge in the Temple will be in safety; he who layeth down his arms and remaineth shut up in his house will be in safety.'

The Prophet (Peace be on him) then said to me: 'O Abbas! bring Abu Sufyan to a halt where the valley is narrow, on the mountain top, so that all the warriors of Allah will pass before his eye.' I obeyed and took my stand with Abu Sufyan on one of the rocks overhanging the outlet of the valley. One after the other passed the soldiers of the Sulaym, the Muzayna, the Banu Ghifar, the Banu Ka'b, the Kinana, the Juhayn, etc., and my companion, despite all his efforts, could not hide the impression made upon him by the numbers of the Believers. When he caught sight of Ashja, he cried out: 'Those tribesmen, not withstanding, were the most inveterate of all the Prophet's enemies!'—'Truly,' I retorted,' but Allah, in His Generosity, instilled Islam in their hearts!'

At last the Prophet (Peace be on him) appeared, surrounded by his bodyguard, the flower of his army, comprising the Ansars and the Mohadjirun, called "Al-Khadra," the green guards. When Abu Sufyan saw these warriors entirely covered in sombre armour, from which the sun caused blinding sparks to fly, he started in affright: 'By Allah! O Abbas, who are those men?'—'The Prophet with his companions, the Ansars and the Homadjirun.'—'None can make a stand against such troops! Verily, O Abbas, this morning, thy brother's son is resplendent with the majesty of a glorious king!'—'His majesty is not that of a king, O Abu Sufyan! 'tis that of a Prophet. And now that thine eyes convince thee that all resistance would be rank folly, hasten back to thy people and let thy good advice save them from misfortune!' Without losing a minute, Abu Sufyan went on his way to the town, where immediately on arriving, he was surrounded by anxious crowds overwhelming him with questions. 'O Assembly of the Quraish!' he cried, 'Mohammad is upon us with such an army that ye cannot hope to resist him for a single instant!'

His wife, Hind, furious at the emotion caused by these tidings, caught him by his moustache to make him hold his tongue and she bawled: 'Hearken not to the old fool and traitor! Kill him!' Tearing himself out of the shrew's clutches, Abu Sufyan went on: 'Woe unto you, if ye let yourselves be led astray by this woman! Again I say to you, ye are lost without fail if ye dream of resistance.' He then added proudly: 'All those who take refuge in the dwelling of Abu Sufyan will be in safety.'—'May Allah cause thee to perish!' was the reply made to him on all sides. 'How can thy house afford security for all of us?'

It was then that he concluded to announce that which he had intentionally omitted out of pure vanity: 'Likewise will be in safety all those taking refuge in the Temple; and eke those who, laying down their arms, remain behind closed doors in their dwellings.'

ENTRY OF THE PROPHET INTO MAKKAH

The Prophet (Peace be on him) stopped his she-camel at Dhu Tawad. At the sight of Makkah, where he hoped to make his entry victoriously without shedding the blood of his fellow-countrymen, he offered up thanksgiving to the Most Generous, bowing down deeply until his beard swept the pummel of his saddle. He then placed his troops for the occupation of the city: Zubayr was to go in by the Kuda

"There is amongst the trees one which is as blessed as the Muslim — the Palm", (Words of the Prophet).

E. DINET.

road; Khalid ibn Walid, by the outlying western districts; Sa'd ibn Ubayda, by the pass of Al-Kada. But as the latter chieftain, in his ardour, let drop this remark: 'To-day is a day of carnage, allowable even in the holy precincts!' Mohammad bade Ali deprive the rash speaker of his command and took charge of the standard in his place.

Zubayr, Ali, and Ubayda met with no resistance and , without striking a blow, occupied the parts of the city assigned to them. As for Khalid, just as he passed through the suburbs, a volley of arrows disturbed his troops and several of his men were killed. The darts came from marksmen in ambush, posted by Safwan ibn Umayya and Ikrimah, behind the rocks of the Jabal Al-Khandama. Without the least hesitation, Khalid called on his soldiers to storm the position. He routed the enemy, massacred many and pursued the survivors, putting them to the sword. Some fled to the Temple; others ran towards the sea.

From the summit of Al-Hajun, which the Prophet (Peace be on him) had just reached, he saw the sparkle of spearheads and swords. 'What's this!' he cried. 'Did I not forbid all fighting?' He despatched an Ansar to Khalid and when he came into the presence of Mohammad, he upbraided him severely for having given battle against his strict orders.

'The enemy were the aggressors. They riddled us with their arrows,' replied Khalid. 'I held back as much as I could, but was obliged to unsheath my sword to defend ourselves . . . And Allah granted us the victory!'—'The Will of Allah be done!' concluded the Prophet (Peace be on him) getting ready to make his own entry into the town.

He rode Qaswa, his favourite she-camel. Behind him, on the same animal, was Usama, the son of Zayd ibn Al-Haris. Mohammad prostrated himself on his saddle and recited the surah of Victory: *"Verily, We have won for thee an undoubted victory In token that Allah forgiveth thy earlier and later faults, and fulfilleth his goodness to thee, and guideth thee on the right way And that Allah succoureth thee with a mighty succour."* (the Qur'an, xlviii, 1, 2, 3.)

Round the red-striped drapery that covered his head, the Prophet (Peace be on him) rolled a black turban, letting one end hang down between his shoulders. He rode to the Ka'bah to perform the "tawaf", and without leaving the saddle, salute the Black Stone by touching it with the end of a hooked stick. He then alighted to enter the sanctuary, but seeing the idols that dishonoured it, he started back in horror. In front of an image of Abraham holding divine arrows, he cried out: 'May Allah annihilate all those who represent our ancestor Abraham trying to peer into futurity by means of arrows!' Mohammad ordered the impious statue to be destroyed. With his own hands he shattered a dove carved in wood and went to proclaiming: 'Allah is Great!'

He then went up to the three hundred and sixty idols ranged round the Temple. Beginning with the biggest: Hubal, he pierced its eyes with the hooked stick, saying: 'Truth hath come, error hath vanished; error is perishable!' The idol fell face downwards, shattered in a thousand pieces.

One after the other suffered the same fate, as he passed in front of them. A single effigy remained standing—the idol of the Khuza'a—fashioned out of bronze and enamel. It stood superbly erect on the Temple's terrace-roof. 'Kneel down,' was the order given by the Prophet (Peace be on him) to Ali. Mohammad mounted on his shoulders. 'Rise!' Ali was unable to do so, despite all his bodily strength. He felt himself crushed by supernatural weight; that the Prophecy. Seeing this, the Prophet got down, knelt in his turn and said to Ali: 'Climb up on my back to destroy that idolt!' Ali, overcome by confusion, but finally obeyed, as Mohammad persisted.

Quoth Ali: 'I stood upon the Prophet's shoulders; he drew himself up erect and I felt myself lifted by some unknown force by which I could have risen to heaven had I tried.'

The idol was fixed by iron clamps, but at the words of the Prophet: (Peace be on him) 'Truth hath come; error hath vanished,' it tottered without the least effort on my part and falling to the ground, crumbled away in dust."

The people, recovered from affright, stole gradually forth from their dwellings and dumb with stupor, looked on while their impotent idols were being destroyed. When the last vestige of idolatry had disappeared, the Prophet, (Peace be on him) turning towards the Ka'bah, proclaimed: 'There is no God but Allah! He hath no associates! He hath kept his word and succoured His Servant and dispersed His enemies!' Mohammad turned to the Makkans: 'O Assembly of the Quraish! how shall I treat you, do ye think?'—'With generosity, O generous brother, son of a generous man!' they replied, devoured by anxiety.—'Begone!' he told them. 'Ye are free!' (According to the laws of war, they were slaves and captives).

The only exceptions to this magnanimous amnesty were made in the cases of eleven men and six women whose conduct had been inexcusable. He ordered them to be put to death, wherever found. The sentence was immediately carried out, and a few of the condemned were executed including Huwarith, who brutally ill-treated Fatimah, the Prophet's (Peace be on him) daughter and Ali's wife, when she went away from Makkah.

In order to establish the new state of affairs firmly, Mohammad proceeded to appoint immediately the two most important functions of Makkah: the custodian of the Ka'bah and that of the Zamzam well.

He sent to claim the keys of the Temple from Uthman ibn Talha who, after having in a fit of fury locked the gates, took the keys away from him to his house. The Prophet (Peace be on him) had them torn from him forcibly, and intended to confide them to his uncle Abbas whom he maintained at his post as Superintendent of the Zamzam well. But a Revelation made the Prophet (Peace be on him) alter his mind and he was ordered to reinstate the former custodian of the Temple. Mohammad, therefore, charged Ali to take the key back to Uthman and say to him: 'O son of Talha, take the keys once more and with them the appointment as custodian of the Ka'bah.'

This official, touched by such generosity, so little deserved, hastened to give the Prophet (Peace be on him) the promise of sincere gratitude and absolute fidelity.

Just then a touching group approached: there was Abu Quhafa, an old blind man, bent beneath the burden of his eighty-seven years, and leaning on the arm of his son Abu Bakr. 'Why didst thou not let this noble old man remain in his dwelling, whither I could have gone to see him?' said the Prophet to Abu Bakr.—'It is only right that he cometh to thee, and not that thou shouldst go to him,' replied Abu Bakr.

Mohammad made the venerable, sightless man sit by his side, paying him great attention, stroking his beard affectionately, and was overjoyed to hear that Abu Quhafa had come to announce his conversion to the faith of Islam.

THE PROPHET AT SAFA

Next day, all the inhabitants of Makkah wended their way towards the hill of Safa where the Prophet (Peace be on him) had called them to receive their submission.

Tranquillized already by the generosity of the first utterances and acts of their conqueror, they did not seem to be affected by the feelings of sadness, shame and dejectedness that usually overcome the vanquished. Was not their conqueror one of their own people? Would not this glory become their glory; his triumph, their triumph; and his empire, their empire? As a matter of fact, despite their hostility towards him, most of them had suffered cruelly at being separated from their genial fellow-countryman;

the man who, in the heyday of his youth, had been called by them: "Al-Amin," the Reliable. They were greatly moved as they called to mind the mysterious charm of his personality and the irresistible allurement of his speech.

For some time past, in secret, they had feverishly longed to join the enthusiastic religious movement that Mohammad stirred up throughout the whole of Arabia, and become converted in their turn. How derisive their idols now seemed; the miserable fragments of the graven images swelling the garbage heaps swept out of the city! Even those men who exploited the superstition surrounding the false gods of wood or stone, were the first to arrive at Safa, being in a hurry to get the fact forgotten that they had been the priests of such a coarse cult. Despite the levelling humility which Mohammad required of all his disciples, those who had waxed fat on the proceeds of commercial idolatry were inwardly proud of the family ties binding them to the Prophet (Peace be on him) upon whom, of old, they had showered the vilest insults.

As for Mohammad, it is impossible to describe the sublime emotion that seized upon his great soul when he saw flocking to him from all parts, their eyes at least open to the Light, all those among his fellow-countrymen who had so stubbornly fought against him and whom he cherished, not withstanding their injustice. Seated beneath the Prophet, (Peace be on him) Umar, as his deputy, received the submission of Makkans who all came, one after the other, to strike his palm, and in the name of Mohammad, he pledged his word to protect them. When this grand ceremony was finished, a most poignant scene was enacted on the slopes of the hill.

An odious barrier, formed by the idols, which for nigh upon twenty years separated the Quraish Mohadjirun from the Quraish dwelling in Makkah, was broken down, never to be set up again, and all the enemy brethren threw themselves in each other's arms, reconciled and reunited in "the Path of Allah."

A third group of brothers rejoined them soon. They were the Ansar citizens of Al-Madinah, the rival town of Makkah; and the two cities, now having become two sisters, called themselves by the glorious name of "Al-Haramani, the two Sacred Cities."

One incident, however, cast a gloom over this unforgettable manifestation that realised so perfectly the dream which had haunted the Prophet (Peace be on him) filling him with superhuman perseverance. The Khuza's, falling across one of the murderers of their brethren, cut his throat. Mohammad caused the guilty parties to be brought before him and after blaming them severely, he added: 'I will compensate your victim's relatives myself, but cease in all reprisals. Too much blood hath been shed already. On the day when He created the Heavens and the Earth, Allah declared the territory of Makkah to be holy; its sacred character hath remained for all before me and shall remain for all after me. Not only shall the lives of human beings be sacred here, but it is likewise forbidden to hunt game, fell trees and cut grass.'—'In this prohibition, O Prophet! the Idhkhir must be excepted,' remarked Abbas. 'It furnisheth us with what which we cannot do without, to wit, fuel for the forge and the cooking of food.' After a moment's silence, the Prophet (Peace be on him) concluded: 'With the exception of the Idhkhir, which it will be allowable to uproot.' Following this declaration, all those condemned to death, and who had not been executed the first day, were granted a free pardon.

Among the crowd of Makkan women who came to declare their devotion, Mohammad's attention was drawn to a female hiding herself behind her companions. Despite the fact that she was disguised, he recognised the ferocious Hind, the wife of Abu Sufyan. 'Aye 'tis I!' she cried, throwing off her veil, 'I am Hind, and I implore pardon for the past!'

The Prophet (Peace be on him) in spite of the odious mutilation of the body of his uncle Hamzah, forgave her. Hind, when she returned to her dwelling lavished insults on her private family idol: 'O impotent idol! How mad we all were to rely on thy succour!' and she smashed it to pieces.

The son of Abu Jahal, Ikrimah, who had organised the ambush that nearly entrapped Khalid, fled to the sea coast. The fugitive's pardon was granted to Umm Kakim, his wife, who rejoined him when he was on the point of embarking. She brought him back, and the Prophet (Peace be on him) fearful lest his companions, remembering how he had been so often outraged by Abu Jahal, Ikrimah's father, might seek to be avenged on Ikrimah personally, declared: "Ikrimah hath come to Islam. Let no one insult his father's memory! To insult the dead is to wound the living!' And Ikrimah, deeply moved by such rare tolerance, became on of the most ardent defenders of the Religion.

Al-Uhayha, the slayer of Hamzah, was pardoned likewise, after becoming a convert to Islam. Habbar who, by a blow of the shaft of his spear, had brought about the death of Zainab, Mohammad's daughter, had fled, fearing deserved punishment; and then, confiding in the infinite clemency of the Prophet (Peace be on him) came and gave himself up, after having embraced the Islam faith in all sincerity. 'Go thy way in peace', said Allah's Apostle. 'Thy conversion doth wipe out the past; but never let me see thee more!'

Safwan, the second instigator of the ambush in which Khalid was to have fallen, profited also by the victor's magnanimity; and as he begged for a delay of two months' reflection before abjuring idolatry, the Prophet replied: 'I grant thee four months.'

Ibn Abi Sarh was the only man who had great trouble in softening the just wrath that his defection had kindled in Mohammad's heart. Ibn Abi Sarh was well versed in the arts of calligraphy and horsemanship. Formerly in the Prophet's (Peace be on him) employ as a secretary, he had shamelessly changed words and altered the sense of the Revelations whilst copying them out, in order to make a mockery of the Word of Allah. When his crime was discovered, he fled to Makkah and reverted to idol-worship. When the town was taken, he took refuge under the roof of Usman ibn Affan, his foster-brother. After having kept the faithless scribe in hiding for some time, Usman made up his mind to take him to the Prophet (Peace be on him) and beg for mercy, but in vain. At each supplication he averted his head. Finally, giving way to fresh and pressing entreaties, Mohammad consented to grant a free pardon, but when the guilty wretch was gone, the Prophet (Peace be on him) said to his companions: 'If I kept silence just now, it was but to give one of you time to kill him.'—'We were only waiting for one glance of thine eyes to put him to death.'—'A sign by a look of the eye is a treacherous act,' he replied, 'ill befitting one of Allah's Messengers.'

From the foregoing examples, it can be seen how carefully the Prophet (Peace be on him) tried to win over his fellow-countrymen by gentleness, but nevertheless never deviating from inexorable firmness when anything concerning idolatry was in question. His mercy led to results which could never have been obtained by sanguinary repression.

He conquered all hearts. With the exception of the Hawazin and the Saquifs, all the neighbouring tribes came in at once and made their submission. From that day onwards, no one could earn the title of Mahadjer by emigration, because Islam was as firmly established in Makkah as in Al-Madinah.

GHAZWAH OR EXPEDITION OF HUMAIN

(6th day of Shawwal Year VIII of the Hegira, 28th of Jan. A.D. 630)

Relying on the solidity of the ramparts surrounding their town of Taif; hoping to be able to take refuge there in case of defeat, the Hawazin and the Saquifs had refused to bow down to the Prophet (Peace be on him). They even got ready to fight him and, under the leadership of two celebrated warriors, Malik ibn Awf and Durayd ibnu's-Simma, they mustered in the valley of Awtas.

Mohammad, being told about their plans, sent Ibn Abi Hadrad as scout. When he came back with positive information, the Prophet (Peace be on him) resolved to set out and face his foes.

His ten thousand soldiers were joined by more than two thousand Makkans, lately converted, and impatient to prove their devotion and fervour. The effect produced by the army of the Believers was so imposing that a voice in the group of Banu Bakr, it is said, cried out: 'Truly we need not fear defeat with such a big army!'

This exclamation of pride displeased the Prophet (Peace be on him) greatly, for vanity weakens endeavour and caused forgetfulness of the fact that victory is granted by Allah. Mohammad blamed the boastful cry in the most severe terms.

On the bank of a "wadi," the troops saw a big green tree, growing by itself, which the idolaters worshipped and looked upon with superstitious awe. Beneath its shade, they sacrificed victims and, on its branches, they hung their weapons, imagining they would become invincible by this verdant contact. Several soldiers, their mind not yet sufficiently purified from the strain of fetish observances, longed to possess likewise a tree. "Dhat Anwat,"—"Carrier of Weapons"—and sent in a demand to the Apostle which made him very indignant.

'Your demand,' he replied, 'is just as abominable as that of the Banu-Isra'il, when saved by a miracle from Pharaoh's hosts and waves of the sea, they asked Moses for an idol in a human shape. Ye are a stupid "qawm" accustomed to adopt without reflecting the vilest customs of your neighbours!'

Quoth Jabir ibn Abdullah: "Shortly before daybreak, we reached the "wadi" of Hunain, at the entrance of an extremely narrow and deep defile. All of a sudden while we were still in the black shadows of the lofty crags, the first rays of the sun, on the other side of the pass, lit up a sight that made our hearts leap impatiently.

"Under the careless guard of a few sentinels, our enemies' tents were pitched in the plain. Between them, women and children passed to and fro. Round the encampment, countless flocks of sheep and herds of camels were about to depart to pasture-land. Without waiting for the Prophet's (Peace be on him) orders, overwrought by the hope of plunder, we rushed into the pass, so narrow that we were pressed together, shoulder to shoulder. No sooner was the entire army in the defile, when a lengthy, whistling murmur was heard in the air and, like great swarms of locusts, clouds of arrows darkened the sky. The darts were showered on us, aimed from two ridges overlooking the pass. We had fallen into an ambush organised by cunning Durayd.

In consequence of the sting of the arrows from which there was no escape, for not one was lost in the soil, all finding a target as they pierced with a hissing noise of flesh of men, horses and camels, mad terror overcame us. Indescribable panic was also caused by our foes, lying in wait, concealed at the egress of the pass and who, with savage shouts, charged into our ranks. Tugging at the bridles of our camels, we turned round, the poor beasts groaning gloomily and shaking their long necks bristling with arrows. In the intextricable confusion of their stampede and fight, they tripped each other up and rolled over on the ground with their riders, who were at once trampled on by fleeing comrades.

Whilst the archers continued to distress us with their darts, we discovered that the entry into the pass was barricaded by another detachment of our enemies who had allowed us to ride through and now awaited our return. At their head was a soldier of the Hawazin, bestriding a gigantic red camel and he was signalling with a spear to which he had fixed a black flag. When a Believer passed within reach, he lowered his lance to run him through, and perchance he missed, he signalled with his flag lifted again to those following him, and they pursued the Mussulman and put him to death."

The defeat seemed irretrievable. Already many of the Prophet's (Peace be on him) old enemies, their hearts still brimming with rancour, began to gloat over the critical situation of the Mussulmans. 'Their flight will not cease until they reach the sea coast!' cried the Abu Sufyan, who busied himself with consulting his divining arrows which he carried concealed in his quiver. 'Mohammad's sorcery is powerless in this day!' exclaimed Kalada ibn Hanbal in his turn. But his brother Safwan, although not yet converted, silenced him with these words: 'May a gag close thy mouth!'

In the midst of the general confusion, the Prophet (Peace be on him) alone was cool and collected. He posted himself on a low hill, to the right of the valley. 'I am the Prophet of Allah and no impostor!' he declared, and urging his mule forward, went to throw himself in the thick of the fight. Abu Bakr rushed in front of the animal and, seizing the bridle, held it back. To try and rally his troops, Mohammad ordered Abbas to shout: 'O Ansars and Mohadjirun, my companions! O ye who took their oath there!' (at Al-Hudaibiyah). When, from the top of a rock, his stentorian voice carried the Prophet's (Peace be on him) cry to the fugitives, they were covered with great confusion. Regaining their self-control, they replied: 'We are here at thy service!'

But what was to be done to stem such a torrent of fleeing men and beasts, crowded together between the two vertical sides of the ravine? The Faithful did their best to lash the camels, twisting their necks by pulling the bridle contrariwise. With great strides, the frightened animals kept on in their flight. It was then that the warriors of Allah slung their shields round their necks and jumped out of the saddle, leaving their camels to go on alone. Unsheathing their swords, the soldiers turned back to begin fighting again.

The Prophet, (Peace be on him) standing up in his stirrups, saw with joy that the situation was changed, and when his gaze fell upon the countless warriors rushing into the brazier of the battle, he cried out: 'The furnace is alight!' Ali, accompanied by an Ansar, resolved to put a stop to the exploits of the Bedouin of the Hazawin, proudly waving his spear adorned with the black flag. With one blow of his scimitar, Ali hamstrung the camel, and at the same moment, the Ansar brought down the Infidel by slicing his leg from the knee to the heel, putting an end to his misery as soon as he was flattened out on the ground.

Mad terror seized the idolaters when thinking they had crushed the Mussulmans, they resumed the offensive. It was now the Infidel's turn to give way. Mohammad ordered his mule to lie down. The animal bent its knees until its belly rested on the ground. Then taking up a handful of dust, The Prophet (Peace be on him) as he had done at Badr, threw it towards his enemies whose flight became a mad rout. It seemed as if they had been blinded by this dust and that their soldiers were dispersed exactly the same as these impalpable atoms.

"Now hath Allah helped you in many battle-fields, and, on the day of Hunain, when ye prided yourself on your numbers; but it availed you nothing; and the earth, with all its breadth, became too strait for you: then turned ye your backs in flight. Then did Allah send down a spirit of tranquillity upon His Apostle, and upon the Faithful; and He sent down hosts with ye saw not and punished Infidels." (the Qur'an, ix, 25, 26)

Harried by the sword during their retreat, Malik and the remains of his army managed to find safety in the fortified down of Taif.

Less lucky, Durayd, the Infidel's second leader, was unable to escape his fate. Ninety years of age and blind, he was unable to direct his camel when abandoned by his panic-stricken fellow-countrymen, and he fell into the hands of a mere lad, Rabi'a ibn Rafia. When he saw the litter in which reclined this celebrated warrior, paralysed by the infirmities of great age, the youth thought he had captured a woman. He made the camel kneel, parted the hangings and was petrified at only finding an old man.

General view of Mecca, the Most Holy, taken from the top of the Djebel Abi Koubeis.

Vexed and disappointed he dealt Durayd a sabre-cut, but the aged fighter did not even seem to know that he had been struck. 'What sort of weapon hath thy mother placed in thy hands, O little vagabond?' he asked in accents of supreme scorn. 'Take my sabre, hanging from my camel's saddle. Lift the blade aloft and hit between the vertebrae of the back and those of the head. That was how I used to strike men down.'

Abashed at his first failure, Rabi'a followed this piece of advice and the famous warrior rolled dead in the dust.

Urged on by the spur of victory, the Prophet (Peace be on him) pursued the fugitives to the foot of the ramparts of Taif and tried to take the town. After a useless siege of twenty days, he preferred to give up all ideas of an attack in favour of other means, slower, but more sure, and instead of invoking the wrath of the Divinity against the inhabitants, he said: 'O Allah! enlighten the people of Taif and inspire them with a desire to come to Thy Apostle of their own free will!'

Despite the disappointment of his troops, he retook the road to Makkah, camping at Al-Ji'rana where all the prisoners were collected, as well as all the booty to be divided.

When the Prophet (Peace be on him) arrived, a female captive, Ash-Shayma, of the Banu Sad, which was a fraction of the Hawazin, was struggling to escape from the brutality of the soldiery. On perceiving Mohammad, she cried out: 'O Prophet of Allah, I am thy foster-sister!'—'Prove it!'—'See the scar on my shoulder where thou didst bite me when I carried thee, a baby boy on my back.'

The Prophet (Peace be on him) recognized the cicatrice. Much moved, he shed tears, spread his mantle on the ground, and asked Ash-Shayma to sit down on it. 'According to thy wish,' he said, 'thou wilt find generous friendship by my side; or thou canst return to thy tribe with all the gifts I'll lavish on thee.'—'Send me back to my people in the desert, O Prophet! Such is my sole desire'. Mohammad set her free, after having loaded her with presents.

A deputation of the Hawazin was presented to the Prophet, (Peace be on him) and Abu Sorada, an old man belonging to the division of the Banu Sa's, spoke in their name: 'O Prophet! among thy prisoners are thine aunts, sisters of the wet-nurses who suckled thee. As for thy male captives, they were the companions of thy childhood—almost of thy race! In the great misfortune which crusheth us, we implore thee in the name of Allah! If, for the same reasons, we were forced to implore Al-Harith ibn Abi Chammar, or Nu'man ibnu'l Mundhir, they would surely take pity on us! Now thou art the best of nurslings!'—'Which do ye prefer, your families or your property?' asked Mohammad, scarcely able to hide his tender feelings.—'O Prophet (Peace be on him) give our wives and children back to us. We love them quite otherwise to our property.'—'I restore to you all male and female capitives belonging to the Banui Muttalib,' declared Mohammad loudly.—'But those who are ours belong to the Apostle of Allah!' cried the Mohadjirun and the Ansars immediately. Thus all the prisoners, numbering about six thousand, were given up to the delegates of the Hawazin.

The family of Malik ibn Awf formed an exception to this ruling. Mohammad however, charged those he had just liberated to make him the following proposal: 'If Malik cometh to me and becometh a convert to Islam, I will give him back his property. Nay, more—I will make him a present of a hundred camels'.

Malik accepted. He left Taif secretly, and when converted, gave such tokens of sincerity that the Prophet (Peace be on him) appointed him as commander over all the Mussulmans of the country. It was the best way to curb the resistance of the inhabitants of Taif.

And so it turned out indeed, for this able leader, proud of the investiture, at the head of the troops stirred by faith, continue to war against the Saquifs. By pitilessly raiding their flocks and caravans, blocking them by hunger behind the ramparts of their city, he soon compelled them to come in their turn and implore the Prophet's (Peace be on him) mercy, when they were converted to Islam. The booty was considerable, consisting of about twenty-four thousand camels and forty thousand sheep. After the emotions of the affair of the prisoners, Mohammad resolved to postpone the division of the plunder until another day, and he mounted his she-camel. But his soldiers were so impatient to share the spoils that they followed and importuned him. By accident, they pushed his animal against a thorny shrub, and its branches tore the mantle of Allah's Chosen One. 'Now, you men, give me back my mantle!' he told them, and yielding to their entreaties he returned to see the booty shared among them.

He tried, above all, to ingratiate himself definitively with the nobles of the city, by favouring them in all ways; and afterwards, they were called "Al-mu'allafa qulubuhum," "those whose hearts have been won over." Abu Sufyan and Mu'awiya his son; Hakim ibn Hizam, An-Nadr ibn Al-Harith, Suhayl, Ikrimah Uyayna, AlAjra, and Safwan, all received fifty camels each. This difference of treatment gave rise to protestations. Ibn Mirda manifested his dissatisfaction in a piece of poetry: 'My share of the booty and that Al-Ubayd have been distributed to Oyama and Al-Ajra. And yet their fathers, Al-Hasan and Al-Habis, never took precedence over my father in any assembly whatsoever!'.

The Prophet (Peace be on him) sent for him and asked: 'Hast thou composed these rhymes: "My share of the booty and that of Al-Bayd have been distributed to Al-Ajra and Oyama?", changing the order of the last two names mentioned, without noticing he had thus broken the metre. In the Qur'an, Allah says: *"We have not taught him (Mohammad) poetry."* (xxxvi, 59.)

Abu Bakr pointed this out to him. 'No matter,' he replied. 'The meaning remaineth the same.' And he gave orders to "cut the poet's tongue" by granting him all he claimed.

An Arab of the Tamim tribe, 'Dhu'l Khuwaysira, dared to say to Allah's Messenger: 'Thou wert unjust in thy division.' Umar started up. 'I'll cut the throat of that insolent churl!' he shouted.—'Nay! let him go his own road,' was Mohammad's simple reply.

The Prophet (Peace be on him) was obliged to resort to most skilful political measures in order to spare all kinds of feelings during the division of these riches; and to prevent dangerous jealousy arising among his disciples. All the spoils, nevertheless, were nearly all allotted and he seemed to have forgotten his devoted Ansars who, naturally, expected to rank among the first to be rewarded. With ever-increasing surprise, they saw no share offered to them and the rich bounty flowing into the hands of the Quraish and the Bedouins.

At last there was no more left to give away and the Ansars exchanged bitter remarks: 'By Allah, the Prophet (Peace be on him) thinketh only of his own people. Now that, thanks to us, he hath returned victorious to his birthplace, we are fogotten and neglected.'

Sa'd ibn Ubada, having heard these complaints went and told Mohammad, who said: 'Good! call all the Ansars together!'

When they were mustered, the Prophet (Peace be on him) came before them. 'O Assembly of the Ansars!' he said, 'I have been told about your talk and the sadness of your souls. Did I not seek you out when ye had been led astray? Hath not Allah led you into the right path? Ye were unfortunate: hath not Allah made you happy? Each man was his brother's enemy: hath not Allah reconciled your hearts?'—'Truly!' they answered unanimously. 'Allah and His Apostle are the most compassionate and generous!'—'And on your part,' he added, 'did ye not welcome me with compassion and generosity when I was a homeless wanderer? Have ye not the right to say to me: 'Thou wert branded as an imposter and we put faith in thee: thou wert cast down and we helped thee to be victorious: thou wert poverty stricken and we made thee rich:"—'Nay, nay!' protested every man of the Assembly. 'We are indebted to thee for everything and thou dost owe us nothing!'—'In that case,' he went on, 'O Ansar comrades! how could you let the least feeling of affection arise in your hearts concerning the fleeting riches of the world, with which I have endowed certain persons in order to strengthen their vacillating faith, whilst I knew that you were unshaken. Know ye not that these people will return to their homesteads with camels and sheep only, whilst ye will take the Prophet (Peace be on him) of Allah back with you and your dwellings?. . . But Him who holdeth Mohammad's soul in the Hands, I swear that if the Arab tribes retired into one valley and the Ansars into another, I would follow into the valley of the Ansars. For me, the Ansars are as shirt on the skin; and for me, the other tribes are as the mantle outside everything. O Allah, show mercy to the Ansars; to the sons of Ansars; and the children of their children!'

These words which the Prophet (Peace be on him) was unable to utter without betraying intense emotion, mollified the entire Assembly. Tears of gratitude flowed from the eyes of the Ansars so abundantly that their beards were wetted. All cried out, sobs causing them to falter: 'Aye, verily, we accept our share of the booty, for the most beautiful portion is ours!'

لَقَدْ نَصَرَكُمُ ٱللَّهُ فِى مَوَاطِنَ كَثِيرَةٍ وَيَوْمَ حُنَيْنٍ
إِذْ أَعْجَبَتْكُمْ كَثْرَتُكُمْ فَلَمْ تُغْنِ عَنكُمْ شَيْـًٔا

Tombs of the Caliphs under whose reign the Muslim Civilisation illuminated the world.

CHAPTER EIGHT — Decorative plate.

وَأَتِمُّوا الْحَجَّ وَالْعُمْرَةَ لِلَّهِ

CHAPTER THE EIGHTH

AYSHAH SLANDERED

Quoth Ayishah: "During my return from the Mustaliq expedition, pressing need compelled me to alight from my hawdaj, (a kind of litter carried on a camel's back). I found a lonely spot and stopped behind, waiting until all the soldiers had marched past. But seeing my camel had halted, and thinking I was inside the hawdaj, they drove the animal forward to ensure it remaining in line with the rest."

"When I came back and found my camel gone, I shouted despairingly; but all in vain, until, overcome with fatigue, I dropped down and fell asleep. One of the rearguards, Safwan Ibnu'l-Mu'attal, catching sight of me, recognised me and cried out: 'To Allah we belong and to Him shall we return!' Having awakened me by this exclamation, he brought up his camel, helping me into the saddle, and he led the animal by the bridle until we rejoined the Prophet." (Peace be on him).

Scandalmongers got hold of the story and ascribed shameful motives to this chance meeting. Despite the accused woman's protestations of innocence, Mohammad felt suspicion gnawing at his heart, and he kept Ayishah at a distance, greatly to the confusion of his father-in-law, Abu Bakr.

At last a Revelation called the accusers liars, and condemned calumny: "*With Allah it was a grave matter*'" (The Qur'an,XXIV,14), thus ridding the Prophet (Peace be on him) of all suspicion and putting an end to a painful situation.

THE BIRTH AND DEATH OF IBRAHIM

In the year VIII of the Hegira, Mary, the Coptic concubine, gave birth to a boy. The Prophet (Peace be on him) who had never found consolation for the death of his sons brought into the world by Khadijah, was beside himself with joy. He gave a slave as a present to Abu Rafi'a, for having brought the news that a son was born, and Mohammad declared that the child's advent freed the mother.

On the seventh day, the baby's hair was shaved off and buried; two sheep were sacrificed and alms were distributed to the poor. All the wet-nurses vied with each other for the honour of suckling the Prophet's (Peace be on him) son, who was called Ibrahim. he was given into the care of Umm Burda, wife of Al-Bara ibn Aws, and she was rewarded by the gift of a palm-garden.

She took her nursling into the country, to the Banu Mazin, where the Prophet (Peace be on him) went frequently to see his son. He used to take him in his arms, unceasingly "smelling him" and covering him with kisses. The affection he felt for the child's mother, Mary the Copt, also increased, much to the great vexation of his other wives.

It happened, too, that he broke his strictly impartial household laws, and granted Mary a night that rightly belonged to Hafsa, Umar's daughter. She was grieved to the heart by her rights being forgotten and reproached Mohammad so bitterly that he promised to cease all intercourse with his freed slave on condition that Hafsa held her tongue. But haughty Hafsa broke her word. She told her grievances to Ayishah, who was likewise furiously exasperated at the favour shown to Mary. It was now the turn of Hafsa to rouse the indignation of the other joint wives.

Scenes, scandal and shrieks caused life to be unbearable; so, renouncing all consideration and refusing to let his spouses dictate to him, the Prophet (Peace be on him) put Hafsa away, after having blamed her severely for her indiscretion. For a whole month, he refused to have anything to do with his helpmates who, although there was now no cause for jealousy, still continued their quarrels; each woman accusing the other of being the cause of their common husband's neglect. All his wives swore that in future they would not pester him with their scolding.

But Mohammad kept his oath strictly. He sought seclusion in a room to which access could only be had by a staircase of palm-tree trunks, and where his sole couch consisted of a mat, of which the rough fibre made dents in his flesh. His meals were brought to him by a black guardian who stood—an inexorable sentinel—in front of the door, which remained closed even to the most beloved among the Prophet's (Peace be on him) companions. At last, on the twenty-ninth day, mindful of the grief felt by Umar and Abu Bakr at the humiliation experienced by their daughters, Hafsa and Ayishah, Mohammad took them both back, and all his other wives as well, after he had recited the following verses: *"If ye assist one another against the Prophet (Peace be on him) then verily, Allah is his Protector and Gabriel and every just man among the Faithful; and the angels are his helpers besides. Haply if he put you both away, his Lord will give him in exchange other wives better than you: Moslems, Believers, devout, penitent, worshippers, observant of fasting."* (the Qur'an, lxvi, 4, 5.)

The joy and hopes accompanying the birth of Ibrahim were not destined to last long. The child breathed its last sigh at the age of seventeen months, under his father's eyes, and Mohammad could not repress showers of tears.

Seeing the Prophet's (Peace be on him) grief and remembering that in cases of mourning he forbade all lamentations, rending of garments, or laceration of faces, Abdu'r-Rahman ibn Awf said to him: 'Thou also, O Messenger of Allah?'—'O Ibn Awf!' he replied. 'Tears arise from compassion. They are not prohibited, like shrieks and lamentations which are protestations inspired by the Evil One against the decrees of Providence.'

Then, as his tears flowed in still greater abundance, he added: 'The eyes shed tears; the heart is full of affliction, but we utter no exclamation displeasing to the Lord. True resignation is manifested at the first shock as, later, time bringeth succour. O Ibrahim, we are deeply saddened by being separated from thee; but we belong to Allah and to Him shall we return!'

Zaira, mother of the wet-nurse, washed the poor little dead body; Al-Fadl ibn al-Abbas and Usama ibn Zayd carried it to the cemetery of Al-Bagi and lowered it into the grave. When the earth covered the son on whom he had founded such great hopes, the Prophet (Peace be on him) prayed over the tiny tomb, and exclaimed: 'Declare, O my son! Allah is my Lord, His Messenger is my father, and Islam is my Religion!'

All who assisted at this scene were shaken by sobs. All of a sudden, their faces took on a livid tint, which, at the same time, spread over the earth, the sand, and the rocks. The azure of the sky changed to a leaden hue; the sunlight paled and gradually faded away, although no clouds gathered to veil it. An icy shudder, resembling that of fever, caused the whole face of nature to be stirred, and the birds, with cries of fright, took refuge in their nocturnal shelters. The last rays, still illuminating surrounding objects with dim and sinister light, began to die away and darkness came on in open day, whilst a few twinkling stars appeared in the sky.

The people in terror knew not which way to turn so as to escape the fearful cataclysm they anticipated. Many in the crowd, struck by the phenomenon coinciding with the death of Ibrahim, cried out: 'O Prophet! the eyes of the sun itself are dimmed by tears and it hath departed to take part in thy mourning!'

The Prophet (Peace be on him) struggling against his grief, drew himself up erect and proclaimed in firm accents: 'Nay, it is not so. The Sun and the Moon are two tokens of Allah's Almightiness. Like everything beautiful in this world, their beauty is liable to be eclipsed by His orders . . . But there is no eclipse for the death of any mortal!'

GHAZWAH, OR EXPEDITION OF TABUK

(Jumada, year VIII of the Hegira, August A.D. 630)

At the battle of Mutah, the Christian Greeks learnt to their cost what it meant to put the valour of Allah's warriors to the test; and in their hatred of Islam's steady growth, they busied themselves in mustering a most terrible army to crush it.

The Prophet (Peace be on him) heard of this. He resolved to be first in the field and attack. Only his unshaken confidence in divine protection could have inspired him with such temerity. How many thousands of soldiers must he gather together so as not to court irretrievable disaster? Now the moment was not in the least favourable: a long drought had withered crops and herbage; flocks were decimated; horrible famine plunged the whole region in desolation; and the torrid heat of the second half of summer destroyed all energy. The harvest of the savoury fruit of each oasis, watered by inexhaustible wells, alone promised to be abundant and invigorating; and it was precisely when the Faithful were about to profit by the only benefits of this lean year that the Apostle issued his marching orders.

Secret discontent invaded every heart and the incorrigible "Hypocrites" hastened to exploit it by hawking about everywhere perfidious remarks, such as these: 'Do you think this war against the Banu'l-Asfar (the descendants of fair-headed Ishaq) will be child's play, as was that against the swarthy sons of Ishmael? Remember that arriving exhausted by the intolerable heat of the season and the superhuman fatigue of the road, ye will have to face the Nazarene soldiers encased in armour!'

These arguments, which would have been logical if the struggle had not been in the cause of Allah, began to weaken the minds of those who were hesitating. As for those who were convinced, they could not get away from the unheard of difficulties bound to be met with in feeding the troops by reason of the dearth of provisions; and means of transport, in consequence of the scarcity of camels. Following the lack of pasturage, the majority of these animals that had not succumbed to hunger, were in a pitiful state of decline. All these circumstances were unfavourable; but no obstacle could stop the Chosen One.

As the "Hypocrites" met to conspire in the house of Suwaylim, a jew, the Prophet (Peace be on him) sent Talha ibn Ubaydu'llah to burn their den. They said, *"March not out in the heat." Say: A fiercer heat will be the fire of Hell! Little then let them laugh, and much let them weep as the meed of their doings"* (the Qur'an, IX 82. 83.)

Caring nothing for his own toil, the Prophet (Peace be on him) spared no pains to impress upon his disciples the grandeur of the goal. So as to arouse general interest, he treated each man differently according to the inward aspirations of his being. If in some he awakened the pure hope of celestial satisfaction, suitable to their souls loving ideality; in others, he did not discourage hopes of material gratification, such as booty and profane pleasures.

Al-Jadd ibn Qays was a man of intrigue. He said to the Prophet (Peace be on him) 'Thou knowest that in my "qawm" no man loveth woman better than I. Now, I fear I shall not be able to restrain myself at the sight of the charming lasses of the Banu'l-Asfar. In that case, wilt thou blame me?'

The Prophet (Peace be on him) avoided answering. Al-Jadd interpreted such silence as showing the Mohammad promised to shut his eyes. The debauchee could not repress a start of joy, despite the presence of his son, who made a gesture of disapproval,and his father threw his sandal in the lad's face.

Thanks to the indefatigable activity of their leader, it was not long before the Believers were carried away by enthusiasm. The difficulties to be overcome, the sacrifices to be made, instead of diminishing their optimism, only succeeded in feeding it, and those who the infirmity of poverty prevented from joining the ranks of the fighters, became so sad that they were nicknamed the "Bakka'un," or "Weepers." Nevertheless, they are excused by this Revelation: *"It is no crime in the weak, and in the sick, and in those who find not the means of contributing, to stay at home, provided that they are sincere with Allah and His Apostle. Nor in those who when they came to thee that thou shouldst mount them, and thou didst say, "I find not wherewith to mount you," and turned away their eyes, and shed floods of tears of grief, because they found no means to contribute towards the expense."* (the Qur'an, IX, 92, 93.)

Moved by their despair, the Prophet (Peace be on him) made an urgent appeal to the devotion of all Believers who, with admirable emulation, replied at once by bringing considerable sums. Abu Bakr placed the whole of his fortune at the disposition of the Prophet (Peace be on him). Usman ibn Affan furnished ten thousand warriors with provisions and weapons. All vied with each other in acts of generosity and women stripped themselves of their most precious jewellery.

The expeditionary force was soon organised and numbered between thirty to forty thousand men; a figure hitherto unknown in Arabia. The troops were assembled at the Sanniyat-ul-Wida pass. Seeing the exaltation of the Believers, the "Hypocrites" considered it prudent to conceal their sentiments, but they arranged to group themselves together in the rear and when the army had disappeared behind the "Farewell Pass", the shufflers dropped out, one after the other, and made their way back to Al-Madinah.

Their conduct was not surprising, but unfortunately their fatal advice had deterred four good Moslems from their duty: the poet Ka'b ibn Malik, Murara ibu'r-Rabi', Hilal ibn Umayya and Ubu Khaythama. The latter, suffocated by the extreme heat and also, perchance, by feelings of shame, went into his orchard, surrounded by protecting walls. It was there; under intertwining palms and vine-branches with leaves and grapes, which stretched like serpentine bind-weeds from one date-tree to another, that two shelters were erected, built of palm-tree trunks and foliage; so impervious to sunlight that the obscurity therein seemed to be the shades of night. To complete the resemblance, the mysterious darkness of each of these arbours was illuminated by a young woman's face, as brilliant as the moon in the fullness of its fourteenth night.

Kindly attentive as well as beautiful, these loving spouses had carefully watered the sandy soil, whence arose exquisite, moist odours. Ingeniously, too, they had hung up, in draughty corners, oozing goat-skins in which water got to be as cool as snow; and they had prepared delicate dishes of which the aroma sufficed to excite the most rebellious appetite . . .

Abu Khaythama, bathed in sweat, powdered all over with sand, experienced a sensation of Eden-like comfort, when he glanced at the delights in readiness and was about to revel in enjoyment by lazily stretching his limbs on soft rugs. But, suddenly, the emerald-tinted reflection of the shade that gently caressed his tired eyes, was furrowed by the flash of a vision:

CHAPTER THE EIGHTH

In a gloomy, wild, boundless pace, beneath the deep azure hue of a cloudless sky, under the unbearable sting of a pitiless sun, a long line of human beings dragged itself along with difficulty, coming into view and then being lost to sight amid yellowish waves formed by rocks or sandheaps . . . He recognised these mortals. They were brethren in Islam. At their head was . . . Allah's Chosen One!

'The Prophet (Peace be on him) leads an expedition, under yon blazing sky! And Abu Khaythama is at rest, in this fresh shade, with fresh water and two fresh beauties! No! that cannot be!' he cried; and turning to his wives, each of them hoping to gain the preference: 'By Allah! I go not into the shelter of any among you! I rejoin the Prophet! (Peace be on him) Prepare my provisions for the journey; and that quickly!'

They obeyed.Releasing his camel, busy just then in drawing water, he clapped on the saddle. Then he took down his sword, spear and shield from where they were hanging, and without a look behind, abandoned fresh shade, fresh water and fresh beauties, to hurry in the track of the army. He rejoined it at Tabuk.

Meanwhile, after having followed the windings of the Wadi'l-Qura, a broad valley where the verdant splashes of colour of more than one oasis, encircling many villages or strongholds, stood out in gay, bold relief on the dull hue of the arid landscape, the expedition had reached the fringe of the frightful desert surrounding Al-Hijr, or Mada'in Salih, the Thamud country. The sight of this inhospitable region oppressed the hearts of the Believers. With its Harra, or burning soil cracked and laid waste by celestial flames that marked it with a distinguishing funeral hue of aches and charcoal, it offered to their view the most startling image of a country cursed by the Almighty.

THE THAMUD COUNTRY

In the earliest ages, the idolatrous and debauched inhabitants of Thamud, proud of the prosperity of their seven towns and massive dwellings, hewn out of the solid rock, welcomed with derision the Prophet (Peace be on him) Salih, sent by Allah to lead them in the right path.

So as to show them that his mission was genuine, Salih implored the Most High to grant him the aid of a miracle. Thereupon, a rock split itself, with a roar which may be compared to that of ocean waves, and brought forth a wonder in the shape of a gigantic she-camel, wonderfully hairy and advanced ten months in pregnancy. She dropped a little foal, already weaned, and bearing an astonishing resemblance to its mother.

Miracles have nearly always been powerless to convert hardened sinners and the only result of this marvel was a recrudescence of perversity among the people of Thamud. To testify how little they valued such a portent, these impious wretches resolved to do away with the prodigy. With sharp blades, they studded the two steep sides of a narrow rocky pass, through which, each morning, the she-camel passed to graze in the plains. In the evening, returning with her little camel, she rushed through and tore her flanks most cruelly. The poor beast, quivering, uttered groans and, it is said, the echo thereof resounds even nowadays, from time to time. She dropped down and died at the egress of the defile that was called "Al-Huwayra,"—the camel-foal—remarkable by the reason of a rock that took on a faithful resemblance to the young animal.

Salih, after such sacrilege, realised how useless were his efforts, and called down the curse of Allah on the head of the Thamud people, upon whom punishment was quickly inflicted: "*And they hewed them out secure abodes in the mountains but they rebelled against their Lord's command: so the tempest took them as they watched its coming . . . So that they were not able to stand upright, and could not help themselves . . . We sent against them a single shout; and they became like the dry sticks of the fold-builders."* (the Qur'an XV, 82. LI, 44, 45. LIV. 31.)

Ever since the wrath of Heaven destroyed its inhabitants, the country of Thamud has been deserted. The abodes of this ungodly people alone were left and are still remaining. Under the brows of their frontals, the wide-open doors look like the pupils of fantastic eyes, dilated by the horror of the formidable mouths distorted by affright and calling out to those who dare set foot in this desolate domain: "Admire by our example, the vanity of mortals' pride and the emptiness of their undertakings. Who can describe the mighty efforts by which our masters carved us out of the heart of the mountain and adorned us with slender pillars and graceful sculpture? Sheltered in our bosom, stronger than iron, were they wrong to reckon that they were in perfect safety?

"How mad were they! In vain their contracted hands clung despairingly to the angles of our walls, the storm of divine wrath passed over them . . . and they disappeared for evermore. Even we tottered on our foundations like unto the limbs of a man devoured by fever whose teeth chatter noisily. If we were spared, it was only so that we might serve as a lesson to travellers straying into our mournful land."

When the army of the Believers penetrated into the midst of strangely-shaped stone blocks, emerging like reefs from a sea of sand, and showing in their smooth sides the dark openings that were the abodes of the people of Thamud, the Prophet (Peace be on him) covered his face with a corner of his mantle, so as to avoid looking at these vestiges of impiety. He closed his mouth and nostrils, not wishing to breathe the impure air emanating from the ruins, and urged on his camel to get away from them as quickly as possible.

Fearing lest irresistible curiosity might lead the soldiers of Islam astray, he exhorted them thus: 'If ye enter these dens of the ungoldy, do so only with tears in your eyes as ye recall their sad fate.' He knew that tears of this kind, welling up by reason of such terrible remembrances, would cause the attraction of curiosity to be dominated by the fear of the Almighty. Impressed, however, by the strangeness of these dwellings, seemingly those of superhuman beings or evil spirits; and by the deathly silence that reigned in these parts where formerly a powerful people lived a riotous life of pride and debauchery, the Faithful sought but to follow the example of their inspired guide and flee from the accursed ruins.

Besides, the soldiers were urged onwards by thirst; and when, in the midst of the sandy plains, the famous well of the Thamud people came in sight where the she-camel of the miracle used to drink, they broke their ranks in the greatest disorder, trying to outstrip each other, racing to be the first to slake their thirst. The Prophet (Peace be on him) who had been unable to restrain them, hurried along with his she-camel, caught them up, and gave his orders in accents of great severity: 'Beware of that water, tainted by impiety. Take care not to use it for drinking purposes; nor for your ablutions; nor for cooking your food! Let all who have drunk of it, vomit it forth! Those who have used it to cook their victuals must scatter those victuals on the ground without touching them!' To put an end to all temptation, he ordered the march to be resumed, without taking into account the fatigue or the thirst of his troops.

His face still veiled by the fold of his mantle, the Prophet, (Peace be on him) obeyed and followed blindly by his soldiers, among whom deception and suffering had not caused the slightest murmur, soon reached the entrance to the narrow, strange pass of the "Mabraku'n-Naqa."

Skirted on each side by crags from one hundred and fifty to two hundred cubits high, the dark defile produced the most sinister impression. The Faithful felt their breasts shrinking as if crushed between the dizzy, dominating walls. What they most feared was to hear the resounding echoes of the miraculous, disembowelled she-camel. In that case, no power on earth could have mastered the mad terror that must have overwhelmed the animals ridden by the soldiers. By dint of wild leaps and bounds, the camels would have thrown off their loads of arms and food, and ridding themselves of their drivers, taken to flight; when, after throwing down and trampling all those who might have tried to stop them, the men must have been abandoned on foot in the midst of the most frightful of all deserts.

The slightest noises, amplified by the sonorous echoes of the rocky heights, made the Believers start and shudder. They went on in the most profound silence, thinking only of how best to speed their camels. At last the lugubrious passage was traversed; the soldiers' breath came and went normally in their breasts now relieved of all oppression, and a wide, open space, suitable for pitching the tents, offered itself to their gaze.

When the Believers had finished the work of encampment, the Prophet (Peace be on him) warned them that a heavy tempest would rage during the night, and he enjoined them solemnly: 'Let those in charge of camels tie them securely and no man leave his tent without a companion.'

They had scarcely time to give a look at the hobbles of their beasts than the Prophet's (Peace be on him) prediction began to come true. The sun had set, covered by a misty veil, contrasting with its habitual sumptuous purple; its rayless pallor was the sign of an extraordinary storm.

All of a sudden, a brownish curtain sprang up from the horizon, to drag in its moving folds the orb of day, and the shades of coming night took on a tarry tint. The darkness thickened to such an extent that each man might have thought he was struck blind. A strange rumbling sound arose from the depth of the desert and approached with incredible rapidity, soon changing its deafening uproar which might have been taken for the hissing of monstrous vipers, accompanied by diabolical vociferation. At the same moment, the camp was crushed by a gigantic whirling spout of sand, tearing away in its gyrations everything that was not securely fastened. The pitchy darkness gave way to yellow obscurity, still more impenetrable to the eye.

Sheltered behind their camels, turning their backs to the tempest whilst shuddering and snorting in terror, the Faithful veiled their faces and covered their arms and legs, so as to guarantee their limbs against the fury of the raging sands that sank painfully into their flesh like thousands of wasps' stings. The soldiers flattened themselves face downwards on the ground, digging in their nails, holding fast in fear of being swept away like flocks of wool.

Despite the horror of the hour, two soldiers forgot the formal directions of Prophet. (Peace be on him) One of them, urged by necessity, left the encampment and at once fell suffocated. The other tried to run after his maddened camel that had broken its trammels and galloped away, only to be caught immediately in the whirlwind, and rolled round and round in its spirals, like a pebble spinning when hurled from a sling; and he was whisked up to the summit of the Jabala Tay. When told of this, the Prophet (Peace be on him) exclaimed: 'Did I not forbid you to leave the camp without a companion?'

He invoked the Mercy of the Compassionate in favour of the suffocated soldier who gradually regained consciousness and came back to life. As for the other victim, the Tay mountains restored him when the expedition returned.

The hurricane, at last, having exhausted its impotent fury against the soldiers of Allah, passed away to ravage other regions and the Faithful had no further accidents to deplore. But they were broken down by their former difficult marches; and that night, instead of granting invigorating rest, only brought them fresh fatigue. The simoon, having dried up the last vestiges of moisture in their bodies, their thickened blood hardly circulated in their veins and the beatings of their temples led to unbearable singing in the ears.

What would become of them on the long road they still had to travel before reaching the first well? The aspect of the surrounding country was not at all calculated to encourage them. They fancied that

E. DINET

Pilgrims at Mount Arafa, on the ninth day of the month of D'zou'l Haddja.

they were tramping through the ruins of a world destoryed by an inconceivable outbreak of fire. A black line marked the horizon: the never-ending Harra, which seemed in some parts to be formed of coal, soot and ashes; and in others, of iron congealed when molten, with enormous bubbles which, in bursting, had laid great crevices open, bordered with scattered slag as sharp as broken glass.

There, at any rate, the flames were extinguished, whereas, on the way they went, fires seemed to be still smouldering. Blocks of rock rose up with sides like a real forest, and by their shape and colour, they could bear comparison with gigantic tree-trunks, partly calcined and partly incandescent. Some were distorted in such strange fashion that, in the eyes of the Faithful, they looked like mouthing demons escaped from Hell and posted where they stood to revel in the torments of Allah's soldiers passing by.

Slippery slabs and pointed black stones of volcanic origin covered the earth, except where it was carpeted by sand of dazzling whiteness which, by its intense reverberation, kindled myriads of white-hot embers under every stone and in all the windings and turnings of the crags and peaks. Even in the depths of the sapphire sky, a hovering vulture and a rare fleeting cloud were tinted with a bright orange hue, as if they reflected the blaze of an immense furnace. To complete the illusion, lofty pillars of sand hung over all these remains, like columns of smoke issuing from a badly-extinguished conflagration.

The Believers' eyes, inflamed by the sandstorm, reddened by the refraction on the dunes, produced—even in their sockets—the effects of burning embers. Each time they put their feet, lacerated by the pebbles of the Hammada, to the overheated ground, their sufferings were unbearable. Their thickened saliva, mixed with impalpable dust, formed a firm paste, which the throat would not allow to pass. Their skin, stretched, as on a drumhead, resounded at the slightest touch, cracking in broad furrows, and split lips made speech impossible.

Some of the soldiers were a prey to delirium, caused by thirst; a sure sign of death. To bring them back to life, the only resource of their companions was to make the sufferers drink the liquid contained in the stomach of a slaughtered camel, and to plaster the dying man's parched breast with the still moist residue.

The Prophet (Peace be on him) endured the sufferings of each of his disciples, but at no moment was his confidence shaken; he knew that if Allah often sees fit to put His servants to the test, never does He abandon them. So Mohammad never ceased to implore His mercy.

Would the day never come to an end? The sun, as if fastened in the sky by invisible bonds, at last seemed determined to come down to earth. The orb was veiled, as on the preceding eve; its ruby disc was swallowed up on the horizon by the dark cloud in waiting and which, travelling fast towards the zenith, covered the camp with an ebony canopy, fringed with stalactites reflecting coppery tints. A series of lightning flashes struck furiously against the sides of this cupola, breaking into a thousand fragments. From between them, large drops of rain escaped, and then came more and more, to be followed at last by a diluvian downpour. The poor, parched soldiers shuddered delightfully in feelings of indescribable comfort when the blessed shower, soaking through their garments, refreshed their racked limbs; and they rushed to quench their thirst at the numerous pools which the waters of the heavens, rolling in cascades on the bare slopes, formed in every depression in the soil.

Thus reinvigorated, and their goat-skins filled again, the Believers joyfully resisted the fatigue of the march between each successive halting-place and finally emerged, safe and sound, from that accursed region.

A vast plain of sparkling sand, streaked by a thin line of a beautiful peacock blue, now spread itself out to the gaze of the Prophet (Peace be on him) and his men. This line, the goal of their efforts, soon

ARRIVAL AND SOJOURN OF THE PROPHET AT TABUK

became notched; and at last there appeared, sharply outlined on the turquoise sky, the slender tufts of the palm-trees of which it was formed.

This was the oasis of Tabuk! No pen can describe the joy of those, who having endured the anguish of thirst, arrived at this safe haven, an oasis of date-trees; nor give an idea of the expression on their faces when, having slaked their thirst and performed their ablutions, they looked down on the crystal water rippling in the "Sawaki;" nor of their satisfaction when they laid themselves down in the light shade of the palm-trees.

The Prophet's (Peace be on him) soldiers had got through the hardest part of their task. They had triumphed over the obstacles opposed to them by Nature, and henceforward could look with deep disdain on any barriers formed by the weapons of the Infidels. Besides, thanks to the fantastic rapidity with which tidings travel through the desert, their arrival at Tabuk soon came to the ears of the Christians and the Syrian Arabs who had formed a coalition to fight the Believers.

The enemies of Allah were overcome by stupor, for they had felt certain that if the Prophet (Peace be on him) should try to carry out his audacious plan at such a time of the year, the bones of all the men of his army would be scattered over the lonely Hijaz wilderness.

Therefore, in spite of their enormous numerical superiority, they concluded that any struggle against forty thousand Believers who had just accomplished this prodigious feat would be madness, and finish by overwhelming their opponents with indescribable disaster. Strife broke the ranks of their innumerable army and each party it comprised fled towards its own part of the country without having dared to face the Prophet. (Peace be on him) The pitiful helterskelter retreat of the allies enhanced the magic power of Islam as greatly as the most brilliant victory; and if Mohammad had not been kept back by the necessity of fulfilling his mission in the Hijaz before any other undertaking, he could have penetrated into the depth of the Palatinate almost without striking a blow.

As it was, established at Tabuk, he received the eager submission of the Arab lords who hurried to him, one and all, coming not only from the vicinity but also from distant regions, such as those of Sinai and Syria. Alone, the proud Prince of "Dawmatu'l-Jandal," an important town situated on the outskirts of the "Nefud" (Desert of Red Sand), having refused submission, the Prophet (Peace be on him) sent Khalid the Terrible to him; and he was brought to his knees at once.

During the few weeks' rest granted to his army, Mohammad never ceased the work of organising the country and teaching new converts.

One event only saddened him in his success, the death of a most devoted comrade, known as "Dhu Nijadayn," (the man with two shoulder-belts). To prove to all in what esteem he held this perfect Mussulman, he insisted in helping, with his own noble hands, the gravedigger to lower the body into the earth, and Ibn Mas'ud, jealous at seeing the dead man so highly honoured, exclaimed: 'Ah! why am I not buried in that tomb?'

THE PROPHET GOES BACK TO MADINAH

The return journey took place without any incident worthy of narration. The hot months having gone by, the army was spared the pangs of thirst; and during the first days of the month of Ramadhan, the soldiers re-entered Al-Madinah.

In such a moment, in the midst of the acclamations greeting the returning, energetic soldiers, the perfidious "qawm" of the "Hypocrites" knew not where to turn to hide their shame. To palliate their meanness, they invoked the most specious pretexts in vain. The Apostle did not even deign to honour them by resentment, reserved for the shaming of the three Ansars, deterred from their duty by the double-faced crew.

Despite the repentant humility of the abashed men, the Prophet (Peace be on him) sentenced them most rigorously by putting them under interdict and forbidding the Believers to have anything to do with them. The delinquents were completely isolated and the Faithful fled from them as if they were plague-stricken. Allah, not withstanding, moved by their remorse, pardoned them:

"He hath also turned in Mercy unto the three who were left behind, so that the earth, spacious as it is, became too strait for them; and their souls became so straitened within them, that they bethought them that there was no refuge from Allah but unto Himself. Then was he turned to them that they might turn to him. Verily Allah is He that turneth, the Merciful!" ((the Qur'an ix,, 119.)

The "Ghazwah" of Tabuk was the last expedition led by the Prophet (Peace be on him). To conclude the conquest of Arabia, he was satisfied thenceforth to send his lieutenants to accomplish a certain number of "Saraya" or expeditions, all fully successful, but which it would take too long to describe here.

He dwelt in Al-Madinah, kept busy in receiving the numerous submissions brought about by the victories of Islam. There were those of the Princes of Dawmatu'l-Jandal; of the Yaman; of the Uman, of Buhayra; of the Yamama; of Taif; of Najran, etc. He also devoted his energies to the most difficult task of governing the Arabs, for the first time united to form a people of brothers; and in his work as legislator, he displayed the resources of as much genius as when he was at the head of his armies.

About this time, the famous chief of the "Hypocrites," Abdullah ibn Salul, died. Seized with remorse in his last moments, Abdullah implored Mohammad's pardon and, despite the objections of the ungovernable Umar, the Prophet (Peace be on him) was not to be stopped from saying prayers over the body of his perfidious foe and burying him with his own hands. After this proof of clemency and forgetfulness of offences, there no longer remained a single "Hypocrite" in Al-Madinah.

In his turn, Ka'b ibn Zuhayr, who passed his life in composing virulent satires against the Prophet (Peace be on him) came to be converted by him, and recited a poem which he had written in his honour. When Ka'b got as far as the fifty-first verse:

"The Messenger of Allah is a flaming sword illuminating mortals; a sword of India, unsheathed by Allah," Mohammad pardoned him, making him a present of his mantle which he threw over the poet's shoulders.

After the return of his victorious lieutenants, the Prophet (Peace be on him) despatched missionaries to the newly-converted tribes, in order to prevent them backsliding by introducing any of their past superstitions into the religion.

One of the principal missionaries was Mu'adh ibn Jabal, who was about to set out for the Yaman. So that all should see the consideration he attached to the mission entrusted to Mu'adh the Prophet (Peace be on him) bound a turban round his envoy's head, helped him to mount his camel, and walked by the animal's side giving final instructions. Mu'adh, confused, made as if to alight, but Mohammad stopped his. 'Remain in the saddle, O sincere friend!' he said. 'I follow the orders of Heaven and satisfy my heart. It is needful that a man performing important duties should be honoured. Ah! if only I had hopes of seeing thee again, I should cut our conversation short; but probably I now speak to thee for the last time.' Much moved, they separated; never to meet again in this world.

In the month of Zu'l-Qa'dah, the Apostle, ever mindful of the religious and political importance of the pilgrimage to Makkah, sent Abu Bakr to accomplish it at the head of three hundred Mussulmans. Scarcely had Abu Bakr reached Zu'l Holifah, when the Surah of "Bara'ah" was revealed:

CHAPTER THE EIGHTH

"O Believers! only they who join gods with Allah (that is to say, those who in any way whatsoever associate Allah the Only One with other divinities or persons) are unclean! Let them not therefore, after this year, come near the Sacred Temple (of Makkah)." ((the Qur'an IX, 28.)

This Surah, remarkable as being the only in the Qur'an without the introductory form: "In the name of Allah, the Merciful, the Compassionate," was of the greatest importance, in so far as the pilgrimage was concerned. It forbad all who were not Mussulmans from setting foot in Holy Territory and even nowadays this prohibition, being rigorously enforced, the pilgrims of Islam are safeguarded against enemy spies, and protected from the unseemly curiosity of foreigners.

THE VALEDICTORY PILGRIMAGE *(Zul-Hijjab, in Year X of the Hegita, March A.D. 682)*

This was also the final blow struck at idolatry among the Arabs who could no longer come to Makkah unless they disowned their idols. Consequently, the Prophet (Peace be on him) charged Ali to rejoin the pilgrims' caravan in all haste and recite this imperative Surah to the assembled Faithful, after the sacrifices had been made in the valley of Mina.

The following year, the Prophet (Peace be on him) determined to lead the pilgrimage to Makkah personally. Since the Hegira, he had only accomplished the "Amratu'l-Qada," or pious visitation, at a time when Makkah had not yet been entirely won over to Islam. Now the "Hajju'l-Akbar," or Greater Pilgrimage, which imposes, besides the visit to the Sacred temple of Allah, a visit to the mountain of Arafa, or of Recognition, (so called because our first parents, Adam and Eve, met each other there after having been driven out of Paradise), is one of the five pillars of the practical religion of Islam.

Mohammad also wished to see his native land for the last time, having a presentiment of his coming end, for he felt himself secretly undermined by the vestiges of poison remaining in his veins. He solemnly announced his intention. The idea of seeing the Apostle of Allah and accomplishing the pilgrimage with him, stirred the enthusiasm of the whole of Arabia, and the number of pilgrims who accompanied him from Al-Madinah or joined him on the way, may be set down at about a hundred thousand.

At Zu'l Holifah, all the Faithful, following the Prophet's (Peace be on him) example, put themselves in the state of "Ihram," as described in the chapter of al-Hudaibiyah, and assumed the robe also called "Ihram," consisting of two seamless wrappers free from any dye likely to stain the skin. One piece of drapery is wrapped round the waist and the other, thrown loosely over the shoulders, covers the chest; the head, arms, and legs being left bare. After the Prophet (Peace be on him) had proclaimed the "Talbiyah," the pilgrims took it up in chorus: *"I stand up for thy service, O Allah! There is no Partner with Thee! Verily Thine is the Praise, the Blessing and the Kingdom!"*

During the journey, two unimportant incidents arose which we note nevertheless, because they show that a pilgrim is obliged to suppress all feelings of impatience or anger. The camel of Safiyah, one of the Prophet's (Peace be on him) wives, was a slow animal, and being heavily laden, did not keep up with the caravan, despite the efforts of its driver. Ayishah's camel, possessing a good turn of speed and lightly burdened, Mohammad, after having tried to explain these facts to its fair rider, gave orders to change the loads of the two animals. But this displeased Ayishah. She lost her temper and cried out: "Thou sayest thou art Prophet? (Peace be on him) Then why not do things justly?'

No sooner had these words escaped her lips, than her father, Abu Bakr, slapped her face; and when Mohammad upbraided him he replied: 'Didst hear what she said?'—'Yea; but she must be excused. The essence of a woman's mind is jealousy; and when jealousy masters her, she is incapable of seeing in what direction runs the current of a wadi!'

"Ed Douâ" or the Invocation.

On arriving at the encampment of Al-Arj, the camel carrying the provisions of the Prophet (Peace be on him) and of Abu Bakr was missing. Ayishah's father laid the blame on the driver: 'How's this? Thou hadst but one camel to look after and thou hast let it go astray?' Carried away by great anger, Abu Bakr, with his whip, gave the man a good hiding. 'Admire the conduct of this pilgrim in the state of "Ihram!" said the Prophet (Peace be on him) ironically. 'Come now, O Abu Bakr, be calm, and rest assured that the serving-man's sole desire was not to lose thy camel.'

The caravan took the same road as that of the pious visitation. The Prophet (Peace be on him) entered Makkah in open day, and made his she-camel kneel in front of the entrance of the Sacred Precincts, called the "Door of Salvation," and on catching sight of the Ka'bah, he exclaimed: 'O Allah, increase the glory of this Temple and the number of its visitors!'

After three ablutions, he kissed the Black Stone, whilst tears welled up in his eyes. He then performed the "Tawaf," and the "Sa'y," in the same way as during the pious visit.

On the eighth day of the month of Zu'l-Hijjah, he went to the valley of Mina where he caused a tent of woollen stuff to be pitched; and it was there he said the prayers of the afternoon; of sunset; and of nightfall. Next day, after the prayer of the "Fajr," he once more bestrode his she-camel, al-Qaswa, in order to reach the mountain of Arafa.

Countless crowds having gathered on the mountain's rocky slopes, as well as on the plain and in the surrounding ravines, the Prophet (Peace be on him) preached, remaining on his she-camel which he had ridden and halted on the summit. Standing immediately beneath him, was Rabiyah ibn Ummayatah, posted there to repeat the words of the sermon, with his resounding voice, during a pause made for that purpose at the conclusion of each sentence.

After Allah had been glorified by the "Takbir," the Prophet (Peace be on him) exhorted the Faithful to treat their wives with the greatest gentleness, and never to forget that the rights of spouses are equal to their duties. He explicitly forbade the exaction of any interest whatsoever on money lent; and no murders committed during the "days of ignorance" were to be avenged. He fixed the duration of the year at twelve lunar months, and declared that the "Nasi," which added a month every three years to re-establish equilibrium and bring the same dates back to the same seasons, was impious and must be abolished.

He then concluded, as he cried: 'O Believers, your blood and your belongings ought to be looked upon as holy to each of you, even as this day is holy and as this land is holy! O Believers, remember what I say, for I know not if ever I shall be with you again on this spot, when this day is past. And, above all, never forget that every Mussulman should be truly a brother to every other Mussulman, for all the Mussulmans in the world form a single people of brothers! . . . O Allah! have I fulfilled my Mission?'—'Yea, verily, O Allah!', replied in unanimous outcry the hundred thousand mouths of the pilgrims, in accents of the most ardent gratitude.—'O Allah! hearken to their testimony!' cried Mohammad.

At another spot, near the summit of the Arafa, and known by the name of "As-Sakhrah," recognisable by being paved with broad slabs, a sudden Revelation came down to the Prophet. (Peace be on him) Under the burden of Divine Inspiration penetrating the heart of her rider, the she-camel, al-Qaswa came nigh to breaking all her limbs, and she fell on her knees.

Here are the words of Allah, the Most High: '*This day have I perfected your religion for you, and have filled up the measure of my favours towards you; and it is my pleasure that Islam be your religion . . .*" (the Qur'an, v, 5.)

This Revelation, terminating the Prophet's (Peace be on him) sermon which had so deeply touched the Believers, stirred up the purest enthusiasm in the whole of the Assembly.

Nevertheless, Abu Bakr, far from participating in the general joy, was seized with a fit of intense melancholy, and was unable to hold back the tears that filled his eyes. He thought that having favour in the eyes of the Almighty, His mercy was bound to decrease. Knowing that his son-in-law's Mission was terminated, Abu Bakr was afraid that the Prophet (Peace be on him) would soon disappear from this world.

The indigo shades of night had fallen over the valley and spread along the slopes of the Arafa. All by himself, on the mountain top, overlooking the great multitude of pilgrims, the Prophet, (Peace be on him) on the back of his tall she-camel, still remained in the light of the last golden rays of sunset. His glance, ecstatic by faith, was resplendent with superhuman brilliancy; but his face, emaciated by illness, had taken on the immaterial aspect of a vision about to fade. The rising shadows reached and veiled him.

It was now the turn of the companions of the Prophet (Peace be on him) to find themselves overcome by the same mournful apprehension that Abu Bakr had felt, although scarcely a few moments before, they were manifesting their joy at hearing that their religion had been perfected by Allah. By degrees, their emotion was communicated to the entire assembly of the Believers and their hundred thousand hearts were filled with the keenest anguish.

The Prophet (Peace be on him) gave the signal of departure; but to prevent the accidents which any haste would inevitably cause among the great masses of such a gathering, he tugged the bridle of swift Qaswa to him, twisting her head round until her nostrils touched her ribs, whilst he slid on to her withers; unceasingly exhorting all: 'Go quietly, O ye people!'

On arriving at Muzdalifa, he said the prayer, "Isha," and next day, after the daybreak prayer, riding his she-camel, led by Bilal, and protected from the sun by a mantle that Usama, riding behind him, held over his head, he went into the valley of Mina, in order to throw seven stones against each of the three pillars of rude masonry, called "Jumurat." This is in commemoration of the pebbles thrown by Abraham to drive away the Devil who thrice tried to stop him at that spot.

After that, the Prophet, (Peace be on him) to prove his gratitude for the sixty-three years of life granted to him by the Creator, freed sixty-three slaves, and with his own hands, sacrificed sixty-three camels, their flesh and skins being distributed among the pilgrims by Ali, acting under Mohammad's orders. He then had his head shaved by Mi'mar ibn Abdullah, who commenced at the right temple and finished at the left. Finally, after having once more performed the "Tawaf" round the Kab'ah, and drunk for the last time some Zamzam water in a vase offered to him by his uncle Abbas, the Superintendent of the Well, he set out again on the road to Al-Madinah.

Such was the pilgrimage called the "Valedictory Visitation," which overwhelmed the Believers with such deep emotion by appraising them that Mohammad's Mission was fulfilled. This pilgrimage serves as a pattern for all the pilgrimages which, during thirteen centuries, have brought annually to these Holy Places, one hundred and fifty to two hundred thousand pilgrims, collected from all parts of the universe.

Any pilgrimage, whatever the religion giving rise to it may be, causes inexpressible emotion by the sight of so many faces beaming with faith; and the most sceptical among the onlookers finds it difficult to escape the contagion of this outbreak of fervour. But, among the majority of the spectators, inadmissible practices soon overcome sympathetic feelings and change them into aversion. At Makkah, doubtless, as in all religious centres without exception, pilgrims are ruthlessly exploited; but in this city, at least, the traffickers may be excused: they dwell in the most inhospitable of all deserts and have no other means of getting a living.

What makes the Mussulman pilgrimage essentially different to any other is the absence of those innumerable chapels, whose narrow arches imprison souls, hampering them as they soar towards the Creator and holding them back on earth at the mercy of the clergy. Here are no fetishes, such as statuettes or miraculous icons, surrounded by their procession of votive offerings; nor that multitude of saints, their worship taking the place of that of the "Eternal," generally neglected on these occasions. There are also none of those monks clad in varied gowns, all jealous of each other, quarrelling over pilgrims and religious resorts for the greater glory of their sect or order.

At Makkah, prayers are said in the vast quadrangular courtyard surrounding the Ka'bah; the ethereal vault of heaven takes the place of the masonry work of chapel roofs and, purified from all its mists, it opens to souls thirsting for ideal good, its lapis-lazuli depths more vertiginous here than in any other part of the world. At Makkah, nothing is worshipped except Allah, the Chosen One, and pilgrims seek the remembrance of Abraham and Mohammad for no other reason than to strengthen the fervour of their faith by following the Prophet's (Peace be on him) example. They never pray to these Prophets in the same way as Christians adore their saints; on the contrary, Moslems pray to Allah for their Prophets.

The gates of the Ka'bah are open day and night. The pilgrim hurries there as soon as he gets to Makkah. At the sight of the temple draped in black, the object of his unceasing thoughts during the severe ordeals of the journey, in the midst of sandstorms or tempest-tossed, he is overtaken by such emotion that in this moment of superhuman ecstasy, he wishes his soul to be snatched away. Sobbing, his breast heaving fitfully, under the influence of remorse, his face convulsed by shame, he approaches the Black Stone to kiss it, exclaiming: 'O Allah! pardon me my sins; free my being from their burden and purify my heart, O Thou the most Merciful among the Compassionate!

When the hour of prayer is called by the Muezzin, the spacious quadrangle is invaded by a veritable sea of Believers; their hurrying waves scarcely leaving in the serried ranks the needful space for prostration. Following one of the "Takbirs" of the Imam, said after him in an immense sigh escaping simultaneously from every breast, a great swell passes over all the Faithful, causing every head to be bowed, like billows breaking.

At another "Takbir", it seems that the ground suddenly gives way under the pilgrims' feet. At one bound, every forehead is pressed to the earth, where the body of each man remains crushed by the threefold weight of Contrition, Gratitude and Adoration; like so many rays converging in the direction of the Temple which seems to be made still taller by the added height of the prostrated Pilgrims. Above them, the black silk veil undulates, stirred by the gusts of a mysterious breeze which many attribute to angels' beating wings.

The Assembly of the Arafa is distinguished by quite as much grandeur. In a wild valley stands the conical mountain of Arafa. Its slopes, bare of all vegetation, bristle with enormous boulders. There is no sign of life on its sides, nor in the neighbourhood; all around is the image of desolation and the silence of death. But every year, on the ninth day of the month of Zu'l-Hijjah, the funereal landscape evokes most strikingly the future Day of Resurrection.

Soil, sand and rocks disappeared, truly cloaked by human beings, enwrapped in their white "Ihrams," and who might be taken for the resuscitated dead, freeing themselves from their shrouds after having lifted the rocks which were their gravestones. As it will happen on that supreme day, all the earth's races are represented in the countless crowds gathered together at this spot, deserted but a short time before. Here comes Arabs, with eyes of eagles, their complexion of a reddish bronze; Ottomans, their features showing them to be energetic and headstrong; Hindoos, with faces clear-cut and olive-tinted; Berbers, fair-haired and rosy-cheeked, their eyes blue; Somalis and Sudanese, their black skins shining in the sun with lunar gleams; refined Persians; bold Turcomans; yellow Chinese, with closed eyelids; Japanese, high cheek-boned, etc . . . Nowhere else in the world can such a variety of faces and languages be met with.

After the prayer of the "Asr," (afternoon), the "Khatib," or the preacher, riding his she-camel, gorgeously harnessed, appears on the summit of the Arafa where the sermon is given forth, interrupted by frequent "Talbiyahs": *"Labbaika! Allahummah Labbaika!"* (I stand up for Thy Service, O Allah! I stand up! I stand up!)

At each "Talbiyah," the pilgrims wave the ends of their white draperies over their heads and the whole mountain seems to be palpitating under the beating of myriads of wings ready to fly, whilst a lengthy clamour rises to the sky from every part of the valley, reverberating in the sonorous echoes of the desert. *"Labbaika! Allahummah Labbaka!"* shout two hundred thousand pilgrims with one voice, neglecting their own idioms, so as to become united in the same tongue: that of the Arabs chosen by the Almighty for the Revelation of His Book.

In that sublime hour, in language as well as by the heart, all these mortals are cordially brothers. They have forgotten all their racial differences, distinctions of rank or caste, and all their political and religious feuds . . . On the Arafa, Islam once more finds its perfect unity and its primitive outbreak of enthusiasm. What great consolation! What balm for some of its wounds!

Quoth the Prophet: (Peace be on him) 'The Moslems are as one body; the pain in any single limb gives rise to fever and insomnia in the whole of the frame.'

On the Arafa, Islam has nothing to fear from enemy spies; it can make good its losses and prepare its future. Despite its disasters, it is more alive than ever! Such is the impression of this unforgettable day, that each of the assistants takes back with him to his own country, as well as the title, so greatly envied, of "Haji," signifying Pilgrim to the Holy Places.

قُلْ سِيرُوا فِي الْأَرْضِ فَانظُرُوا كَيْفَ بَدَأَ الْخَلْقَ

CHAPTER NINE — *Decorative plate.*

إِنَّكَ مَيِّتٌ وَإِنَّهُم مَّيِّتُونَ

CHAPTER THE NINTH

ILLNESS AND DEATH OF THE PROPHET *(Rabi'u'l-Awwal, Year IX of the Hegira, June A.D.632)*

Quoth Abu Muwayhiba, the Prophet's (Peace be on him) serving-man: 'One night towards the end of the month of Safar, my master woke me up,' "I must go and implore the blessings of Allah," said he, "for those at rest in the tombs of Baqui'u a'l-Gharqad. Come with me."

I accompanied him. "Blessed be you, O dwellers in the tomb!" he exclaimed, when we reached the cemetery. "Rest in peace! Allah hath spared you terrible ordeals, like unto the anguish of a dark night, more terribly black at the end than at the beginning. Such are the torments in store for those who are still upon this earth!"

As he finished speaking, the whole of his body was shaken by the palsy of fever, and he wended his way back to his dwelling with difficulty; his temples racked by the unbearable pains known as "Suda".

Quoth Ayishah: "When the Prophet (Peace be on him) returned from his visit to the cemetery of Al-Baqi, he came to see me in the middle of the night. I was suffering from violent headache and as I complained, he said – 'Ah! 'tis I who ought to complain of pains in the head and not thou!' He went on, jokingly: 'Would it not be better for thee to die whilst I am still in the land of the living? I could implore the Mercy of Allah in thy favour; with my own hands I could enfold thee in thy winding sheet; I could pray over thy body and place thee in thy grave.' 'Of a surety thou doest me great honour in apprising me that thou wouldst act thus in my favour,' I replied; 'but I fear that after I was buried, thy sole consolation would be to bring back with thee, into my room, some other of thy wives!' At this sally, a smile returned to the Prophet's (Peace be on him) face and, for a brief moment, he forgot his pain."

As time went on, his illness left him no rest; nevertheless, mastering his sufferings, his mind was busier than ever, and he occupied himself with the future of Islam, for he felt that the effects of his management would soon be lacking.

Thinking that Syria was one of the gates through which the warriors of Allah would have to march to conquer the world, Mohammad's gaze was unceasingly turned towards that country and he resolved to organise a third expedition against the Christians, in whose power it was.

Great rivalry at once arose with regard to commanding such an incursion. Of heroes and generals having been put to the test, Islam had enough and to spare. The most famous among them, Ansars of Mohadjirun, anxiously awaited the Prophet's (Peace be on him) choice.

To the stupefaction of all, however, Usama, barely twenty years of age, was chosen. It is true that this lad was the son of Zayd ibn Harith, the martyr of Mutah. Mohammad placed greater reliance on the revengeful ardour that Usama would show in fighting the murderers of his father on the very spot where he gloriously succumbed, that on the experience and warlike valour of the Mussulman generals.

This selection caused deception and gave rise to murmuring. The Believers hesitated to put boundless confidence, such as is indispensable for success, in a chief so young and inexperienced. Having been told about this, the Prophet (Peace be on him) rose and cut short all disputes by these words: 'Ye criticise my choice of Usama, even as ye formerly cavilled at that of Zayd, his father! Listen! To you I swear, by Allah! that Zayd was truly worthy of the post of command with which I did entrust him. I cherished him above all other men; and after him, his son is the man I prefer. Go, carry out my orders, and have confidence!'

These simple words, uttered in a tone of inspired conviction, banished all hesitation, smoothing away all jealousy as if by magic; and the noblest and most famous among all the chieftains, together with the most humble soldiers, came enthusiastically to obey the commands of the stripling. When the expedition marched into the "Farewell Pass", the Prophet (Peace be on him) was deeply moved as he saw his troops disappear. The superhuman faith animating the warriors at the parting hour proved to him that no obstacle could bar their way on the road to victory and that the irresistible torrent of Islam, like unto the salutary overflow of a wadi, was about to inundate the world and bring it the prolific germs of its new civilisation. Meanwhile, it was not long before the alarming news, relating to the Prophet's (Peace be on him) illness, stopped Usama's forward progress, bringing him back to Al-Madinah.

About that time, the Apostle received a letter, couched in these terms: "Musailimah, the Prophet of Allah, to Mohammad, the Prophet of Allah. Peace be with thee, I am thy associate. Let the exercise of authority be divided between us. Half the earth is mine, and half belongeth to the Quraish. But the Quraish are a greedy People, and will not be satisfied with a fair division."

The author of this epistle, Musailimah, Prince of the Yamama, had recently been converted to Islam; and then, fully appreciating the majesy of the part played by the Prophet, (Peace be on him) this pretender planned with monstrous pride to play some part in his turn.

To the envoys bringing the impudent missive, Mohammad replied: 'Were it not that your situation as ambassadors causeth me to look upon your lives as sacred, I would have you beheaded.' And he handed them this answer: "Mohammad, the Prophet of Allah to Musailimah, the Impostor. Peace be with those who follow the right road! The earth is Allah's and He giveth it to whom he will. Those only prosper who fear the Lord."

Both Musailimah and Al-Aswad, another impostor, soon found out the danger run by those who enacted the part of Prophet without having been called by Allah. They expiated their temerity most cruelly.

The Prophet's (Peace be on him) illness became daily more serious. He grew so weak that he could only move about by dint of the most painful efforts.

Being the house of Maimunah, he sent for his other wives. His usual habit was to pass the night in turn, impartially, at each of their dwellings; but feeling himself weighed down by intense suffering, he begged them to let him remain with Ayishah alone for the duration of his illness; and to this they consented.

Quoth Ayishah: "The Prophet (Peace be on him) left the abode of Maimunah, thanks to the assistance of Al-Fadl and Ali, who held him in their arms. A bandage was bound tightly round his head, and his weakness was so great that he had no sooner set foot in my room than he swooned. When he came to, lancinating pains tortured his temples; and hoping to soothe his pangs, he asked: 'Pour over me six skinfuls of water drawn from a very cold spring, so that I may be in a fit state to go forth and preach to the Faithful. We set him in a stone trough, borrowed from Hafsa, and poured water over him in abundance until he bade us stop, by a wave of his hand, saying: 'Enough!' "

Momentarily invigorated, Mohammad went out through Ayishah's door which gave on to the Mosque; and again supported by his cousin Ali and Al-Fadl, he had great trouble in mounting the steps of the pulpit, from which he made the following declaration to the faithful assembled: 'O Believers, if among you there be one whose back I have beaten, here is my back so that he may do himself justice! If there be one whose honour I may have wounded, here is my honour, let him be avenged! If there be one whose property I may have seized, here is my property, let his satisfy his claim! Let no one hesitate in fear of my resentment, for resentment formeth no part of my disposition.' After having stepped down to give out the noonday prayer, he went up in the pulpit again and repeated the same declaration.

A man arose and claimed payment of a debt amounting to three drachmas. The Prophet (Peace be on him) handed them over at once, adding: 'It is easier to put up with shame in this world than in the other.'

He then evoked the remembrance of the martyrs of Uhud, to whom he devoted the best part of his prayer, imploring Allah's blessings in their favour. He wound up as follows: 'Allah hath offered one of His servants the choice between riches of this earth and those that are to be found at His side.' At these words, divining that the Prophet (Peace be on him) was alluding to himself and the state of his health, Abu Bakr burst into tears, and exclaimed: 'Ah! why cannot we offer our lives as a ransom for thine?' – 'O Believers!' replied Mohammad, 'it hath come to my ears that ye fear your Prophet may die; but before me hath any Prophet been immortal as he accomplished his mission? How can I dwell eternally among you? Every soul is doomed to die. I must return to Allah and ye likewise will return to Him.'

Quoth Ayishah: "After this effort then the Prophet (Peace be on him) came back to my room, he fainted away again. When the call of the Muezzin was heard: he rose up and asked for water wherewith to perform his ablutions, meaning to lead the prayers. He swooned three times.

As the Faithful awaited his coming in the Mosque, he sent Bilal to fetch Abu Bakr, so that he could perform the duties of Imam instead of the Prophet (Peace be on him). The crowd, guessing the reason of this change, broke out into fits of sobbing.

The Prophet (Peace be on him) was frequently seized with delirium. One Thursday, whilst all his companions gathered round his bed, he said to them: 'Bring hither to me ink and parchment. I would place on record a book for you which shall prevent your going astray for evermore. – 'Allah's Messenger is burdened by pain,' said Umar; 'have we not the Qur'an? Allah's Book sufficeth for us.'

Several of his companions, accustomed never to argue about anything said by the Prophet (Peace be on him) and remembering that he was illiterate, thought that in this supreme moment a miracle was about to be accomplished. Therefore they wanted to give him what he asked for. They were opposed by his partisans sharing Umar's opinion, and a quarrel began. The Prophet (Peace be on him) recovering his senses by the noise, He told them reproachfully: 'It is not seemly to quarrel thus at a Prophet's bedside. Go away!'

To soothe his unbearable pain, he dipped his hands in a pitcher of cold water and passed his wet palms over his face, as if to wipe it: 'O Allah!' he cried, 'help me to support the terrors of the death struggle!'

He had Fatimah, his beloved daughter, fetched to him twice and spoke to her secretly, whispering in her ear. The first time, Fatimah's face was bathed in tears: the second time, her features were lit up by a smile. We asked her the reason of her changed expression, and she told us: "The first time, my father warned me that he must soon succumb to his illness, and I could not repress my tears. The second time, he informed me that of all his family, I should be the first to rejoin him, and so great was my joy that I

View of El Madina the illuminated.

could not stop myself from smiling.' "

On the Monday, the twelfth day of Rabi'u'l-Awwal, Abu Bakr was saying prayers in the presence of the Faithful, when Ayishah's door giving into the Mosque, was thrown open. Supported by Ali and Al Fadl, the Prophet (Peace be on him) appeared. His turban was twisted tightly around his head, and his benumbed feet dragged along the ground. On seeing him, the Faithful were comforted by a ray of hope and a wave of emotion stirred them all. Without turning round, Abu Bakr guessed that only the arrival of the Prophet (Peace be on him) could have given rise to such a manifestation while prayers were being said, and he moved away to join the ranks of the worshippers and let his place be taken by Mohammad. But he made Bakr go back, pulling him by his garment, as he said, 'Continue to lead the prayers.'

He then sat down on Abu Bakr's right hand, under the pulpit, and his face beamed with happiness, at the sight of the piety in the congregation. When prayers had been said, he spoke to the Believers for the last time; and in tones firm enough to be heard outside the Mosque, he preached a sermon predicting terrible ordeals and charging them with the strictest observance of the principles of the Qur'an, for such would be the only way leading to Salvation. Leaning against one of the palm-tree pillars, he chatted familiarly with some of his companions, and then went back to his room.

Quoth Ayishah: "After this last effort, the Prophet (Peace be on him) was again overtaken by greater pain than ever, and covered his face with a black garment, which he threw off again, as it stifled him.

Just then Abdu'r Rahman, son of Abu Bakr, came in holding in his hand a small twig of green "araq", with which he was picking his teeth. The Prophet (Peace be on him) stared at the little stick and I made out that he would have liked it. So I took it out of Abdu'r Rahman's hand. Cutting off the end of the toothpick, I shook it, cleaned it and gave it to Allah's messenger who immediately made use of it, picking his teeth more carefully than ever before. When he had finished, he let the little stick drop from between his faltering fingers. He raised his eyes to heaven repeating three times: 'O Allah! with the Compassionate on High . . . !' And I felt his head, resting between my chin and shoulder, grow heavy on my arm.

I guessed that the Prophet (Peace be on him) had chosen the eternal dwelling and that his noble soul had just been taken by the Angel of Death. I placed my head on the pillow and uttered a great cry of distress. His wives came running in; and all together, we went down on our knees, and tore our faces with our nails."

On hearing these lamentations, the Believers filled the Mosque. They were dazed, like sheep straying on a dark, wintry night; but not one of the Faithful would admit that the Prophet (Peace be on him) was dead. The disappearance of the man who led them in every way seemed an impossibility.

'How can he be dead?' they cried. 'Did we not count upon him to be our witness on the Day of Resurrection? He is not dead? He hath been carried up to Heaven, even as was Isa (Jesus).' And through the door they cried, 'Beware lest ye bury him!'

This met with Umar's approval: 'No, verily, the Prophet (Peace be on him) is not dead! He hath gone to visit the Lord, even as Moses did, when after an absence of forty days, he reappeared to his people. In like fashion, Mohammad will be restored to us. Those who say he is dead are traitors to the cause of Islam. Let their hands and feet be cut off!'

At that juncture, Abu Bakr, who had been fetched from the As-Sunah quarter where he lived, arrived on horseback, galloping as fast as possible. He alighted and making his way through the crowd in consternation, he went into the Mosque without speaking to a soul, and from there, passed into the room of his daughter Ayishah in order to see Allah's Messenger. A piece of striped stuff was thrown over the body; Abu Bakr uncovered the Prophet's (Peace be on him) face, kissed him, wept and then broke down under the weight of his great grief, 'O Thou for whose ransom I would have offered both father and mother,' he cried, 'thy career is well accomplished!'

Tearing himself away from his sorrowful contemplation, he covered up Mohammad's face again and went out, going straight up to Umar who was haranguing the people. 'Sit down, O Umar!' he said. Umar refused to obey him. In the meantime, the majority of the Faithful left him by himself, and gathered round Abu Bakr who told them: 'O Believers, if ye adore Mohammad, know that Mohammad is dead; but if ye adore Allah, know that Allah is alive, for Allah cannot die! Ye must have forgotten these verses of the Qur'an: *"Mohammad is no more than an Apostle; other Apostles have already passed away before him; if then he die, or be slain, will ye turn upon your heels? Thou truly art mortal, O (Mohammad), and they truly are mortals."* (The Qur'an, III, 138, and xxxix, 31.)

Quoth Umar: "By Allah! scarcely did I hear Abu Bakr recite these verses than I felt my legs give way under me. I was near falling down, for then I began to understand that the Prophet (Peace be on him) was really dead!"

Before thinking about the funeral, it was urgent to guard against the pressing danger threatening Islam, totally broken up by the loss of its inspired guide.

ABU BAKR ELECTED

The man who had succeeded in bringing together in religious fraternity families and tribes at loggerheads for centuries having disappeared, what would become of this brotherhood? The immediate nomination of a Caliph, or lieutenant appointed to continue the Prophet's (Peace be on him) task, could alone prevent irretrievable disaggregation. This urgent necessity stirred the tribes tumultuously; a tragical conflict between Ansars and Mohadjirun was imminent, each party claiming to have the Caliph chosen from among its adherents. Happily, Umar's energy and spirit of decision easily averted the crisis. Having succeeded in gaining a few moment's silence, he called upon the Believers to take notice that during the last days of his life, Mohammad had designated Abu Bakr, his companion during the Hegira, to take his place as "Imam" and doubtless the Prophet (Peace be on him) would have chosen him for Caliph.

This opinion carried the day. When the sun rose again, all the Believers, forgetting their disputes, came and took the oath of fidelity to Abu Bakr.

THE PROPHET'S BURIAL

This important question being settled, the Faithful were free to arrange the Prophet's (Peace be on him) funeral and give way to the despair that racked their souls.

At first, they were embarrassed, not daring the strip of his garments so as to wash the body according to the usual rites. Respect forbad them to look on his nakedness, as if it were sacrilegious to do so. After long discussions, irresistible sleep weighed down on their eyelids, their chins rested on their breasts, when suddenly, a voice proceeding from the chamber of death was heard. They awoke at its sound and replied what was passing in their minds: 'Wash the Prophet (Peace be on him) without undressing him.' That was the solution they sought, and without further delay, they acted on the suggestion. With striped stuff of the Yaman, Abbas erected a kind of tent in the room, so as to keep the crowd away from the body. By the aid of seven skinsful of water drawn from the well of Al-Ghars, at Quba, preferred by Mohammad to any other, Ali, Usama, Abbas and his sons, and Shukran, the freed slave, proceeded with the ritual washing. Abbas, assisted by his sons, Al-Fadl and Qutham, turned the venerated body over. Usama and Shukran sprinkled it with water and Ali wiped it without removing the shirt.

The first washing was done with plain water, the next with an infusion of lotus-flowers; and the third, and last, with camphorated water. Abbas and Ali then perfumed every part of the body that comes in contact with the earth during the ceremony of prostration; forehead, nose, hands, knees and feet.

'How sweet is thy smell, O Prophet!' exclaimed Ali, and all marvelled at not finding on Mohammad's frame any of those horrible traces of decomposition following the separation of the soul from the body, with the exception of a slight bluish tinge appearing on the nails.

Instead of a shroud, the Prophet (Peace be on him) was wrapped in the garments he wore at the moment of death: his shirt, which after the ablutions was wrung out and allowed to drip; and a double robe woven at Najran. It was then that Ali and Abbas, having replaced Monhammad on his bed, allowed the crowd to enter.

The room was at once filled with as many Believers as it would hold, and after they had said: 'Peace be with thee, O Prophet, and also the Mercy and Blessing of Allah!', they got ready to pray without an "Imam" to lead them, for the real "Imam" was present, although his soul had been called back to the side of the Almighty.

Abu Bakr and Umar were in the front rank of the worshippers, and they concluded the prayer by these words: *"O Allah! we bear witness that he hath accomplished the Mission Thou didst entrust to him. O Allah! grant peace to those among us who follow faithfully the orders Thou hast revealed to him and hasten to reunite us with him. Amin!"* And all the people, stirred to the innermost depths of their being, repeated: *"Amin! Amin!"*

Fresh difficulties now arose, concerning the place of burial; some wanting the grave to be dug in the Mosque; others, at Al-Baqi, among the tombs of the Prophet's (Peace be on him) family. A few mentioned Makkah, his birthplace. Abu Bakr silenced them, affirming that he had heard Mohammad say: 'Allah only taketh the soul of a Prophet on the spot where it is fitting that he should be buried.'

The bed was accordingly moved away and the grave dug in the ground underneath it. This task was allotted to Tahla, the gravedigger of Al-Madinah. He strengthened the sides of the grave by means of nine unburnt bricks, and carpeted the bottom with the red blanket that served the Prophet (Peace be on him) as a rug for his camel when travelling, and which was not be used by anyone now that he was dead. Ali, Al-Fadl, Quthan and Shakran lowered the body into its last resting place.

Al Mughira ibn Shu'ba affirms that he was the last man to have the happiness of contemplating the face of the Chosen One before it was covered with earth. 'I let my fingering drop into the grave,' he says, 'so that when I regained it, I should be the last to address a farewell salute to the Prophet' (Peace be on him).

The sad ceremony was concluded in the middle of the night between Tuesday and Wednesday. On the morrow at dawn, when in his call to prayer, Bilal, the "Muezzin", proclaimed: 'There is no God but Allah, and Mohammad is the Prophet (Peace be on him) of Allah!' He could only shout the name of Mohammad through his sobs. The whole town replied to him, as by an echo, in a long moan of despair which rose to heaven from every door and window of the houses.

Ever since that day, the twelfth of the month of Rabi'u l-Awwal, Year XII of the Hegira, (June 8th A.D. 632), this extraordinary man who was, to say the least, the equal of the greatest of all Prophets, monarch, general, theologian, legislator and philosopher, and whose religion counts at the present time three hundred millions of disciples, rests in this spot where his noble soul was carried aloft.

A sumptuous Mosque, erected over the room where he died, has taken the place of the humble temple of raw bricks and palm-trunks that he built up with his own hand. A visit to the tomb is not one of the pillars of Islamic practical religion, but nevertheless there are few pilgrims who, after the severe trials endured during their journey to Makkah, hesitate to undertake the twelve days' caravan travel, so distressing and dangerous, between Mohammad's birthplace and Al-Madinah, in order to salute the Prophet (Peace be on him) piously and enthusiastically . . .

Even the learned men of Europe are beginning to forget secular prejudices and do justice to the founder of Islam. 'If a man's value is to be estimated by the grandeur of his works', declares Dr. G. Le Bon, 'we can say that Mohammad was one of the greatest men known in history'.

وَمَا مُحَمَّدٌ إِلَّا رَسُولٌ قَدْ خَلَتْ مِن قَبْلِهِ ٱلرُّسُلُ
أَفَإِيْن مَّاتَ أَوْ قُتِلَ ٱنقَلَبْتُمْ عَلَىٰٓ أَعْقَٰبِكُمْ

Final decorative plate.